After Ithaca
Journeys in Deep Time

Charlotte Du Cann

After Ithaca
Charlotte Du Cann

Cover Design: Christian Brett, Bracketpress, UK
Interior Design: John Negru
Cover art: *On the Edge of This Immensity*, Meryl McMaster © 2022

A Greenbank Book
Published by
The Sumeru Press Inc.
PO Box 75, Manotick Main Post Office,
Manotick, ON, Canada K2J 5W3

Library and Archives Canada Cataloguing in Publication

Title: After Ithaca / Charlotte Du Cann.
Names: Du Cann, Charlotte, 1956- author.
Description: Essays.
Identifiers: Canadiana 20220134030 | ISBN 9781896559834 (softcover)
Classification: LCC PR6104.U2 A78 2022 | DDC 824/.92—dc23

For more information about Greenbank Books
and The Sumeru Press
visit us at *sumeru-books.com*

For all the places I journeyed to in these years: for Australia, for South America, for Turtle Island, for the First Nations, for the coyotes that howled outside my door, for the eagles and owls; for all the old activists who lived out in the desert in Arizona, who kept singing and gathering medicine plants; for all the young activists in Oxford and Norwich who fought for the trees of England, who burrowed under roads and kept dancing and laughing. For those who did not make it out of the city: the beautiful men who forgot how to dance, the smart women who forgot how to laugh, for everyone that got institutionalised, caught up on the wheel.

For those of us who left and live on the edges: all the writers and artists who have held the fire and sing through the dark times. For all those who are in the long game, for the Earth and the ancestors who stand behind us.

Preface

The pieces in this book all follow the shape of an ancient myth of descent. They were originally written as solo essays and can be read either by themselves or in sequence. Many were first published by the Dark Mountain Project, a network of writers and artists I stumbled upon in the woods on the edge of the Hampshire Downs one August night in 2011. I had been documenting grassroots changemaking in the face of ecological and social crisis, but as I sat round the festival fire listening to a Siberian tale told under the stars, I realised that no one had ever mentioned creativity or the Earth.

Change is a messy thing and doesn't happen at once. When a butterfly is formed inside a chrysalis, it first dissolves its old caterpillar form. Out of that sticky collapse the imago emerges. Most calls for responding to planetary breakdown are based on climate science or behavioural studies. They are all tidy outer affairs discussed in rooms. But the kind of shift needed to navigate times of collapse requires us to undergo a difficult inner change with our feet on the earth, to hold fast as a known world falls about us.

Looking back at these pieces I see they make certain shape, a pattern of opening and closing doors, a set of moves, leaving one way of life and forging another. I've called these moves *deep time journeys* because their direction of travel does not go forward, following the modernist story of progress, but downwards through different layers of time and place. These journeys intersect and overlap because this is a non-linear inquiry, how we learn language, how we dance and weave fabric, how people have practised culture for thousands of years.

Around that Uncivilisation fire the story repeated itself as its characters met different challenges in the forest, the way fairy tales always do. Their rhythm is how we remember the story. The story of how human beings change form, as one of the species who undergo transformation on this planet so life can continue.

So we remember our way home.

Charlotte Du Cann
Suffolk, December 2021

Contents

✦

The Kist

❦

'I like your story,' said the vicar, 'but I think you should forget about the myth.' In a church that doubles as a dance studio, I am packing up my costumes: a red coat, a turquoise jacket, a green shirt, a cook's apron, several wands of reeds and a teapot. I've just finished a performance called 'Divesting for Beginners', based on the Sumerian myth and Underworld journey of Inanna, Queen of Heaven and Earth.

It's late September, autumn equinox, in the town of Reading, a key moment in the ancient world, as the year goes into 'fall' and tips towards the dark.

The reeds in my hand are from the marshland where I live in East Anglia and the mythical reeds of the Tigris and the Euphrates; the teapot held a tea of flowers that we drank as we sat down with the audience in small circles and discussed the topic of divestment. What connects a 4000-year-old myth and the modern fossil fuel industry? we asked everyone. In Sumer, birthplace of the first Fertile Crescent civilisation, now the oil fields of Iraq, both these stories happen underground.

The myth follows the descent of Inanna, as she steps into the *kur*, the Underworld, in search of her sister Erishkigel; the fossil fuel is crude oil, that bubbles up from beneath the desert floor and now runs in (mostly invisible) pipelines across the world; the power that fuels every aspect of modern life and is a principal driver of climate change and the Hadean crises it brings in its wake.

The performance follows Inanna as she goes through the seven gates of the 'Great Below'; and also the track of my own life, as I begin my own 'divestment', the shedding of a high consumerist culture. At each gate we have to leave an aspect of our upperworld power behind.

It's a fairy tale turned upside down, a widdershins, Cinderella story.

But it is also a physical and imaginative encounter with the planet and the transformative forces that Inanna forgoes her privilege and authority to secure. I forgo my place in a city-based world to discover a relationship with the Earth, and with a self that has been suffocated for years, and is now waiting in the dark with the clock ticking.

The question we asked the audience, the question that begins this book is: how do we do that as ordinary people, in our actions, in our hearts, as individuals and together?

What kind of people do we need to become for the future to happen?

Entering the kur

The myths of the ancient world came to me during the last decade as an infrastructure, a way to underpin a *cultural* divestment as our civilisation enters a time of fall. Divestment is commonly understood as an activist campaign that pressures institutions to take their financial investments out of corporations, but the urgent task this book looks at is how we 'power-down' our own lives and ways of engaging in the world. The performance begins when I stop being a community activist and realise we cannot 're-set' our civilisation because its shiny stories of ascent were holding us in thrall. No matter how many articles I might write about the 'new narra-tive', how I might pile them up with scary data about ecological collapse or joyful community projects, something was trapping us in an unkind grip. Something wasn't getting through.

The myths took different shapes: they emerged as essays and work-shops and performances and took the form of a set of instructions, as powerdown revealed itself to be more a series of shifts of direction than a linear story. These moves take place in the Underworld because change needs to happen at a deep inner level to make any kind of effective change on the outside. This existential process was once integral to the ancient mysteries or initiations, which provided a core encounter with the forces of life. They happened in caves and kivas, in the dark, at key times of the year, like the Eleusinian Mysteries at this equinox, and often at adolescence.

This descent however is for the grown-ups. Inanna is no ingenue: she is both lover and mother, who in her youth outwitted the god of Wisdom and procured the *Me* (attributes of civilisation) she wears at the outset of the tale. She knows however that some part of her essence is missing, some depth, some meaning without which she is not whole within herself, or for her people. Inanna goes to find that part buried beneath the walls of the new civilisation of Sumer. She can hear her dark sister bellowing, and knows somehow she is responsible for her wrath and suffering. When Inanna finds her, Erishkigel puts her bright sister's naked body on a hook.

One of the reasons it is hard to face the hard truths about the climate crisis is because we lack any story that can help us see and feel its urgency: there are almost no imaginary or real life stories about powerdown in our culture. There are plenty of success-through-adversity stories, hero stories, princess stories. You could say there is success in the Inanna story, as she is rescued by her back-up team and is restored to the Upperworld. But it is her downward path that grabs us now as we hear sounds of lamentation all around us for which we are accountable. Because here is a figure who deliberately divests herself of power, not knowing either the territory she enters, or the outcome of her passage. And somewhere in the bones of ourselves we know this is a key to our future: we don't know the outcome of the play. Or whether backup will arrive. We go in anyway. Something is pulling us. It's time.

Among the reeds and on the mountain

On a mountain in Wales in the teeming rain, five of us sit on hay bales in a yurt tightly-packed with people, dressed in men's black suits and bowler hats. One of us has a pack of cards up his sleeve, another an African folk tale, another a guitar and a love song by Nick Drake from the 1970s. I have oak leaves in my hatband to signify I carry an instruction circa 600 BC from the Sibyl who once guarded the door to the Underworld in the Campi Flegrei outside Naples. The Cumaean Sibyl, one of several in the ancient world, is a link to the pre-patriarchal 'uncivilised' world in a time of autocratic gods. She guides a lineage of poets to the territory under the volcano where all creative transformations take place: Virgil, Dante, T.S. Eliot, Mary Shelley, Sylvia Plath.

Refusing to submit to Apollo, she has been denied immortal youth by the solar god and her unviolated body is kept in a jar, becoming smaller and more desiccated by the centuries.

Now only her voice is left for us to follow.

Dougie stands up and invites the audience to take part in a demonstration of two figures from that ancient world: one is Chronos, the embodiment of the inexorable march of linear time; the other a young man with a lock of hair over his forehead, who intervenes and interrupts his passage. His name is Kairos, and sometimes 'Possibility'.

We're giving a performance called 'Testaments of Deep Time' to introduce a creative project called Dark Mountain, itself an 'uncivilised' intervention into the linear narrative of ecological and social calamity. During the last decade we have all stumbled upon it in similar ways, in tents on mountains, around fires, in the inner caldera of ourselves.

'Cracks in the narrative have begun to appear,' I tell the audience, as the thunder claps above us and the wind whips through the thorn trees. 'Through these cracks in time, archaic, indigenous knowledge, hidden by empires, has begun to slip through. Glimpses of another future are revealing themselves.'

Kairos is their messenger.

The fleet boy is not a god but a daemon. When he enters the room, the winds of heaven blow through your house, throwing your desk papers into the air. Startled, you look outside the window and feel the enclosing walls around you. You find yourself in time's prison. He crosses your path at strategic points, a young man with a lock of hair over his forehead, interrupting a line made by the old timelord Chronos with his relentless ticking clock and calendars. You stop, and time opens up, revealing past, present and future all at once. Suddenly you realise you can take a different direction.

Like all daemons, embodiments of the human condition, Kairos, the force of destiny arrives in a moment of crisis, unexpected. His moment of appearance is quick and you have to seize him by the forelock. If you hesitate, the time for that split-second all-moments-now encounter will be gone. You will lunge to grab him from behind, but your hands will slide down the back of his smooth shaven neck. You will fall back into linear time. Afterwards you have to make time to realise what has happened and integrate that all-at-once moment into everyday life. When Kairos enters our Chronos-ruled civilisation, the official story of progress, by which our worth is measured, is shown to bear false promise, you realise there is a place outside the house of history and a road that leads to nowhere we have gone before, yet feels like home.

For the last 17 years I have made my home beside a slow, salty river in East Anglia, gathering the strands of a lexicon that might make some kind of guide to the 'forgotten' mythic language human beings speak. It is a work of memory that was not transmitted by anyone or any lineage but I had to forge myself, with my companions on the road, from a set of practices I developed with my partner Mark, in glimpses from my own inner archaeology. It did not rush but came like this river, slowly over time, with the salt of the sea, with the steely patience of the heron who stands at its bank. A place of bird hides, and whispering reeds that boom in the spring, and cry with curlew and geese, a big sky, its grammar arising like a flash of silver fish in the water, needing me to dive and seize the moment of clarity.

This is a Kairos book, that sets out to capture and explore these moments and this lexicon in a time when the world itself appears to be unravelling. A time when I set out as a writer to document what happens when you follow the Sibyl's voice and step through the cracks in the conventional narrative. It records not the big moments of a linear life, but the small quicksilver ones that make you change direction: moments of a soul life, the encounters that change everything, that tell us what we are doing here, the work we need to accomplish within what was once understood as destiny.

The shape of this book follows the four Underworld tasks of Psyche from the Roman myth of Cupid and Psyche. Her name means soul and butterfly, both of which need to undergo radical change, from being a devouring creature to becoming another creature entirely – a winged pollinator for the world. Psyche is a human girl but the instructor in her quest is the goddess Venus, who in ancient Sumer is also Inanna.

Each section uses the structure of these four tasks to explore a journey of divestment I began after I left England to travel in 1991: what I had to leave behind, how I had to re-engage with the human world on my return, what the gods showed me and what the ancestors require us to do in these times of unravelling, chaos and loss. What moves we need to make as Chronos tightens his grip.

Sacred run

'Can we speak with you for a moment?' asked the girl with blond hair sitting at the table outside the Betsey Trotwood. It's midwinter and we have been at a book launch at the literature house Free Word in Clerkenwell. 'We loved the way you started your talk about being a know-it-all journalist in London when you were 35. We're 35!'

I looked at them, two young city women, smart, sassy, with sharp tailoring and a curiosity that could not be satisfied by the whirling world of Farringdon Road. I realised I was talking to myself 25 years ago. 'You have to go!' I laughed. 'You won't regret it.'

Twenty five years ago I had interviewed a Native American activist called Dennis Banks. He was running to the USSR with a band of young warriors to deliver a message of peace. I had persuaded the news desk it was a good story. By a poisoned lake in Milton Keynes, a man called Mark I had just become friends with was singing at a gathering for the warriors. As the band began an Irish ballad about transportees. I advanced towards the makeshift press office.

'Why are you running?' I asked the chief runner.

'I run to remind the world the eagle is still the eagle and the owl is still the owl,' he told me.

'Does the world want to know?' I asked.

He looked at me, French designer jacket, Japanese tape recorder, London attitude.

'It doesn't matter who gets the message,' he replied. 'What matters is that the message is delivered.' 'Well,' I said. '*Thousands* of people will read this tomorrow.'

But as it turned out they didn't. The photographer didn't find a good shot, so the story was never published. But I got the message anyway. Six months later I was on the road to Mexico. With Mark.

A year later, after the Sacred Run, the Berlin wall fell.

At some point all our empires end. The ones that hold dominion inside us, the corporate machine that strides the Earth, the parts we play to keep it going. The encounter seemed a small thing at the time. But it wasn't. It changed my whole world.

Shift

There is a small hexagonal space in the Natural History museum in Oxford in the rocks and minerals department. When you step inside it is entirely dark, except for the glow coming from several crystalline chunks in a psychedelic host of colours. In front of you there is a switch. When you flick it something extraordinary happens: a different set of colours lights up. The minerals emit fluorescent light according to the wavelengths of UV light they are exposed to. The switch changes the frequency.

In the dark of the Free Word theatre I am flashing up coloured images from two books published by the Dark Mountain Project. Twenty five years after I left working for fashion magazines in the 1980s, I have become an art editor for this small 'uncivilised' publishing house. *What is this man in a suit doing on a raft on a Swedish lake?* I am asking the audience. *Why is this woman's face covered in a mask made from heritage wheat?*

The images are modern but they are also archaic, rough, made from riverwood, roadkill and storm debris. Glaciers in Pataonia are juxtaposed with broken glass in Walthamstow, the rain on a cherry tree in a gale on the Ligurian coast and a red door leading to a curious wooden house in the Hampshire woods. They are paying attention in places where we do not, stopping the world so we can see inside its workings, so we can see what lies outside the city walls.

Art is like a strange attractor, I am telling the audience, that breaks a limit cycle and brings chaos into play. When it comes to climate change we can talk about sustainability and resilience and finding A New Narrative. We can discuss environmental and social justice – but still we are at the same table moving pieces on a chessboard in a losing game. The new story turns out to be the old story only with different vocabulary.

Sometimes though the barbarians come to the city and appear on the edge of our civilised lives with a message.

Sometimes that barbarian is you.

Divestment

In 1990 my life changed direction when I met a Native American activist. What I learned from Dennis Banks in that Kairos moment was that unless I had a land to belong to I would not have a message worth delivering. To find that territory I had to become a different kind of person, operating on another wavelength. When I later stumbled upon a lecture about Aboriginal dreamtime in California, I found that the mystery of life on Earth can be found in our ordinary dreams. When I met a road protester called Heather in Oxford, I discovered that the medicine of plants can be found in the weeds that grow outside your door, that there is living consciousness in every tree and flower.

Each of these encounters blew the dimensions of my small world open. Each meeting sparked something alight in me. But the question remained: how do we flick the switch in the dark room as a collective? How do we change the frequency, so that the low hostile hum of Empire is turned off and different parts of ourselves are lighted up?

How can we move the conversation away from the game on the table to feel the currents of the Underworld below our feet, to hear the spirit birds above our heads, when we are boxed in by language, by class, by prejudice, by untempered inner forces, when only the lucky and the rich hold the microphone and most of us feel dumbstruck?

But if we remember we are the People in the same way the eagle is the Eagle, and the owl is the Owl, then it matters that we keep delivering that message come what may. The untempered forces are strong because they are encouraged to prevent people from saying what they really feel, what we know in the core of ourselves to be true about the Earth, about social justice, about freedom, that human beings are meant to radically undergo change in their lives.

The uneasy chair

There is a writing class I have taught in these years called The Uneasy Chair. The Uneasy Chair is not about being a writer, but about writing as an existential practice, as a way of perceiving the world and our place in it, about putting our feet on the Earth, involving collaboration and time and imagination. I could say my whole life has been about sitting, or avoiding sitting, in this chair, which is the paradox position all writers have to put themselves in in order to find their true material. You don't want to sit there of course, but you don't get the story if you don't. This is the dual position where you sit in the chair and experience everything going down in the room, and also stand behind the chair, directing and making sense of what you-in-the-chair are experiencing. All chair position, and you lose the plot, all observer, and you lose the reader.

In 2020 when the pandemic appeared, the lockdown interrupted our lives like a *kōan* and discombobulated time. It began a process past seekers might recognise as alchemy, not of the individual soul, but of the collective. We were hemmed in in small spaces, like battery hens, but felt more connected to the people and planet outside the door than ever before, to the birds and the mountains showing their snowy faces for the first time in decades. The more we were held tight in our crucibles, the more our imagination reached out, the more we remembered, the more we reached out to touch others in our longing. The paradox of the hermitage and monk's cell. Of not moving and yet moving.

The old gods and governments do not want us to sit on this uneasy chair, to consider this paradox, to reach out to our fellows in what social theorist Jeremy Rifkin calls the shift towards an empathic civilisation, where we become biospheric, in tune with the planet and all its denizens. When the individualist 'psychological' dynamic of the 20th century cedes to the 'dramaturgical' age of the 21st, we are able to step into another's shoes and feel their joy and suffering because we have not denied our own. But, no matter how strong the oligarchic resistance to this shift, we have stepped into those roles already, seeing ourselves as players within a global tragedy, whose small scenes were enacted each day on screen in our kitchen-sink theatres. The chorus and spear carriers, all who stood in the wings, had taken the stage. We cheered them from the balconies.

Once you have seen, you cannot unsee. Once you have sat with the trouble on that uneasy chair, you can see what lies outside the door. You remember how it feels not to be alone, even when you were alone.

Nothing will unseat you then. The unstoppable power of transformation is what Kairos brings to your attention, what Inanna goes through the seven doors of the kur in search of, the gift Psyche brings from Persephone, when she emerges from the Underworld, the switch we hold out for inside, hearts beating, as our new colours unfurl.

I

SEEDS

After Ithaca

❧

I am standing in front of a wall covered with small yellow notes. There are connections between the names of people and places and myths on those pieces of paper that I keep moving around – like suspects in a crime drama. Only I am not sure if I am the detective or the murdered girl here. Or maybe I am both.

The window is open and a fresh breeze blows in. Here I am, living in a damp cottage on the edge of the kingdom, having travelled for a decade and stopped, having worked for a further decade and neglected this case. The sea bounces like a silver mirror on the horizon beyond the marsh. Why even look for links between these names? Because they tug at me. Something is missing and I know if I don't solve these connections, I won't be able to sleep.

Underneath every case you can find a buried woman. I don't know if we need another story about how she got there with her throat slit, abandoned in a city skip, buried with her face down, her skull adorned with mammoth teeth and hemp seeds.

Maybe I'm looking for myself, or part of myself, hidden from view, no story from my empire world, or psychology can reveal to me.

What is clear is that there needs to be a search, a kind of archeology, for the pieces that lie missing beneath the storyline, like the sherds of a pot.

In the cities that lie beyond this house, there is a clamour for a new story to make sense of a world that is falling apart. But maybe what we need is not a new story with a beginning, middle and happy-ever-after end, but an ancient curvy one hidden beneath our feet. One that can give us instruction at a time of calamity. That can show us how to make moves in a culture that has become rigid and stuck.

Psyche

In a time when the story falters, the golden story of human promise and progress, the myth reveals itself, like broken bones in a midden. For the last decade I have been unearthing them to see what they can tell us about our obligations to the Earth that succours us. Not the aspiring hero myths that bring glory to civilisations but the downward ones that connect us with the non-linear forces of the planet: Kairos who brings the intervention that cracks open our small worlds of time; Inanna who takes us down through the seven gates of the Underworld; the hamstrung Wayland who waits, slowly crafting his swan wings that will allow him to escape captivity; Ariadne who shows us the labyrinth is not a prison but a dancing floor.

But as the world falters, one myth emerges. Not the tales of gods and glory but an upside down Cinderella story of a human girl and her struggle with the alchemical forces of love, beauty and justice. Her name Psyche means soul or butterfly, the creature that transforms itself from caterpillar to imago in the hermetic space of a cocoon.

Tasks are the stuff of a female initiatory process, sometimes called kitchen work, because the changes they demand take place amongst the ashes and pots and pans. Male initiatory quests depart on shining horses that head into the forest and the mountains; female initiations bow our heads, cut off our hands, put a cape of rushes or moss around our shoulders. We are forced to take off our princess dresses and challenged to sweep the floor before sundown. Either way, everyone goes downstairs.

The myth

The myth which holds these tasks is particular. It surfaces not in Homer, nor any of the Greek classical works, but as an inside story of a 'novel' written by the Roman writer Apuleius in the second century AD as the Roman Empire was ceding its earthy pagan structures to a rootless Christian story. The love story of Psyche and Eros lies at the heart of *The Golden Ass* (originally titled *Metamorphoses*) and is told by an old woman to give courage and strength to a younger one. And inside the metamorphic tale, like the final Russian doll inside its layers, you find the four tasks that Psyche is set by Eros's mother, the goddess Venus.

The tasks, the kernel of that story, are part of an older mystery story, here hidden by the Berber storyteller, an initiate of the star goddess Isis. But deeper still lies a more ancient earthy female initiation, embedded into the fabric of the tale.

So the search begins here: not at the start of the story related by the old bandit woman to her captive, nor when the favourite daughter of the King agrees to be devoured by a dragon on the mountainside; nor when the beautiful Psyche falls in love with Eros and is betrayed by her elder sisters. But at the desertion of the human girl by her divine lover who has taken flight after she has disobeyed his instruction never to look upon his sleeping face. Distraught, Psyche pleads with his mother to restore her to the god she has fallen in love with. Venus gives her four tasks, each one more challenging than the next. If you succeed, she tells her, I will reconsider my verdict.

Psyche has to undergo change to earn the love of the winged boy she has lost. This love is not given freely, even to the most beautiful girl in the world. The mystery of metamorphosis lives underground, in the dark, and to learn the deal we have with life, to be symbiotic with the Earth, rather than a parasite on its bounty, we have to undertake that journey into the place some call the Underworld.

The first task Psyche is set is to sort a vast pile of grains and pulses. These are the seeds that have sustained civilisations for millennia: chickpea, lentil, poppy. Psyche is a foolish girl. She is beautiful but she knows nothing about life or love. We are the most technologically advanced culture in history but we know nothing about obligation or relationship with anything apart from ourselves. I have been a food editor in one of the most sophisticated cities in the world but knew nothing about industrial farming or the seeds that now grow outside my window in the arable district of Britain: wheat, barley, field bean.

These myths from the ancient world ran alongside civilisations for thousands of years. Like the Ancient Pueblo culture of the South West, they housed a spiritual relationship with the corn and pulses that sustained them. And with a tiny flower seed that reminds us how we must go underground, and die to the husks of our former lives, before we discover the kernel of life inside.

In each of the four tasks Psyche is helped by a small voice that speaks to her as she despairs of completing them. My sisters can help you, a kindly ant whispers in her ear, and the colony sorts the jumbled seeds into piles. A swaying reed offers her advice, an eagle battles dragons on her behalf. When Venus gives her a box to take to Persephone, Queen of the Dead, and bring it back unopened, a stone tower tells her how to undertake the perilous journey. How the rules of the Underworld are not the same as those that hold sway in the upperworld, where good looks and privilege count for everything.

The long descent

No one likes to go down. No one wants to be humble. When I endure my own downturn after years of freewheeling travel, I have to learn to love the dun colours of East Anglia and no longer yearn for the turquoise *cenotes* of the Yucatan, or the roar of the Pacific Ocean. I will have to open my eyes to the realities of an unravelling planet. This was the world, this was life at the end of Empire, the thing we thought could not happen. I would no longer be a person who could be smart and clever at parties. I will wear a sec-ond-hand coat, and work very hard to make myself at home in a country where I no longer have any value. When I speak of descent in response to these ecological crises, people will tell me 'we will be ascended and pow-erful in other ways'. No, I reply, we all have to go down.

Dale Pendell, the great plant metaphysician, once wrote that the opium poppy affected the brain in such a way that it enlarged the imagi-nation and brought visions of palaces and cities of splendour. Without the poppy, you were bereft of access to these glittering places and felt their absence keenly. I am bereft of access to places and people I once loved. But I know this loss is part of the payback, the great sobriety, the pivotal act of relinquishment in the work to stay this unravelling, known as Deep Adaptation: 'what we need to let go of that is making the crisis worse'.

The Underworld is where you come up against the consequences of your actions, not only as an individual but as a citizen. The decision to give up the attributes of civilisation is a hard, hard task. Not only in the physical world, but in terms of our perceived greatness, our reputation, our sense of agency, our immense privilege that can only come at the cost of violence to the Earth, its creatures and to populations of people we never have to care about.

We hesitate at the banks of the great Styx, where the sterile willow trees lay down their branches, avoiding the baleful eye of Charon. But we hold a box in our hands, two coins in our mouth, and barley cakes to deceive the three-headed hound of Hades.

How much does it cost to know the love of the Earth?

When Psyche opens the box and dies, Eros, the primordial creator of the universe, raises her up. When the year turns, the sun returns, the seeds burst open their casing. The women rise up out of the Underworld. The world starts again.

One answer I have searched for in these years: anyone can fall into the Underworld but who can tell us how to return?

Venus

This is not a love story, nor a family story, the stories that underpin most Western literature, but a story about undergoing change. It's about the tasks given to a girl who knows nothing, so she encounters the deal you make with life, and how you earn love if you pass the test. It is about a relationship between two female beings: one an ingenue who knows nothing and one who knows everything. The instructor is not the wise La Que Sabe, the bone-collector of fairy tales whose territory is the desert, nor the wild demanding Baba Yuga of the northern forests, but an alchemical goddess, the goddess of love and beauty whose husband is the smith Vulcan, though she sleeps with other gods. Eros her son, was fathered, it is said, by Mars, the god of war. But others say his roseate fast-spinning wings were bequeathed to him by Venus' other lover, her fellow alchemist, Mercury.

The territory of change is a geography never taught us by our teachers and families, who follow the roadmaps of obedience and tradition (and their counter actions, rebellion). The alchemical territory is where the base of yourself and your relationship with life is radically altered because you have agreed to become a different kind of human being. To suffer, as the mystic philosopher Gurdjieff once said, consciously. To change in this way you have to recognise you are working with materials that need refining – to undergo an inner process, symbolised by the transformation of lead into gold. To start you have to agree you cannot evolve unless you do the work. Human beings have to agree to evolve themselves, either because they belong to a culture that recognises the necessity, or because their individual soul pushes them towards such an undertaking. The latter, which is the normal route for people living in industrialised, individualistic societies, is a rocky road.

The purpose of the myth is to complete the tasks, or to go through the seven doors of the kur, or to bring back the fire in the skull to your dark sisters. Whatever tale you follow, work is required.

Eros's wings touch you when you are young and romantic, full of lightness and possibility, then as age sours you and brings your feet into land, that fleeting moment goes and he departs. Alchemy brings the boy back into your life but not in the way you might imagine. To become a butterfly, to return to that lightness, you have, like Psyche, to undertake the tasks that demand courage and fortitude and openness to instruction, to learn from your heartbreak and small failures. The myth acts as a crucible for that kind of soul change in a time when such transformations are not admitted.

All archaic and Indigenous peoples have these forms of change embedded in their cultures, to break childish ties with family, to break open a fixed sense of self, to reveal the cosmic nature of life on this Earth, and what it demands in return. Their myths and prophecies remind them that there are consequences to not honouring life. And in these years, when I have been recording the cases on yellow paper on that wall, a litany of catastrophic consequences now surrounds them: climate change and deforestation, fires and floods, extinctions and a host of biblical plagues and locusts that currently beleaguer us.

The deal

The seeds Venus asks Psyche to sort before sundown are the ones that can be found inside the ruined larders of every civilisation, in the Fertile Crescent, across Europe, and now stored in vast silos across the world. Civilisations are dependent on these cultivated seeds. But when we sit down to eat bread or drink beer, hummus and dal, we do not see the arable fields that fostered them that now lie under flood water, drenched with fossil-fuelled pesticides and fertiliser. We have forgotten our original deal with the plants and the soil in which they are grown. We do not even recognise their green and golden forms, staggering under the summer heat, as our cars from the city speed by.

As agriculture advanced out of the Neolithic age, we knew we would lose sight of our contract with the Earth, unless we made reparation and rituals that still honoured the wild nonlinear planet. And for a long time, up to the time *Metamorphoses* was written, the mystery schools ran alongside the empires of the ancient world to remind its citizens of those obligations. Unlike the democracies on which Western governments are founded, they were open to everyone: to foreigners, to slaves, to women. Their initiations were not for the benefit of the state but to tend to the business of being alive and to the meaning of our brief human lives together on this Earth.

Ah, you might say, but these schools are all gone now. We have forgotten. Listen, you don't need a mystery school to go into the Underworld, or to converse with chthonic gods. The stories are still here, like a map we trace with a nervous index finger, and then feel impelled to follow. And the writers are still here, reminding us, sometimes annoyingly, of our contract with the wild world. It is the writers who know you need the structure of a story in your hands, as you advance to the gates of Hades and face the threshing of the Underworld – a grinding process in which you lose or die to your tough conditioned husk and discover the germ within. The germination of the seed is the core of every spiritual practice and encounter. It is a metaphor for soul work, and it is also the physical seed itself: without these seeds, embedded in grain-based civilisations as we are, we perish. A deep relationship with these seeds remembers us: who we are as a people, and our place on the planet as a species.

These stories delve into deep time and put us back in touch with the shapes of the world when we were still kin to its breathing, with its cave paintings and kiva, longhouse and tumulus, the spirals on stones across the world. They lie hidden at our feet, in myths that break up our linear moment and stretch it outwards in all directions.

But mostly they take us down into the dark.

Our 200-year-old industrial civilisation wants to keep the lights on, but millenia-old cultures don't think like that. Because they know that dark matter is the primordial stuff of the universe, and this world of appearances is a brief moment in time. The dark is where everything is born, animal and human, where seeds burst their casings before they emerge in spring. This is what the seed mysteries tell us – the corn and the beans of the Hopi mesas, the barley of the Eleusinian mysteries, the wheat stalk in the solar chamber in Newgrange in Ireland.

Underneath the patriarchy, another body of knowledge remains that we sometimes unearth, like the Gaelic female poets buried face down, or women buried with hemp seeds and horses, swords and coloured skirts, on the far steppes of the North. We find it hidden, sometimes like this story, the kernel of the Roman writer's novel, disguised as a fairy tale.

Apuleius depicts the goddess as a hussy and her son a naughty rosy-cheeked boy, but we know that this is a clever device: Apuleius, an initiate of many schools, is hiding a phial of quicksilver inside a ribald tale. Venus is a planetary force and Eros is the primal creator, sprung from a silver egg at the beginning of time, who sets the universe in order. So she is not the shrewish mother-in-law, but the matrix of a dynamic between these stellar forces and the human Psyche.

Venus knows being beautiful is not enough, being high-born and a daddy's darling is not enough, there is no beauty of soul unless it is transformed. You need to open the kist and find the ledgers on which are written what you need to look at, your lineage, your nation, the legacy of being human in an industrial empire and learn how to put a crooked thing straight.

Can we break out of our individualism and listen to instruction about how to sort the seeds, how to honour the animals and the spring, how to enter and return from the Underworld? Can we resist the plaintive pleas of the souls of the Underworld, and steer our own passage? Can we take the coins into our mouths to pay Charon and the barley cakes for the three-headed hound of Hades? And can we then, finally do what every female being does in their infinite curiosity, disobey the order from our elders and betters, and open the box?

You need a strong memory and imagination to undertake these tasks, neither of which are ever encouraged by the village, city neighbourhood or nation state you find yourself in. We live in superficial times. The tasks ahead are all about depth and return. The older and more fixed you are the harder it is to fulfil them, but the richer and more rewarding also. When you are younger you feel you have more to lose, but when you are older, you lack desire and feel you have lived your life already. Either way, it is tough. Either way, it's not just about you. You don't do the work for just you. That is what gives you strength, what stops you from despairing, staring down from the cliffs into the foaming sea, or into the obsidian waters of the Styx.

You engage in these tasks to cohere the fragmentation of the collective you see and feel all around – its broken heart, its confused mind, its twisted and enraged will. You do it to remember what was once called Original Instruction, the right way to engage with earthly life. You do it for the luminous planet that hosts you.

The work is exacting and challenging and can give you every shred of meaning you might have longed for in a world that has lost its way, but it comes at a high cost: the loss of a self you and everyone you know once knew.

My own search took me to many places on Earth, into inner and mythic landscapes, far away from everything I had once known and loved. But as I found out, this journey is not about going out or away. It is all about coming back.

Return

The Nostoi were the ones who returned from the ten year siege of Troy. It took another ten years for the commanders to find their way back to their homelands. Most of these returns were calamitous. The last of these was the fabled return of Odysseus to Ithaca, his island kingdom, which marked the end of the second and arguably most famous piece of Western literature, Homer's *Odyssey*. It also marked the end of the hero cycle and the mythic structure that made sense of people's lives in the ancient world. His journey across the seas is a farewell to the fabled creatures, sorceresses and monsters who lived in a string of islands across the Aegean. Odysseus is killed by his son who does not recognise him through his disguise. Afterwards history took the place of the mythic world he seemingly vanquished but we live with the legacy of the hero – half man, half god – famous for his cunning, his outwitting of dangerous creatures and for his wife Penelope, who waited patiently for his return for a decade.

So this search, this inquiry, begins here at the death of the heroes, in a time which still worships them as Olympic champions, as garlanded laureates, as crowned victors of parliaments and battlefields. The restless and clever leaders, with their patient wives, their doubting sons, are still the figures who fascinate us. The Greek heroes were destroyed by Zeus and his pantheon because they weighed too heavily on the Earth. The Trojan war was waged for the gods' amusement. Because gods like to be amused. It is their cruel and heartless nature that we mimic in all the high and bellicose places.

But the gods were not there at the start of things, as most creation myths will tell you. There were other forces that formed the *terra* beneath our feet. The gods were keepers not creators of life, though they liked to pretend they were. In a time of return, you have to go back to another order to start again. We do so not because there are wives waiting for us, or because the war is over, or because we are great poets laying down tracks that all writers will follow. We do so because of an ancient obligation that gnaws at our hearts, like a little mouse.

Somewhere we know Ithaca was not the end because it was not the beginning.

This casebook fell open with the morning star rising outside my window before dawn, the time Mexicans call *la madrugada*. The planet shone bright and behind her the tiny speck of the star Spica, the grain of the constellation Virgo, a celestial body once considered beneficent in the days people looked into the heavens for guidance. I couldn't sleep so I got up and looked out at the light that shone through my yellow curtains. Venus appeared above the oak trees in the lane and beneath her a crescent moon the colour of tangerines that hung like a boat above the sea. It was cold, almost December. I had not written in a long time – but looking in the luminous sky I suddenly felt I had no choice.

Fava

❧

Here is the story of the first task in a pea pod, the story that is not yet told. Psyche goes to the island each summer, lured by Eros. Eros leaves her in the white house with the lemon tree. Inside the stone room it is dark. The sea is blue, he tells her, the wine is rough, the sky is hot. Some years, she stays with her sister when he is no longer around. In the long hot afternoons the curtain blows out and in, and she watches it, feeling the vastness of the stones the wind blows over beyond the small window: the brightness and the sea that wrinkles like a piece of material, this ancient inky sea. There is a table and a chair in the room, a jug of water and the skull of a horse by the door. The wind is blue, Eros writes from the mainland, and the sea is rough.

Yanuklari comes to visit after he has returned from the stony fields. *Area* is one word she knows in Greek. *Poli area.* Big wind. He smiles and raises his glass. *Whiskaiki.* Small whisky. The young girl and the old man sit together in the dark limewashed house, with an oil lamp burning and the wind outside. The *melteme*, the north wind that presages the end of summer and the beginning of autumn, is howling in the chimney. All the visitors have departed the island now, only she is left. When she goes this time she will not return. She will stand on the boat and wave the island goodbye until it becomes a dark speck on the horizon.

And yet this place will remain with her all her life, the place of light and dryness. The place with the wells in the courtyard and the talking under the vine, the *clack clack clack* of the beads the men who do not smoke hold in their hands. It is a place she wanted to live in but cannot. It is not her destiny.

Throughout her life Psyche will feel abandoned by people, or forced to leave places she loves – but the truth of the matter is more complex. People took her to places and then left her to work out what she was doing there. Often it does not occur to her until later that she was on a return mission.

31

What she does not know at this point is that Eros will not return in the form she once knew him, as the boy with the spear among the dark rocks, appearing as he did there, laughing, a line of fish around his waist, an octopus in his hand. It is as if his territory were broken into a thousand pieces and she had to collect them all, in the small moments in the decades that followed. The lightness of the sky will fade and the depths of the indigo sea become shallow. For ten years she will be yoked to a life in the city, cataloguing the shifts of markets and dressing rooms; for another ten, on the road, in search of desert places and high mountains; and yet another forging grace in a time of fall. The light of the Aegean will be dimmed, the doors that were once open will slam shut and she will be forced to remake and remember these things inside her.

Here is our story, my story and yours in ways we do not know yet.

Terroir

You may ask why Greece, when my native land is neither dry nor light. Why at the beginning of things did the autumn wind, the time of departure, tug so powerfully inside me, in places I had no words for? Some territories pull you: they give you an entry point into the landscape that speaks to what people used to call the soul. Destiny or fate is a Greek concept, built into the vast mythological landscape of rock and sea that still existed, even in the 20th century, on this small Cycladic island. It was a direct encounter with forces that were both physical and metaphysical. It was mine and also not mine. The time of departure was also the mood of the late civilisation I was born into.

I chose this ancient Mediterranean myth (or did it choose itself?) because in the Western hemisphere everything in our educated minds comes from the classical world; our mathematics, our philosophy, our literature, our political debate. Our reason is underpinned by the *logos* of Athens, our laws and soldiery dictated by Rome. If you need to find the way out of a conundrum you need to go to the territory where it was forged. You use the *technê* of the master's house to get out of his house. Keep what is important and discard the rest.

Because the first lesson that caught my eye came from a book with a pink and green cover called *The Legends of Greece and Rome*. When I was eight years old I knew everything about Persephone and Zeus and Pan. So when I stepped off the boat into the bristly arms of the harbour master, it felt like coming home. Like coming out of the Underworld for a brief summer.

Because leaving was always a key move I was to make.

Island

Yanuklari had a herd of goats and here he is carrying the evening milk in a pail made of an old olive tin. Later he will sell us some of the fresh cheese he makes. For some reason I am transfixed by the ingenuity of this bright blue and green bucket with its carved wooden handle. Sometimes he comes round in the evenings with Yanuko, his burly friend with a wide Cretan-style moustache. Yanuko's big hands have fashioned the skin and horns of a goat into bagpipes which he plays ferociously so the walls shake. For some reason I have been given the drum to keep the rhythm. After several *whiskakis* and *ouzakis* we wend a Dionysian path down the stone steps towards the main village in the darkness. People wave and laugh as we enter. I don't notice that I am the only female being in the cafe.

One night we take our music to the threshing floor on a cliff top outside the village for the annual celebration of one of the island saints. It is a round plaza made of stones where the wheat and barley are trampled by the hooves of mules, and then tossed into the air, so the chaff is blown away by the salt wind. We drink a lot of rough pine-flavoured wine and dance around the circle, arms around each other's shoulders. The men wave white handkerchiefs, leap into the air and hiss like snakes.

Afterwards we fall asleep in a pile. I have never slept outside before and the stones are hard and unyielding. Just before dawn I see the priest and the singer in a doorway of golden candlelight, chanting in the small chapel, swinging a silver necklace fragrant with frankincense to and fro. The people of the village are sleeping, stacked like sheaves of corn under the stars.

When we wake the sky is blue, the sun is hot.

Larder

One year I came to the island in spring. There were few boats in those days and no harbour, so when the sea was very rough you had to disembark on the northern side of the island. Small fishing boats came and went from the anchored ferry and piled up people and suitcases, families coming home for the Easter celebrations, clutching orange peel to ward off sea sickness. Half-drenched we walked up the steep goat path to the village above, as the donkeys came down to collect luggage and supplies.

There was a different mood to the village when we arrived: there had been fasting for weeks and there was no food to be had in the one taverna. Famished after a ten hour boat ride, we went to the *kafeneon* and asked if there was anything we could buy to eat. Then a woman with a pale baby appeared at the door. The baby, her fifth child, was famous for never sleeping, and stared at us with her large sea-glass eyes. The women disappeared and then came back with two plates of *fava* – yellow split peas – with halved boiled eggs on top, and bread. She smiled and told us to eat. We fell on the food.

There are meals you have that are delicious, that are artfully cooked, feasts that remind you of places or people. But the food you eat for which you are truly grateful is the food that really matters, that sinks into the memory in a place you don't forget. The woman was from the poorest family on the island, and yet her instinct was to feed two hungry visitors, who were almost strangers. It was there that the germ of a different larder began. The yellow peas. The smile. The sleepless child. An island covered in daisies.

In the evenings I would watch the sun go down from the upper village. The women would sit in the doorsteps beside the basil plants, and a donkey raised its lament to the sapphire-coloured sky. They would talk to their neighbours as they sorted the rice, or beans or other pulses, discarding any small stones. Sometimes the women would tell stories that began: today is a yellow day.

Sometimes I woke to find a basket of grapes left on the doorstep.

The cooks

Into the post-war dining rooms they came, the travelling cooks, from the South of France, Alexandria and Rome: they brought with them the scent of the *marais* and harbour quays, and their paperback guides were soon to become stained with olive oil and red wine in the aspiring households of Northern cities. Their books liberated our pale and snobbish cuisines and made us all yearn for the sun. I learned to cook in their generous shade, visiting those fields and terraces in my imagination – and then one day when I was 20 I went there. The Mediterranean food I knew came from the painterly slopes of Provence or Tuscany – but Greece was a wild unknown, rocky, barbarian. It came with the odour of goat and salt fish.

Patience Grey writes her seminal cookbook, *Honey from A Weed*, following her husband, a sculptor, to the marble quarries of Tuscany, Catalonia, the Cyclades and Apulia. In Greece she lives on the island of Naxos, documenting the cycles of fasting and feasting in a culture that has not changed the way it harvests and eats since the Bronze Age. While the sculptor and quarry men sing and get drunk in old-fashioned piazzas and anarchist bars, around shepherds' fires in the hills, his wife observes how the women cook and gather, noticing how different woods are selected for each dish – apple wood, chestnut, dry sage cistus, lentisk, vine cuttings.

'The secret of cooking is the release of fragrance and the art of imparting it,' she writes and starts her treatise with a recipe for *soffrito*, the finely-chopped herbs and vegetables that underpin many of these dry, stony-land dishes.

Pulses form the staple diet in these places, especially in the lean months (which coincide with the time of religious fasting). The core cooking vessel, the earthenware two-handled *pignata* holds the beans or chickpeas, carefully simmered over four hours with hot peppers, tomatoes and garlic, ready for the return of the men from the fields. It is the details of the hearth and kitchen table that pull you in: 'The best frittata is made with wild asparagus shoots', she declares. 'The tomato paste only dries with the help of the North wind, and if the sirocco is blowing it is no good'.

She writes a whole chapter on collecting weeds in spring: the early shoots of thistles and daisies and mustards, picked before the flower heads formed to cleanse the body after winter. Dandelions are prized for their bitterness especially – the whole plant washed thoroughly in the village fountain, boiled then and eaten with lemon and olive oil.

Thus did an imaginal taproot described by these writer-cooks anchor a culture where food could be 'life restoring not just the satisfaction of appetite'. Food that galvanised not just our bodies but also our etiolated souls and connected us with an inheritance we shared across geographies in deep time.

The larder that formed the soffrito of my life began on the island: something became etched in my bones forever, in the technê of those earthenware pots, the dusty neighbourhood store with its bags of rice and flour, the spiny lemon trees, the lessons on how to chop an onion in your hands and prepare beans in a great tin to bake in the communal oven. The feeling of a place where everything was connected, hospitable, open.

'Whenever independence flowers, austerity and fellowship combine,' Grey wrote of her times among these tough Mediterranean and Aegean communities. When austere times return and the larder become bare, it feels necessary to remember the conviviality and rhythm of these ancient places, to search in our imaginations for these caches of corn and chickpeas, hidden in desert rocks, among the ruins of Babylonia, Turkey, Sumeria, Palestine and Greece.

One morning she went south with Eros and his companions in the blue caïque. They anchored for the night in a cove, where the first naked statue of Aphrodite was carved by the sculptor Praxiteles. The next morning at sunrise as the men lay sleeping below deck, Psyche steered the boat with her bare foot on the tiller out into the open sea, the dark rocks against the sky, dolphins leaping, following in their wake. She did not think the world would ever be more beautiful.

Ground state calibration

I look at my hands and they are holding a paper bag of dried brown beans, grown in East Anglia where I now live. The year is 2016 and I am introducing a discussion about the future of food at a summer gathering. The beans, I am telling the audience, are a magical ingredient. The foolish boy in the fairy tale plants a handful of coloured beans and his fortunes entirely reverse. Next to me are an activist called Molly Campbell who holds a bag of wild rice from Minnesota, and an artist called Anne-Marie Culhane a bag of heritage wheat grown in a community-sown field in Lincolnshire.

These hands once held dead hares and fish and fowl and now no longer do. These hands have written in these last ten grassroots years about a powerdown kitchen, about food that keeps the *navoti*, the spirit of life alive. Whenever I have stood up to speak in those years the shape of that island village I once loved would come to me with its intactness, the smile of the woman whose name I no longer remember. As we sat down at our community meals, learned again to bake bread, to ferment cabbage in

winter, to forage for wild leaves in spring, to eat a humble dish of gr.
I saw the caper flowers that grew between the stones, the fig tree by tι.
bridge. One day when a group of us set about the task of reimagining the
world, we drew maps of dishes we had brought to share for our supper,
listing the provenance of each of the ingredients. My own was fava. The
bowl of golden peas was sprinkled with olives I had bought from a Palestinian refugee in the city market, sliced red onions from a smallholding by
the coast, fresh eggs from a neighbourhood roadside stall, parsley from my
own garden.

When he chose to map inheritance, Mendel selected the humble pea
to work on in his monastery garden. He discovered one chromosome difference in their genetic make up made either yellow or green peas. When
we chose to map a new world that might arise from this old one, we looked
for the seeds that could give us resilience in hard times, that allow us to relinquish an old story, and most of all restore ourselves and the wrecked soil
of our homelands. The legume family of which fava, the yellow pea is one
member, is a key nitrogen fixer, which means it gives to the soil, rather than
depletes it. Just by being present it nourishes the land and all who crop it –
the four- and two-legged and the winged, who feed from its copious nectar.

The island was one of the most stripped-down places I ever visited,
and the most nourishing. There were no cars, few houses had electricity
and everyone drew water from wells and a communal spring. The diet was
rough and plain, archaic: vegetables and pulses, with meat and fish on feast
days – Easter kid, snails, sea urchins, octopus and bream. Food was dried
and stored on the rooftops of the white houses, the bread baked in a communal oven in the side of the hill. The people were largely self-sustaining,
their olive oil and thyme honey the most fragrant I would ever taste. It
was food with meaning, grown with roots that sank deep into the earth, in
time. The food of the cities, produced by industrial agriculture, has none
of this connection, neither with place nor people, nor the memory of the
heart. So we have needed to remake those links in our imaginations and
find another kind of provenance.

'These beans tell a different story, a Jack and the Beanstalk story,
about a boy who exchanges his mother's cow for a handful of beans that
reverse their fortune. These beans have been grown here since the Iron
Age and formed the staple diet of early agricultural people across Europe
to the Middle East.'

g the gathering how these beans have been returned into
rn production, followed by red, blue and black peas, then
ot in the Andes but in the flatlands of Essex), lentils,
barley and oats, where they would normally be imported,
nields that would normally host monocultural commodity crops
for the global market.

We spoke of moves by small farmers and co-operatives to return the land to its proper use, to put the tools of growing back into the people's hands, about land rights and fossil fuel dependence, and many of the counter-stories a regenerative food culture can bring to share at the table. Molly tells her story about helping the Ojibwe people harvest wild rice and prevent oil companies from destroying the Northern lakes where their heirloom food plant grows – and in South Dakota how she and others are working to bring back the buffalo to the prairies that once hosted millions of them. All the flowers start returning as they do, she says. The creatures hold all our stories, their hooves regenerate the land and the people.

Fava

When you recover yourself, you yearn for the simplicity of that white room, for those afternoons that once stretched out, a sense of the future that existed like the vast wrinkled sea beyond the island. To gain a right relationship with food means to regain a relationship with place, remember the part of ourselves that knows about seeds and earth and rain. Sometimes this memory is hidden away somewhere we don't want to go, down a path in time, that bites sharply like lemon and brings with it a pain to the heart.

In June the night is filled with the thundering of the pea harvesters, as the fields are stripped by vast machines, and the sweet green smell of crushed pods hangs in the dark warm air. I've taken to sleeping outside most nights in a tent under the greengage tree until the big frosts come. I like to feel the hard ground under my body, hear the sounds of birds above my head in the morning, their whirring of wings, the sound of the sea when the wind is in the east, the rise and fall of temperatures. The body holds a different story to the one we tell each other. Our hands know things our minds do not. You can pick up an axe and without being told, know how to chop wood, as you know how to knead dough, wrap the dead or hoist a sail. When I was 29 and ran away to Italy, a man placed an egg in my hands. It was warm and smooth. Listen! he said. *Tap tap tap*: a chick was pecking its way out of the shell into the unimagined vastness of the world. I had been wrapped up in myself, far away from Earth and suddenly I was looking into his eyes. 'I wanted to get through to you,' he said.

To break out of the small spaces we need an encounter with life, with the terra beneath our feet. When you put your hands back into the earth, you burst into laughter or tears, filled with feelings that have no name. Then those hands start to work: searching out roots, pushing seeds, pulling weeds, throwing out flints. Something happens when your hands take charge: something unsusceptible to the eye, that thunders inside you and breaks. You think it is your heart. But it's not. It's your isolation.

Can you sing praises to broad beans and yellow peas?

The Israeli poet Aharon Shabtai sings praises to cucumber and spring onions:

> *Times are bad. I take an oath of loyalty to the table*
> *coated with white Formica.*

His fellow countryman, the Palestinian poet, Mourid Boughati, advises us to speak of real things in these times, to hold everything dear. In a world steered by abstractions, by the high-flown rhetoric of Empire, to cherish the concrete with words is the radical act of writers and chroniclers. To acknowledge time and place, to engage in the physical breathing and growing world is radical. Cooking is radical. Tasting the fruit of the earth, knowing where it comes from and whose hands grew it.

I take a stack of peapods grown by Malcolm Pinder in his smallholding in Darsham and sit on the doorstep by the southernwood, and start shelling the peas into a small bowl. The evening sun is in my face. *Tack tack tack.*

Today is a red day.

The Tea Houses of Osaka

❦

*L*ondon 2001 Standing in a changing room in Kensington in cherry blossom time, I am wearing an outfit I once saw in a dream. It's an elegant jumpsuit made of crinkly dark grey material, the kind a fashionable extraterrestrial might wear, or a modern Joan of Arc. It fits my body like a glove. But when I look into the mirror I cannot find myself. It feels as though the dress is wearing me, and not the other way round.

This soft armour was created by the Japanese designer, Issey Miyake. When I was still working as a journalist in London at the end of the '80s, I was invited by Issey Miyake to visit Japan, along with other fashion editors from around the world. We arrived in Tokyo and were entertained like nobles on tour of a foreign kingdom. When we walked into clothes shops we were told to help ourselves. Special visits were arranged to red and gold temples. Beautiful meals were constructed in our honour: elaborate dishes based on the theme of autumn, adorned with small maple leaves and twigs. We were chauffeured in limousines, put on luxury trains and hosted in mountain lodges with paper windows and cedarwood baths.

One day in Osaka, I was asked who in Japan I wanted to speak with and when I hesitated, my host suggested I met the architect, Tadeo Ando.

I am visiting the architect who is making a theatre shaped like an egg in an old stock exchange in Paris. Yesterday I visited the bare church he built where the only light comes from a cross carved out of concrete. Something in that bareness pulled me. The lame priest explained to me that you do not need a show of wealth in a church because all the riches are in your mind.

But the architect is not at home. I am being shown instead a trio of tea houses he built for his own amusement in a side street. They are in a tiny house where he lets his student lodge.

The first is a tea house of stone, the second is a tea house of veneer and the third a tea house of glass. When you close their sliding doors, there

40

is nothing inside, except the materials of which the rooms are made.

'Because there is nothing', says his assistant, 'there is everything'. The third tea house is on the roof. As we climb up the stairs, one of the students clambers past us and quickly places a twig in a stone pot that sits for no apparent reason on the tiles.

It is evening and from up here you can see the commercial city merge into an industrial landscape that stretches all the way to Tokyo, 300 miles away. You cannot see the sinking sun. But the floor of the tea house has a red liquid underneath it, so when the white blinds are pulled down, you find yourself in a perfect square whose light is the colour of sunsets.

杰

In the conference on the future of fashion, Miyake talked about the Earth and the fabrics that are demanding such a high price from the natural world – realities which I had never considered when I sat down in front of my typewriter, or with my notebook alongside the catwalks of Milan or New York.

The Japanese relationship with materials is quite different from that of Europe. It has a rigorous abstract aesthetic that Miyake felt was being undermined by the coarser narrative and glamour of the West. This aesthetic you can encounter everywhere in Japan: from the simplicity of Zen gardens, to the innovative, elegant way parcels are wrapped, the reverence with which everyone sits underneath the cherry blossom at springtime. The Japanese are also phenomenal consumers of rainforest wood. Rayon, made from wood, is their principal fashion fabric.

One night in Kyoto, we went to a traditional restaurant to dine with a company of businessmen. We sat on the floor and behind each of us kneeled a geisha girl in her rigorous attire. Occasionally they would serve us food and pour out sake in perfect silence. Their stiff clothes and their painted faces and submissiveness made me feel uncomfortable. All the visitors exchanged glances with each other, not knowing quite how to respond to this part of our tour. I am remembering this moment, as I stand here in South Kensington in my fashion suit. As the cherry trees outside sprinkle the London pavements and lawns with pink and white blossom.

No one except a Japanese craftsmen could have created this suit. It is made from the material that made Miyake famous in the West. Only

41

Mario Fortuny in the 1920s had worked with this crinklecut fabric be-fore. Evening dresses that could be squeezed into a small shape in your hand, that never needed ironing, that always make you look like a million dollars. The material hugs the body instantly and lends your physical being a certain elegance and shape, making you shimmer in the metallic hues of gold, silver, copper, bronze, like a classical statue.

My dress was pewter-coloured, just like my dream. It fitted perfectly. It was not even very expensive. But as I looked at myself, I suddenly felt overcome with something I could not name. When would I wear such a garment? I thought.

It was then that I no longer found myself in the changing room: I was paused on a stair, held in a certain moment. It was the stairway of a grand hotel, and there was a dark man on the dining floor below. There was a place at a table set for me, and he was waiting. It was the moment when he saw me, would afterwards rise, greet me and allow me to sit down.

But I am not that woman. This dress was designed for someone who would serve a man, and whom a man would formally make a place for, as she descended the stair, shimmering in all her metallic colours, in all her jewels. There was an ancient agreement between them, except that I have never made it.

'It's beautiful,' I said to the shop assistant. 'But I am going to leave it.'

"It looked good on you,' she said simply.

'Yes,' I said, 'I know. But I don't have any occasion to wear it.'

That was the last time I tried on a fashionable garment. For years, I had worked in this world and known it in so many ways. And now suddenly it had lost all its meaning, all its allure.

Later I walked home through Holland Park. There was a peacock amongst the cherry trees and flowering camellias and as I walked by, he opened his glorious multi-coloured tail. There is such beauty in the world! I thought, and was filled with all the excitement of spring. When the pea-cock unfurls his tail, when the blossom of a tree appears at the end of a street, when you put on a new dress, you feel for a moment transcended.

There is a lot of power in that moment. It is a moment that millions of women fantasise about. That one moment of blossom, where the man is waiting, beholding you, finding you beautiful. Millions of dresses pour out of the factories all over the East to fulfil that one moment. The geisha mo-ment. Hundreds of rivers run with poisons, forests denuded, fertile land sucked dry, creatures destroyed. The moment is repeated again and again. Never quite reached, never lived out. Then the tail descends, the bloom fades, the dress doesn't fit, and you search for another, and then another.

I am not going to be in that moment.

Because beauty in a cage is not real beauty. It is a glamour, a moment where we are stuck and doomed eternally to repeat; beheld by another, but possessing no qualities of our own, except that we adorn and serve some business that is not ours to question.

In this world, no matter how beautiful you are on the outside, no matter how many dresses you wear, or how many times the man does or does not wait for you at the bottom of the stair, there is a price to pay and someday you will have to pay it. If you are smart you will pay this now. While you can. You will put your dress aside and think about the inside of your being, what treasures lie in your bones, what transformative power lies deep your cells.

Tea ceremony

It was only later I found out what those tea houses signified, when I met a Zen practioner called Valerie. She had gone to the Louvre one day and encountered a *raku* pottery bowl. 'I saw my own beauty in its imperfection,' she told me. 'In the West we are always chasing perfect images that are far away from us. For the Japanese everything is about remaining humble before nature. They are more interested in craft than art.'

The tea houses were a teaching tool but they also housed an intrinsic part of Japanese culture: the tea ceremony. Once an aristocratic art practiced by the nobles of Japan at the advent of Zen Buddhism in the 8th century, the ceremony became a way for monks to develop rigourous attention. The ritual was designed to focus on the aesthetic of the season: the changing colour of the raku bowls, the *ikebana* flower arrangement, the kōan offered for contemplation by the master of the tea house. You entered by a small door, to signify that you were entering a ritual space. In that space you sat and admired the polished impliments, followed a strict codification of actions and gesture: the whisking of the green macha tea: the thick one that is passed around in a bowl, the thin one that is shared later.

The families of the firekeepers who curate this 'Way of the Boiling Water' stretch back centuries. As you adopt the gestures of the tea ceremony, you align with the ancestors who also sat in this way, and with those who will follow you. It is a method of positioning yourself in time and space, with the teaching of the Way.

Because it is empty, it is full.

When Japanese fashion arrived in the 1980s it confounded the West, clothed as it had always been in narratives of hierarchy and privilege, and the colourful rebellions against them, the punk and street clothes, that were being played out on the catwalks at that time. Almost overnight, the desire for the princess ballgowns of Britain, American WASP raincoats and Italian power suits, was intercepted by the sober abstractly-tailored lines of Japanese design. Houses became emptied of chintz and clutter. Minimalism shaped the menus of city restaurants. These were the monochrome years, the years when less was more, when I interviewed Yohji Yamamoto in Paris and he told me: 'Black is the colour of hysteria'.

Maybe it was stepping into those tea rooms in Osaka that made me question why our Cinderella world so yearned to be filled with palaces and princes. Was it capitalism, or was it something else? How could I find that humble engagment with the fabric of life?

A year after I went to Japan, I began to empty my own rooms. I sold and gave away my black Japanese labels, my French *batterie de cuisine*, my Greek pottery, 3000 books, a whole apartment of objects, culled from the markets of the world. I began to unstory myself.

I would not write a fashion article again.

When the party is over

Norfolk 2007 'Would you like to try some pollen from the Himalyas?' the man in the kitchen asked.

Intrigued I took a small carved pipe into my hands.

'Let me introduce you to the Deva of Cannabis,' he says and lights the bowl. And though not a devotee of marijuana, I close my eyes, draw a deep breath and inhale the smoke of the burning flowers.

It was as if, in that precise moment, a force came out of the shadows and pushed us apart. The next thing I knew I was in the garden walking across the lawn. Everything in the shrubbery was shifting all around me, I could feel all the plants and trees breathing, moving closer, as if investigating my presence. I laughed and lost my balance. Behind me in a square of light there was a figure moving around to the 'music' in the house – words intoned by politicians, declaring the end of the planet with a forboding tone like large aeroplanes. The sound boomed out into the dark garden.

In front of me, I could hear sparks from a fire and the murmurings of invisible guests. It was during that time as I moved – it seemed to take an aeon – away from the house, toward the fire, that I remembered a young Indian drummer I once knew who had organised a music festival called the Ras Lila. The *ras lila* is a game organised by the *devas*, the demigods of India, for their amusement. Nothing matters in the ras lila, because everything goes round and round and nothing ever changes. It is the game that devas play with humans.

Some disappear into imaginary worlds when they smoke cannabis, others start talking like politicians, but however you respond, something in you has gone numb and no longer cares about your present circumstances. Here we are swirling in strange music, plants are shifting about us, feeling we are in the thick of the party. But the truth of the matter is we have been pushed far apart from one other. The sound of our stoned voices drones like aeroplanes.

It was the best party I had been to in years. There were fireworks and birthday cakes, speeches and poems and a film celebrating our hostess's 50 years that flickered against the faded wall of the Elizabethan house. It had been orchestrated by her husband, who had spent a lifetime conjuring photographs, fairs and travelling circuses. People who had travelled all over the country to come to the party were camping under the fruit trees in the garden beyond the fire.

As everything drew to a close I stood in the French windows and breathed in the night air, my bare feet feeling the cold stone of the floor. The sounds of farewell were echoing in the drive. Then I put down my empty glass on the table and left the house, moving through the dark garden towards the car where Mark and I were sleeping under the cherry trees. One by one the little tents in the orchard extinguished their lights, the voices in the house faded away, and there was just the starlight left, as I shifted my position on the car seat, under our coats, and heard the cry of peacocks in the dark.

That summer, when the party sailed into the view, like a liner with strings of coloured lights and a band playing, we were facing a complete financial crisis. 'Tonight,' I said to Mark, 'We will forget everything and just enjoy ourselves.' So we put on our best frocks and shirts and jumped into our scarlet car and set off.

At the hardest time she came, the Deva of Cannabis, like a fairy godmother and blunted the pain of that moment. Because we could, for a while, just be as magnificent and as beautiful and successful as everyone else at the party. Not wanting to see us suffer among the sculleries, the god-mother descends with her sparkling favours, her ballgowns, her charming princes, her golden slippers and silver wand. But she cannot help any of us in the real world, for she cannot help herself, deva such as she is.

At the age of 22, I was instructed by the editor of *Vogue* to always consider the sufferings of Our Reader – in one hand, a Hoover and in the other, a gin bottle.

'Tell her there is more to life than that,' she said.

So I did. I told the readers of glossy magazines where they could go, what they could wear, how they might remain forever young, forever beautiful. They might be prisoners of their circumstances, but in their fantasies they could travel around the world, own paintings and designer furniture, eat caviar. Life is just like a party! I said.

For a long time I could not understand why I had worked for so many years in this world of glamour, as a beauty editor, fashion editor, design editor, style editor: why so many of us, poured our lifeforce and creativity into an endless whirl of photographic shoots, interviews with designers, models and stars, cataloguing the latest whims of would-be princesses, all their frocks and fairycakes. And then I remembered Tommy Roberts and what he said about taste. *What is taste?* I had asked various arbiters of style, owners of grand and opulent properties. Tommy was once a designer of natty suits in the 60s when he was known as Mr Freedom but at that time had a shop under Centrepoint in London, full of brightly-coloured modern furniture.

'Taste is the Japanese room with one beautiful vase in the corner,' he told me. 'A lifetime of taking away makes that room. It's what you don't have that defines taste'.

To find your way out of the ras lila, you cannot be lured by its fascinating glamours. You do not resist its powers because you are innocent but because you know every trick of the trade and will not swerve in your task.

One thing I learned from those fashionable years: the devas are not the ancestors.

Going down the mountain

'We will have to grow down,' Mark said.

There were four of us on the mountain, gazing towards the sparkling blue bay of Santa Barbara, at the Californian resort shimmering before us. The glamorous town and the sail boats had grabbed all our attention. But the still presence of the ancestral Santa Ynez mountains behind us was stronger. It held us in its stern embrace and finally we looked away. On the mountain, it would have been easy to grow down, amongst the sage bushes and the hummingbirds. But could we do this when we awoke instead in beautiful Santa Barbara? When we awoke with the sound of peacocks under cherry trees and felt the tug of the ras lila in our veins? Oh, the show, the music, the laughter! We talked about that party for days. It hung about us and lingered, like a tune, a fragrance, an ache you cannot bear because it is gone, so you replay it endlessly in your mind.

We go to parties because we love parties, but if parties are the only thing what then, when we are left abandoned in the cold, outside the theatre, in the streets at night? Do we then fasten our coats and hurry home, carrying the intoxication of parties and theatres in our minds, wishing secretly for the next time and the next?

We do not like to grow down, for that is to forget the games of the gods, to leave the theatres and our sailing boats behind. It is to eat humble pie. It is to wear hempen cloth rather than the silken garb of peacocks and princesses, to eat the nourishing seeds of the hemp plant, rather than smoke its flowers.

To return means the escapes and distractions from our hard industrialised lives have to go, everything that numbs our feeling the heartlessness of a culture that only values money. It means you stand at the door and love everything the godmother brought that made that hard moment bearable – the glasses of wine, the beautiful dresses, the old scarlet car with its fine chrome lines – and then you let it all go. You allow your suffering to speak to you. You let the lines of life reorganise within your being on a summer's day and begin to live without the taste of theatres and shows in your veins.

Finding the door

London 2016 Years after that party, I went back to the place that gave me my first job in fashion journalism when the Japanese aesthetic was beginning to enter the marketplace. I stood in the Condé Nast board room with a glass of wine, surrounded by the women and men I had shared typewriters, taxis and parties with 30 years ago. Most had not left this elegant, glittering world. We were celebrating the memory of our former editor, Beatrix Miller, who had once instructed me on my duties toward Our Reader. I learned the tricks of my trade here one day when I was given the task of writing captions for the main fashion story. 'Miss Miller' sent me back to my desk, hour after painstaking hour, until they were perfect.

You have a duty to tell her there is more to life.

It's true: there is more to life than gin and housework. Just as there is also more to life than vintage champagne and houses where maids do the hoovering for you. More than Mozart and *Jerusalem* sung in your memory at St George's Hanover Square; more than the rayon and silk dresses I once praised in cleverly-stitched copy. These are lovely things, but they all come at a price, as every fairy story will tell you. And it's a price you have to pay one day (or your descendants will) – with your body, with your mind, in the part that was once called the soul.

Every descent myth tells us that to become a real people, we have to relinquish the self-obsessed material life we grasp and cling to, and radically change our ways. Somewhere we know this in our bones. Somewhere I knew this when I was writing those captions, when I entered the tea houses in Osaka. But to deconstruct a story you have to know first how it was conjured, the spell that keeps us there.

It takes a lifetime to live in that room.

After the memorial drinks party, I went into Oxford Street and was immersed in a sea of ordinary people. It was a big relief. Nothing in me wanted to go back through those glass doors.

Because that's the real duty of writers. Showing you the small door to the place that has everything because it has nothing.

Lilies

❧

*H*alesworth 2004 I am standing in the darkened theatre of a small town in East Anglia. It is five o'clock and I am alone. Outside the wind is howling and it is freezing cold. Snow has been falling all day and we had thought of cancelling the performance – but in the end we didn't.

I have been working for this theatre all winter. Bracing all kinds of cold weather to keep it open – the frigidity of neighbours, the chilliness of the local council – and now it looks as though things are turning around, that spring might be coming after all. I go to the lighting desk and switch on one of the spotlights and then stand in its beam on the stage.

It is a warehouse theatre with rough brick walls and seats for 200 people. As I face the shadowy rows, my voice booms out loud, breaking the silence: *When the Blue Hare Jumps!* And I smile when I hear my own voice. I haven't done any performance for years and it feels like the moment when you first enter the sea or put your feet on the ground on a warm day. You know it so well, you have been doing this for an aeon, and yet it feels like the first time. I read through some marked passages and then I put the books down on the piano, and sit on the stool, looking at the tiers of empty seats.

How many strange performances have I watched from the back of this theatre? Tibetan monks blowing giant horns, arch-druids playing fairy harps, virgin choirs singing about loving Jesus, preachers playing cinema organs, Christians emasculating the words of Dario Fo, the immaculate words of Dylan Thomas twisted in the mouths of fools. A failed magician struggling through his last trick, children maniacally toe-tapping as their dancing teacher shouts: *You can be special! You can be a star!* Hundreds of nameless people filing in and out, watching these bizarre acts, sometimes a full house on a music night but mostly a handful of souls in anoraks, watching a smaller amount of people, doing their special thing, having their moment of stardom.

All these months I have been standing by the doors, turning the house lights on and off, watching in the aisles, turning the heaters on in the dressing rooms, pulling and pushing monitors, screens, wires, and now for one night, it's going to be the other way round.

'Where do you want the mikes?' asks Trevor the lighting technician, as he bursts through the stage doors in a whirl of snowflakes. 'Just here where I am standing,' I say. And go downstairs to change into a red dress.

II

Everyone loved the show. It was an open mic evening. I hosted, Mark was the compere. The woman who worked in the cafe turned into a singer who sang about a drowned fisherman, the administrators of the poetry festival became poets who spoke about love, the man at the box office sang a Venezuelan song about the planet Venus, the usher who was also an antique seller recited a classical poem about Eurydice. For one evening we were all so much more than we were in the day in our shops and offices. And there was a feeling, perhaps because it was such a cold evening and everyone had made this special effort to come out, perhaps because we were all together in this business of going to and fro from the stage, one minute audience, the next a performer, that something was *happening*. There was excited talk in the interval about doing more evenings. As I thanked everyone for coming at the end of the show a huge bunch of lilies was thrust into my hands. Thank you, I said, and bowed.

'Everyone liked the singing, Charlie,' said Mark as we waved goodbye and started to lock up the building. 'Yes,' I agreed. But no one had mentioned my poems. Those poems the theatre manager had read about silence and the desert, the kind of silence when you can hear the stars, the leap of the salmon, the wind in the apple tree, about the time when the ancestors of the snow-bound north wait for a cat to arrive and tell them who they really are.

I put the lilies in a vase and left them in the office. And then I turned out the lights.

III

Stargazer lilies are the kind of flower you get as a performer. Waxy blooms with pollen-covered stamens that command the stage like opera stars with giant candy-striped throats. They sit on pianos, in hotel lobbies, in funeral parlours, perfectly shaped for weeks on end, permeating these public arenas where sentimentality and artifice are at their height, with their strong and urgent perfume. These lilies arrive in great container lorries from the glasshouses of Holland each week, one of those cosseted hothouse flowers that poison and suck dry the water tables of Colombia and Africa, and enslave thousands of people everywhere. And all because we can't quite look each other in the eye, at a time when we should be looking each other in the eye: the mother we wish to butter up; the lover who we want to get into bed; the friend we want to keep for our own reasons. The women we pretend we adore. The flowers that are a substitute for the feeling of the heart, that say Sorry and I love you and Goodbye and all the things we can't say, because we don't really mean them.

The reality is these lilies are expensive, where you are cheap.

IV

Flowering plants are divided into two principal categories by taxonomy: the monocotyledons and the dicotyledons. The vast majority are the dicotyledons. The monocotyledons are a small and distinctive group. They are not just different botanically, that is in their structure; they differ in their mood and vibration. This is because they are governed by the reflective nature of the moon, rather than the sun. You can sense this in the way they appear in the darkness of a wood and possess a liquid nature that feels mysterious and indefinable. Hidden. Still. Many store their energy in reserves underground, in corms and bulbs and rhizomes. Lilies are mono cotyledons, as are orchids and irises, gladioli and saffron. All flowers that are all highly sought after, prized, collected, presented. Special plants that need special attention. Flowers for special occasions, for special people.

I had not felt special that night. Even though I had enjoyed performing, I felt no one was listening to what I was saying. We had been able in that hothouse moment to sing our song and pretend we were other than we were. But somewhere we were fooling ourselves. And some part of me would not let that go by.

When the stargazer lilies fell into my hands, I was very far from being a star. I was working a 60-hour week in the basement office for £2.50 an hour, without overtime. Each night as I stood in the dark, as the people flowed in and out, as the galleries changed pictures, as the wine glasses filled and emptied at the theatre bar, I sensed these movements as if the building were part of my own body. But one thing I did not realise: this open mic evening was to be my farewell performance, my one and only appearance on this stage. I had poured all my life-force into revitalising this theatre and all that will come back from these endeavours is a powerful reek of lily flowers.

Is this all we have at the end of our time? I will wonder in a few days time, gazing at their frigid beauty, and imagine if that is how departing spirits feel as they look back at their earthly lives and see a pile of stinking glasshouse flowers perched on top of their corpses.

V

'Those flowers are just too much,' said Jo. I laughed. The office was filled with the perfume of lilies and amidst the grinding machinery of the computers and coffee cups, the ceaselessly ringing telephone, the delivery men arriving, their grandiose forms seemed somehow ridiculous. I gave them to the volunteer in charge of the front-of-house flowers and she used them to brighten the underworld of the ladies toilet.

I felt ungrateful for putting them in the toilet.

'What are you looking at?' snarled the lilies. 'This is where we belong. Have a good look. You are looking at yourself.'

I didn't want to look at myself. I didn't want to face the fact that no one gave a damn about whether I wrote interesting poems or worked all hours in this office, so long as they could get their entertainments, have their one shiny moment on stage. I didn't want to face the fact that no one seemed to give a damn about anybody or their creativity, that there was no place for our hearts, for anything splendid that might occur in that theatre if we did. Only that the star-making machine went on and everybody played their roles and remembered their lines and made the correct curtsey and bow when they were expected.

I had stood there and felt splendid in a red dress, but no one was listening to a word I was saying. I could stand and hold everyone's attention, but the Earth of which I spoke could not enter the room. The words evaporated even as they came out of my mouth. I could have just stood there (perhaps we all could) and made gestures. It would have been enough, sufficient.

It was a small moment in a small theatre on a cold night, and it was also all theatres, every night, as the Earth turns on her axis, as these hot-houses let out their sounds of lamentation into the air: fiendish fiddlers, shrieking sopranos, the moaning of choirs, the groans of orchestras, actors, dressed in outlandish costumes, repeating the same lines endless-ly through the centuries, ballet-stars hiding blood-stained feet, sad-eyed comedians making us laugh, or what passes for laughter. What was I doing there, in those arenas of heartlessness?

Sometimes we caught each other's eyes as we passed by on the stairs, as I handed the performers a cheque or brought them a drink on the house. We exchanged our looks of exhaustion. Some part of us was ashamed.

VI

I stood by the lilies in the toilet, by their impeccable stillness, and remem-bered a party that had taken place upstairs one night the previous October. The building had been packed with people. You could not move on the stairs. As the band struck the first chord in the theatre, pandemonium had broken out, as a hundred adolescent children released from years of good behaviours in their houses and schools, jacked up with alcohol and am-phetamines, suddenly let rip. The building roared. Mark and the fathers rushed outside. 'Get back in!' they yelled. But the youth of the town took no notice. They were pouring out into the streets, shrieking and laughing and vomiting and crying and dancing. The event was out of control and for a moment, as I leaned against the brickwork, I felt the foundations rock and laughed.

It was mayhem, a consequence of repression, but at least it was alive. Soon enough they would become like the people in the audience, watch-ing the flickering screens, listening to the singers and the piano players, the stiff, the anoraked, the dead moving through. Then I realised I was in charge of the house and they were bringing ruin down upon it.

'What shall we do?' cried the mothers in distress, as I went upstairs. 'You will have to stop the music,' I said, 'you will have to pull the plug,' and went to talk with the neighbours who at that moment were hammering on the glass door.

I had to look at myself, in the red dress, in the ladies toilet, packed with the young and the reckless in the dark. Lilies are all fierce flowers, moon flowers, and the moon does not let you get away with anything much, especially when you stray too far from the path. Underworld stories recount how foolish starry-eyed females who fall down there by accident, find themselves on a hook, and learn to get smart and get out. Lilies are the flowers given to the Madonna just before she is ravished by the angel, the flowers gathered by the daughters of Earth just before they are raped by the lords of darkness. The flowers signal some kind of recompense for an action illegally taken, their scent covering up a crime no one can quite detect. Or really wants to.

But we should find out about these things, look at ourselves in the Underworld mirror and see what lies inside this bouquet a stranger has just delivered to our door. Because as we sit gazing up into the stars, into the spotlights, adoring the divas and the divas stand adoring all our special attention, a price is being demanded from all of us, and if we were wise, we would all take notice of what this price is.

And start refusing to pay it.

VII

The cherished flowers of the English spring are all wild members of the lily family. As the winter wanes they set the woods and meadows and gardens alight with their underworld lamps – narcissus, bluebell, snake's head fritillary, Solomon's seal – and every window in the land shines with the golden hue of daffodils.

The weekend after I handed in my resignation, Mark and I went to see some acquaintances who had come by the theatre and invited us to see their snowdrop display. They had retired to an old house in a village about 25 miles away. We had a love of flowers in common and wild birds and poetry, and, so I thought, shared a kind of egalitarian outlook on life.

It was a perfect house with everything in its place. Small chairs with writing desks. Renovated fireplaces. Collections of china and paintings. Larders full of home-made preserves. Glasshouses full of interesting plants. A successful stargazing house. When we arrived I talked animatedly about what had made us resign as managers of the theatre but something made me stop. I was out of place and out of order. 'I thought you cared about the workers!' I joked with my host across the dark oak table. 'I don't anymore,' he said without a smile.

So the mood shifted and everyone began talking instead about so-and-so's review of so-and-so's book, what was happening on television and in the cinema, what their various children were doing working for various charities in the city, and how the British Empire was actually a very good thing. I grew quiet and my hands grew cold. There was a fire but it seemed very chilly. Afterwards we sat in the drawing room like characters out of a Sheridan play and drank small cups of coffee and made even smaller conversation. A former theatrical agent spoke about the humanist funeral services he conducted in which the end was really The End, none of this Christian nonsense about the afterlife. No soul. No spirit. No karma. No Underworld. No scales. There was a celebration of the human biographical life, a relevant poem recited or song sung, and then, curtains! As if our human appearance were just a show and we were actors without any kind of other life.

Afterwards we went into the garden. It was the end of February and there were all kinds of green-flowered hellebores in the beds and a daphne bush with its sharp pink blossom. But most of all there were snowdrops, the first wild lilies of the year, sprinkled about the meadow, under the trees, shining in that immaculate way they do, even on a grey Sunday afternoon. There was something about their purity, the way they hung their heads quietly, gazing inwardly at themselves, perfect, self-contained, the very opposite of the actress and her gaudy artifice. And I loved them in that moment and knelt down on the wet ground to inhale their sweet fragrance.

As I did, something in me rebelled. I just couldn't say what I knew I was *supposed* to say. I was there to admire the garden but I couldn't admire the garden. *Never underestimate the power of the small,* the snowdrops once told me. For the want of a nail, the kingdom was lost.

'Hello snowdrop,' I said as I knelt down, as my hosts stood beside me. There was an awkward silence.

I had forgotten my lines.

What happens when we forget our lines? What happens when we stop admiring the perfect house with its perfect collections of objects, when we stop worshipping the shiny divas and thrusting scented lilies into their hands, when we no longer wait to sing our one and only song in an empty theatre, with the snow whirling all about us?

Will we come out here on this winter's day and kneel in a garden by a wild flower and remember somewhere quiet, deep inside us, about another kind of show?

Varanasi

❦

It is hard to know that this magic carpet exists and that one will no longer fly on it.
– Jean Cocteau (Opium)

'The way these people are living is not what I had in mind'
– Sun Father, Zuni creation myth

I'm sitting under the peepal tree in the Deer Park in Sarnath. Dark-tuniced Tibetan students, white-clad nuns, orange-robed monks, many-coloured tourists move around the tree, and contemplate the statues of the Buddha and his five disciples with their piled-up Aryan locks. It was here the Buddha delivered his first teaching. His words are carved in slabs of stone in different gold-scripted languages. The inscription reads that after declaring the Four Noble Truths and the Eightfold Path, the devas in all the invisible circles above the Earth shook with fear.

Nirvana is sometimes translated as a 'return to the shining void' or 'extinction', in the sense of blowing out a flame, no longer fuelling the fire. By ending the anguish and desires of the ego, the Buddha's path to extinction introduced death into the eternal world of the devas. It meant their realms would cease to exist, because human beings would not be clothing and feeding them anymore. If people could liberate themselves from the wheel of karma, the devas' shows would come to an end. They would lose all their hiding places.

Afterwards I go to Varanasi, leaving the calm of Sarnath for the crowded streets of India's oldest city. Rachel told me: 'If you don't go now, you will never go.' It is 2006 and I have just received the last of the inheritance from my dead father. I don't know it yet but a whole way of life is about to come to an end.

In Varanasi I get out of the tuk-tuk and walk towards the river.

Suddenly the narrow street opens out to the vast opal-coloured stretch of the Ganges – the pitted ochre buildings of the teeming ghats and the emptiness of the shore on the further side. It is shining in the morning light and the light suffuses everything. 'Here I am!' I say, half to myself, half to the river, and feel, in that moment, complete.

'You are thinking too much,' says a tall young man behind me. 'A man will approach,' Rachel had instructed. 'Go with him.' I smile and agree to follow his guided path, down the steps, towards the burning ghats, to his friend the astrologer, up to the towers where he points out the view down the river with its steps full of devotees, boats, bullocks, monkeys and the morning.

At the ashram of Kali, we sit in the shade of a mango tree and smoke hemp flowers.

'When I saw you, I was dazzled! How beautiful,' he whispers, and runs his hand up my back, as if I were a horse. 'You are tired and I am a young man. You need some of my Shiva power.'

'No, I don't,' I said, and laughed.

I might have gone with him in another time, for the adventure, to have lain in Kali's rose garden in Shiva's city. But something is coming to an end. The boy said: I will take you out onto the Ganges and sing to you. We took the boat into the middle of the river, and as he rowed towards the empty shore, his face grew suddenly sulky and dark, like all men who do not get what they desire. The City of Light hovered before me. The most beautiful city in the world. The shining hub of the wheel where all things began, and where all things come to an end.

Here I am, I thought. A great humming arose from the ancient city, three thousand years of human karma coming to an end, as the boat drifted past the shore on the further side. For years I had wanted to come to Varanasi. And here it was. Everything I had ever dreamed of. And then it was time to go home.

You will dream of me, the boy said, as we parted company on the bank. I smiled and wished him well, because I knew I would not. I would not even remember his name.

When we fly over London, the buildings below the plane appear grey and oppressive. No one smiles at the train station. It is silent, cold, hostile. My head fills with antagonistic thoughts. But wheeling our suitcases down the lane, the night wind stirs the ash and oak trees above us, I can smell the spring, the feel of the ground beneath my feet, a force pulling me towards the earth.

'Almost there Charlie,' says Mark.

Selva

How did this begin? Lying in a hot leafy hut, frogs croaking in the Peruvian rainforest, a certain line comes to me: *My circus life unclawed me.*

I am 'on location' with a fashion team and the two models have gone on strike because they feel (as African-Americans) they are being exploited by the 'indigenous is hip this season' story. The German photographer is arguing with them. He is not pleased with our abundant backdrop. *Selva* is too green, he says. Tonight we drank a strange alluring brew the lodge owner had made and swam naked in the Amazon, heedless of piranha, crocodile and electric eel, and watched a slim boat go out and point its prows to the full moon. I am writing another line in my notebook that is not a caption:

Tonight there are no dreams because there are no dreamers.

I went to South America by mistake: Eric Newby was supposed to cover the story but he had fallen ill and so I went to Lima as the replacement travel writer. After that I was sent to New Mexico with the team and wrote a story about beans and adobe and Georgia O'Keefe – and somehow, between the forest and desert and mountains, those big spaces got inside me. Afterwards I could not fit back into my box-shaped London life.

🔆

When I left the city I found out how plants can open up your imagination in a way no book can ever do, how mountains can speak to you in your dreams. I encountered people I would never have met in the bars and offices of my own country. People who were learning about the indigenous spirit of things, who tussled with their nation's karma, who walked an ancestral path in their own way.

Though we longed to be the people who could love the Earth with song and dance, with feather and prayer, we were not born those people. We had work to do in the places we least wanted to go. Turtle Island, Madre Tierra, Pachamama, pushed us all out like birds from the nest, into an unmapped territory that felt like a kind of Antarctica. Go back to where you came from, they said, and deal with your shit.

What I hadn't realised was that the people in the canoe in the rainforest that night were on their way to an ayahuasca ceremony, and that when the planet makes contact with you and shows you its inner splendour it demands something in return that you are not sure you know how to give. That when Georgia O'Keefe said 'New Mexico will itch you for the rest of your life', she wasn't talking about holidays.

Terra

How did it stop?

'Your carbon debt is massive,' said Josiah. I am writing about a low-carbon group that has decided to cut its personal emissions by half the national average, which in 2010 is eight tonnes. Last night we gathered around the kitchen table with our transport bills. I can just about make the target if we use the car for short journeys but taking a plane anywhere blows it completely. We are eight people who have read the data, we know the facts about climate change. We know we are among the five per cent of the world who have stepped on a plane and that one return flight to New York would take up one of those four tonnes and then some. Across the sky, contrails from 100,000 planes leach out carbon monoxide, nitrogen oxides, sulphur oxides, lead and black carbon into the atmosphere each day and we know that no amount of creative accounting can reverse the planetary feedback loops that say what goes around comes around.

And yet in spite of this the dissonance is palpable in the room, as the prospect of NO HOLIDAYS ANYWHERE INTERESTING OR SUNNY is veering into view. When you realise that even travelling to that small island in the inky Aegean would take four days by train and boat. Even if you did have the money which, this being the *kali yuga*, you no longer do.

My carbon debt is massive. I have touched down in La Paz and New York, in Tokyo, Kingston, Santiago de Chile, Kauai, Hong Kong, Sydney,

Delhi – but now in a small town in East Anglia I am learning to love the patterns of neighbourhood, of reed bed and market square, to build a culture of sharing and humble return. We meet to unpick our fossil-fuelled lives and find ourselves at the place that stops all our endeavours – a realm that hovers on every magazine page and screen, luring us into its world of turquoise seas and swimming pools, of white tablecloths and limousines. Come, fly here, a voice whispers in our ear.

I don't know about Buddhism but I know all about devas. I am someone who used to drag huge Globe-trotter suitcases full of fairy frocks across the planet, I know what devas like to eat and what sparkly places they like to go, and exactly what it takes to blow out that flame. I know that illusions are the last thing you give up when you are up against it: your special moment, your little winter break, that romantic destination. What would life be without these treats?

It is the flying and not just the flying. It is the technology of flight, the ease, the speed, that fits the pace and dominion of the capitalist pleasure-dome. But it is also the ancient illusion that we can treat the world like a plaything, as if we have a right to reward ourselves for our slavery to GDP with a visit to the market at Marrakesh, or a trek in Nepal, a quick trip to Iceland, or Bali, or Florida. A never-never land culture without ethical or spiritual constraint.

Industrialisation has made us restless and dissatisfied. We live in terror of missing out and finding ourselves in the wrong hotel. We want all our journeys to be outer ones, full of leisure and luxury; none of us wants to go inside, unlock the Pandora's box of our small histories and suffer. We would rather sacrifice any number of wild creatures or trees than extinct our adolescent selves, let whole kingdoms of fish and people fall, so long as we can keep holding that boarding pass in our hands, our sense of entitlement, our five per cent exceptionalism, our trophy holiday.

The reality is we don't want to land.

Karma

In the backrooms of England some of us despair: we have become no-fly-zone outcasts, enemies of promise. The initiative that had once cut its teeth on radical energy descent has settled into a cosy community haven, where you can hold conversations about carbon reduction and still fly to

Copenhagen for the day to go swimming.

The taboo-breaking marks us as 'the difficult people' in the room, the people who ask awkward questions. Sometimes we are unable even to ask the question, an invisible force preventing us from opening our mouths.

Silently we face our friends who justify 'love miles' (he was dying, she was getting married); artists who justify exhibitions (I have to share my work); climate scientists who justify conferences (I have to exchange ideas); yoga princesses who justify retreats (I have to be with my guru) in a civilisation where governments can hold conversations about emissions targets and still keep building runways and not taxing aviation fuel (we have to serve the economy). We did the offsetting, the flyers chorus, absolving themselves in the way medieval sinners once paid for indulgences. We're not good like you.

Sometimes I want to say very loudly: YOU ARE ASLEEP AND YOU NEED SOME OF MY KALI POWERDOWN, and stick out my very long red tongue.

Selva 2

Rachel no longer stays in the room on Dr Jain's roof terrace that overlooks the Deer Park in Sarnath, among the drying sheets and pots of holy basil. She lives in a small wood on the edge of the neighbouring market town and runs her own guest house. I remembered the story she once told us about her friends who lived on an ancient pilgrimage route in India. The path ran by a river she said and it was the most beautiful setting you could imagine, full of trees and flowers and birds. One year however her friends moved to an ugly industrial city. 'How could you leave?' she asked them. 'Our work is here,' they replied simply. 'This place needs us.'

Last summer our paths crossed after many years, and the three of us had an intense conversation in the way we used to when we could all afford to travel the world. She told me in India there are five ages, that begin with our youth and end with the time of 'Going into the Forest'. 'What happens before old age?' I asked her. 'Preparing to Go into the Forest,' she said and we laughed.

Casa

I lived out of a suitcase for ten years. I gave up many things to be on that road – a house, a family, a career, some kind of reputation – and I regret none of it. I got to see the Earth in all of her loveliness. I went to break out of a restricted city life that hemmed in my real self like a Victorian dress. After I broke the stays I became like a lover who could never have enough of wide open spaces, of the pepper trees leaning towards the red sand of the Elqui valley (the boys riding horseback down the street), or the roar of the Pacific at Mazatlán, bus stations on a tropical morning, the volcano rising above the hot spring, hummingbird and cactus. It was in these places, those borrowed houses, I could empty myself, bring a silence and a space that had been full of ghosts and other people's words.

But at some point you have to be in relationship, you have to settle down and give up your interesting freewheeling life. You don't want to, but it is time, your time and the times you live in, the payback time, when all our small karmas come to roost and that joystick is no longer in our hands. To love a country that is Not-Home with all its breathtaking geography and sweet fruit costs nothing; to love this polluted, crowded island with all the responsibility of descent on your shoulders costs everything.

So you go home. And home is not a place you want to go, or that you like even. Here I am on the east coast of a country I spent a lifetime getting away from and have not moved for 16 years. In the seatown there are 1400 houses and only 500 of them are lived in: the rest serve wealthy weekenders who pay nothing for the roads or cash-strapped libraries, or the feudal history of place that weighs down invisibly on those who inhabit the region. The visitors are having a 'Southwold' experience with local beer and fish and chips, and £100,000 beach huts. A perfect backdrop. No strings attached. A hideaway where you can step out of the door and feel free.

Except you learn, when you come home and live in a place, that nothing is free. Some person, some bird, some plant, some insect is paying for that weekend, that fortnight, with their lives, and now that person is you. Yes you, renter, with your second-hand coat and low-income lifestyle, who cares for you anyway?

Nothing has ever said you belong here, or anywhere you have found yourself. You were always the wrong class, the wrong gender, too white, too privileged. You went to the wrong university, didn't write enough books, wrote too many of the wrong sort. Never knew the right people, or maybe you did once, but then you missed the party and it was the wrong time. It's always the wrong time. At some point you realise it's not about belonging, it's about being at home in your own skin, on this Earth, wherever you land, and deciding to pay the debt, your family's debt, your culture's debt, stretching back through the centuries. The buck stops here, you say. I'm not going anywhere.

Nirvana

'We could go to la Casa de los Azulejos,' said Mark, as we both in that moment find ourselves in a dark-panelled dining room surrounded by businessmen in suits and chattering families. It was where we liked to go for breakfast in Mexico City in our travelling years. There are white table-cloths and waitresses with paper wings the colour of sugared almonds flying past with trays of *huevos rancheros* and *pan dulce*. A glass of *maracuyá* juice sits on the table in front of me and for one moment time stands still. Outside the blue sky arches above the Alameda, above the megalopolis, stretching out towards the Sierra Madre, backbone of America, towards the forests of glowworms and jaguars, towards the ever-moving oceans of the world.

'Ah, yes,' I say. 'But after breakfast, what would we do?'

II

HERD

Walkabout

❧

I have begun to dream about tidal waves. The first one was in Japan. 'There will be 50 more,' the dream informed me. 'This is the beginning of the big weather.'

These tidal waves took place in South America, in North America, and in countries I did not recognise. Some I plunge through, some I flee from and seek refuge in the mountains. Sometimes they are fast and clear and people freeze in their wake, others are slow and black, as if made from volcanic sand and poisonous. From deep space they appeared like great waves of light pouring down on the Earth.

After these big wave dreams I developed strange aches. Pains I did not have names for filled in my body. And it was then I realised that in order to change the way I engaged with life, my physical being also needed to change. We have returned from Australia at the end of a decade of travelling, determined to live freely in our own lands, and this was where the breakout needed to begin.

In the small cottage in Oxfordshire the rooks circle about the village over the thatched roofs, gathering up the dusk in their beaks and returning to their nests in the great pine trees. It is a time of slow return in middle England as the millennium turns.

I had a stomach ache for six months. There is nothing you can do. You expand and it is a growing pain – a release from a confinement you have been living in all these years. My whole body ached and groaned and rebelled and grew allergic. Everything that had been held captive and constrained had started to release itself: in my physical will area, my guts, my womb. I found myself drinking water, moving in a different way, changing what I ate, giving up everything artificial, sweet or addictive.

I weaned myself off a lifetime of relying on the flesh of animals and fish and had to change an entire way of cooking, which took me six months.

It is tough to not eat meat after eating it for so many years, because our Western bodies are reliant on this powerful food. Not only do you have to work to gain the same kind of sustenance from plants but also to withstand the antagonism from fellow diners. I gave up eating meat the day I walked through a field of cows and began dreaming of slaughterhouses. Afterwards, I felt a kinship with the animals I have never experienced before.

I knew I had not to get obsessed about my physical body – something I had always taken for granted and been quite happy to live in all these years. Complaining about aches and pains is the easiest way to get attention. Female beings evince a good deal of sympathy for these physical dramas and indulge in a lot of self-pity about their imperfect looking, imperfectly-working bodies. But none of this leads to freedom. It only leads to the invalid room, to the obsessional mirror. So I let the transformation happen to me. And worked out how best I could help myself.

Years before this, I had a vision that took place undersea. In this the sea-green oceanic god Neptune showed me a way out of the circle of karma: it took two routes, the way of the pool and the way of the mirrors. The pool was a swimming pool filled with poisoned water, which you had to drink and transmute within yourself, and the way of the mirrors was to go through an arcade of crazy mirrors and amusement machines, to see yourself beyond every distorted image, and not to be distracted by the amusements. The pool was physical and emotional, the mirrors related to the mind. The pool was the female challenge, the arcade of mirrors, the male.

Individual freedom depends on how much you are willing to undergo to break the binds that hold you, not knowing when the suffering will end or whether it will end. For years, I suffered physically as I expanded, never badly but chronically, through each part of my body, as my history, our history, exacted its toll – through my womb, my vagina, my spleen, my intestines, my bones. When these parts of me began to move, everything moved. Dreams threw up terrible scenarios, relationships I rather wished had been forgotten, my mind ran round in circles like a fevered dog, emotions would howl and roar through my being. I would explode in furious tempers, erupt like a volcano, throwing tidal waves of bath water on the floor, as my will started to move and allowed me to express all those things that had been repressed. Sometimes I was laid low for days as the poisons of the world of my former life ran through my very blood and sinew. Terrific headaches would appear and then disappear. I wept for everything, regretted every missed opportunity, ranted for every misunderstood scene. Strangely, though I had always led a very rackety kind of life and had drunk and smoked since I was 19 neither my liver nor my lungs ever hurt. My heart never missed a beat. The male parts of my physique were strong; it was the female parts that had suffered, atrophied, taken a dark toll.

As I changed what I ate, I forced myself to assimilate plants – their leaves, roots and flowers. I began to ask my dreams questions and the answers were always given to me: the energies I needed to change, the attention I needed to pay. These adjustments took time but they worked. I was re-tuning myself, to live at a different tempo, to slow down and assimilate experience, in order to be swift, light. You need a lot of energy to perceive and encounter the world in an expanded way. You need to train yourself as fiercely as an athlete, jettison any heaviness from the past that is weighing you down. Anything that I conceived as comfort food I threw out. I didn't want to live in a cosy nursery world full of babyland treats and sweets, cakes at four, little glasses of wine at six. I wanted to be real, alive, dynamic. I trained myself to walk into shops and let my body choose the food it wanted not what my mouth desired. And after a while it didn't want anything else.

And then in line with the dreaming practice we were engaged in each day, I began to move my body. I started to walk.

Walking West

> I dream I am in a hotel in London waiting for a visa to go to Australia. I have to take two journeys. One is a green road that goes from Hyde Park Corner to Cornwall, and will take five days walking to get there. Hyde Park is a heart shape with arteries going in and out which are the green tracks of the land.

When did it begin? The night at Dorchester Close where unable to sleep deeply because of the noise of the ring road, jet-lagged, exhausted from travelling without reason, from living in hotel rooms, I waken to see in the glaring night light which I cannot shut out with my flimsy curtain, there in the car park, shiny with the night rain, a toad waiting outside my door.

'Maybe if we go for the deeper things, the rushing will run out,' said

Mark. Underneath the earth there is a different pace, a different time. Here in our temporary lodging, new houses had been built over an ancient wood, the toad's territory, but it was still his. Even though there was all this concrete and brick and artificial light in the way, he was still there. 'Tomorrow I'll visit the wood that is still there,' I thought. Over the bridge a track led to a hill covered with trees, and to escape the noise I went there.

At first I just walked because I couldn't stay in this uneasy house all day. Because there were no longer any seas or pools to swim in, because my feet had become accustomed to the feel of the ground in Australia. I walked over the bridge and up onto the hill where the craggy English oaks commanded. And I felt the presence in the wood of the creatures that lived there. The rank smell of fox. The singing of birds. I came back muddy and exhilarated without knowing why. Something about the hill, something about the wood, something about the spring I had forgotten and my feet were reminding me.

And then I walked because something was happening to me. For years where I had felt cold and shivery inside something began to burn in its place, so I could walk for hours and not freeze. I walked in the twilight, at dawn, at moonrise. I walked in the dark over the wet meadow with just my senses to guide me. I learned to distinguish the trees by their barks, the birds by their flights. And as I walked I became stronger and more flexible. I walked through thunderstorms, learned to wait in the woods, climbed trees. I ate damsons, smelled the rain, discovered swans nesting, rabbits that ran in and out of gorse bushes. I realised I was not alone; walking through the lanes, along the cornfields, the beanfields, the scent of camomile and hawthorn, I called out greetings. Hello fellows! And later these beings – these places, these trees, these waterbirds – came into my dreams.

I did not know why I was walking except it felt necessary to move after so much close scrutiny with the practice each morning. I did not plan where I went. I let my feet, my instincts choose. Some days I never went out. Sometimes it was not easy. I had begun to notice things I had never seen before, walking through fields of cows, past the pig farm, past the shuttered hen house, through the sterile fields of green wheat where no birds sang, where only nettles grew. Farms were eerie places. Rivers stank. I began to ask myself questions. I walked down pathways covered with dead field mice and voles, brutally torn hedgerows and razed wild places and an anger began to burn in me I had not felt before.

In the town I took every alley, went through every park and graveyard, along every canal and river towpath. I walked through places and I learned to immerse myself in the feel of them, like a fish in the sea. I learned to feel the mood and nuance of the streets. I experienced a strange delight in wastelands burgeoning with flowers whose names I did not know. And sometimes I would see strangers on my path who lived in canal boats, in caravans, in trees, on the streets, who smiled at me in a way I had not been smiled at before. And later these people, these flowers would come into my dreams.

Sometimes I found myself wondering, why do I not want to go down that street? Why did I feel cold, spaced out, afraid in some places? Sometimes I shivered as if someone had walked across my grave and realised that the town was full of ghosts: the brilliant young students who had gone cold in the wars, in the cruel world of men, and had come back, searching out for some temporary warmth in a passer-by. And these young men too came into my dreams.

You want to walk because you have to get somewhere. You want to walk because you need a bit of fresh air, but I was walking because I had to feel the kingdom under my feet, I had to sense it, smell its sewers, its coffee stands, its outsiders, ghosts, the people waiting at the bus stop. And I had to know what it was like to live on the rim, to observe and then be observed by those who see everything and belong to nothing but themselves. To see the world without referring to anything that went before. To let myself be unknown, unrecognisable. The University's men and women in their gowns and party dresses from the other side of the bridge on a summer's evening never saw me. The shoppers in the street never saw me. But I was not completely invisible.

'You I know you,' cried a tramp laughing as he rode by on his bicycle, 'You're that girl!'

I am a girl walking, walking open, not with a purpose to get to a place, to work, to shop. I have to start somewhere, I have to go somewhere else and I don't know where it is, won't know where it is for a long long time. I am walking from Hyde Park to Cornwall to Australia, along the green track. I have to walk down different paths, paths that I have never taken before, I have to taste things I do not like and see things I would rather close my eyes to. I have to feel anger, shock, exhaustion, defeat, fear; the blankness of the small roads, of the empty buildings; the presence of a severed tree, the torn body of a mole in my hand. I have to wait in the pouring rain with bitterness in my heart. I have to know time, know its slow measure, of empty hours: by the clock of my years passing by without result; then I have to know the time of the cherry tree, of twilight, of myself in the fall of my life. I have to make connections, make meaning of what I experience, unravelling one road and winding up into another place. And always I have to keep moving, keep walking, going out, from a small place into a larger place, from a room into the world, house to house, land to town, from wood to marsh, from hill to valley, from west to east. Walking.

My life is emptying of people I knew, there are childhood dramas that are coming to an end, I am being filled with other things, things I used to know as a child, things of a solitary beauty, of a swan flying past at sunrise on a misty day, the light of sunset on green trunks.

I am walking home. Walking myself from a stranger into one that feels at home. It's a long long road.

Walking East

Along the sandy dunes and shingle banks of the East Anglian seaboard there is a front line of wild ancestor plants – wild carrot, wild cabbage, sea beet, sea pea, sea kale, sea rocket, oraches, sorrel. The largest, most resilient of these ancient vegetables is the wavy-leaved seakale, with a tap root that sinks deep into the shingle.

The plant marks a territory that runs along the salty rim of England, from the Norfolk broads to the Kent marshes. It's a geographical, ecological territory, but also a place you can map in time, in the ways that make meaning of our human presence on the Earth since our forebears first ate those sharp-tasting iron-rich leaves.

We came here to this eastern edge because of the sea, drawn by its tides and slow rivers. After travelling in the wide open spaces of Australia and the Americas, these sandy, heathy flatlands, with their watery horizons and giant skies, gave the feeling of openness and light we had grown used to.

When you face an uncertain future there needs to be space for what Dale Pendell calls a *Ground State Calibration*. You need to find the existential basis for all your actions that lie deep inside your being. There have to be different coordinates by which to navigate your ordinary lives. We have to know what kind of creatures we are and what is being asked from us in return.

I always thought this ground state meant you needed to have your feet planted on terra firma – but when I came here I realised it meant being at home in another state, rooted in something more shifting and fluid. Where you can, like the seakale, hold fast in a rocky and uncertain time and weather a storm.

🜊

At night when the wind is in the east I can hear the North Sea heaving and sighing on the shingle, and sometimes there is a tang of salt that drifts across the marshes. It's not a clear brochure-blue sea, it's mostly a gun-metal grey, whose silvery shine can take you by surprise on a winter's day. But it holds mysteries beneath its workaday exterior. The sanderlings and turnstones that run at its edge are not part of a fixed territory like the inland country of limestone, chalk or clay.

In 1992 the writer, W.G. Sebald famously walked along this shoreline from Lowestoft to Dunwich. I sometimes sit in the Sailor's Reading room in Southwold where he once wrote, in the cold months, watched over by long-gone fishermen in sepia photographs, the model boats they crafted preserved behind glass, the clock ticking behind me. We are in a sandy place, where time shifts and unmoors you, and you can glimpse the past and future of things.

Sebald was reminded of the horrors of history as he walked along the crumbling cliffs and heathland of coastal Suffolk, the Yazidi circle we are all stuck in, doomed to repeat the cruelty of Empires. He gazed out across the German Ocean (as he called it) from Gun Hill and watched the warships of Britain and Spain battle for Sole Bay. He was always looking backwards; we are always looking forwards, equally in horror.

A fret creeps over the fields and covers the land, a lone curlew calls. Undersea, a country called Doggerland is tugging at our dreams. The men look at you with sea glass eyes out of the photographs, the men singing in the back room at the Eel's Foot, mending the nets down at Blackshore. Without realising it, you forget which century you are in.

🜊

David Moyse's grandparents once lived in the house we now live in, a brick cottage tied to the local farm. His grandfather was in charge of the horses that ploughed the surrounding beet and barley fields, his father was the village blacksmith. For a decade we talked with David over his gate. About the weather, about flowers, about making wine from rosehips in a bucket. I had found his leeks one winter dusk on a stall made from an old pram and something in me felt exultant, as if I had suddenly found harbour after a storm. The following autumn he gave me a bag of his home-grown green tomatoes, and I made chutney for both our larders. It was the first direct exchange I made in my new neighbourhood. David gave us wood when he chopped his trees, he lent us his mower when ours broke down. But most of all he was always there at the top of the lane, like a guardian of the place, the church steeple keeper and key holder, the history man of the village. We always waved at each other, as we cycled by. *Here we are, here we are!*

For years I yearned to return to the countryside I had once encountered when I was young. For a long time I thought this was a nostalgia for a summer seaside childhood – an escape to a rural idyll from a cynical city world. When I came to the lane, I realised it wasn't a personal longing for a familiar territory but about becoming a real human being again at home on the Earth. This wasn't just about having a relationship with the land. It was also about recognising the people who were already anchored in the territory.

David was like the country people I knew when I was a child, who were fierce and yet kindly, who grew cabbages and dahlias in their gardens, who knew the names of the birds and kept their tools in good order. And although we were from a different generation and different backgrounds, we loved the same place.

When he died, it was as if a great boat had been unmoored, and you could no longer hear its mast stays rattling in the wind. That's when I realised at some point you have to become the kind of people you want to see in the neighbourhood.

ぇ

Making yourself at home is a task. Because there is a big restlessness in the world. I am one of millions of disconnected people yearning to drop anchor, who at the same time, are pulled and pushed by a culture that demands that everyone moves all the time.

What happens when you stop? What happens when you don't leave? What happens if you go to the place where your heart leads you to go and don't move away?

𝔁

In the woods I walked: gathering bitter cherries and meadowsweet.

Across the heaths I walked: down silvery paths, listening for night-jar in the moonlight; down the flinty pathways, in the gorse-covered sandbanks that were once rivers, in the quarry pits where elephants once roamed, watching the starlings gather above the marshland in the winter dusk, the sand martins at the departure of summer.

Through the flower year I walked: making pilgrimage to the snow-drops on the cliff top among the yews, wild daffodils and bluebells under black poplar and sycamore, a bee-loud goat willow on East Hill, lime-flowers, heather, wormwood on the scratchy dunes on a hot July morning, naked silver birch on a bracken-covered tumulus, edged with snow.

Along the paths and trackways I walked, surprised by the living and the light: a sleeping adder beside the broadwalk, tadpoles teeming in a woodland pond, a nightingale singing in a gorse citadel. The sea in the distance, a mirror, a streak of deep blue, pewter, flecked with foam, al-ways moving. The sky, huge above me, hurling rain, or pure azure, piled with mountainous clouds, throwing sunlight like copper against the oak trees.

Along the lanes and roads I walked: encountering the dead, the spiny, feathered, antlered, furred, scaly. An otter, her body heavy and stinking, a weasel, his tail tipped with snow, the speckled breast of a song thrush in my hands, a baby rabbit dying against my heart. Grass snake, hedgehog, owl, hare. Laying them to rest in a verge among the alexander and cow parsley ghosts.

Through weather and time I walked: smelling snow and mist and rain coming in on the wind, the scent of sweet violets as the winter turns, hedgerow flowers ribboning the lanes. Climbing into the long arms of sanderling oak and pines, tasting wild pears and damson, scuffling for chestnuts at the end of the year. Body thirsty for river water, salt and frost.

Ice on the lane cracking underfoot, paw marks in the snow – fox badger, bird – a huge moon above the barley field in May. Balancing a dead elm for firewood on my shoulder.

Past the reedbeds I walked, by the grove of ash and dark-tasselled alder: keeping tempo with my feet, with the rhythm of my heart, keeping time with the boom of bitterns in the spring dark, the stag roaring at leafall, golden celandine, toadstool and bulrush. On either side of this track, the legacy of history – gamekeepers, guns, dogs, fertilisers, derelict farm buildings, dying trees, emptiness, hostility; here on a track of flowers, a state of lightness, possibility, beauty, freedom, colour, vibrancy. Here the land doesn't care whether you have friends or have succeeded in business, or own a big house. Here your presence is everything, your participation, your communication is everything.

I walked myself home, back to a country I loved, but I could not connect with the people, or rather not in the way I wished to, which is to say equally. I felt awkward in the suburban houses and gardens, adrift among invisible currents of antagonism, or haunted by the past. I stood by poets and performers in the art centres where I worked, recognising their words, but feeling their presence like ghosts passing me by. It was as if I could not properly appear in any of these places. In the land, I feel vital and alive, in this social world I am invisible. I go to talks and plant sales and Greenpeace fairs, but there is something about joining in with these ventures I can't quite *do*. There is something in the women's faces, the ones who serve the tea and cake, as if their natural intelligence and creativity will never be allowed to burst out of them

One warm August evening in 2004 a small old lady approached me at a garden party. Her name was Pam Ellis and for the last 25 years she had run a botanical show at the local museum. 'You are going to take over from me,' she said. 'Do you know the Latin names?' 'Yes,' I replied. 'Good,' she said. And carried on talking to the others.

Of course I had no intention of taking over. I had a horror of becoming one of those Women Who Did the Flowers I had seen at the church jumble sales. But when the museum curator rang, I found myself saying I would do it so long as I could write a paper each week to go with the exhibition.

'You can write what you like,' he said, and told me where I could find the key and the water.

Here I am getting up with the hares and foxes, cycling through the dawn, roaming meadows and riverbanks and heath, collecting plants, placing life and colour amongst all the dry fossils and facts on the windowsills of the Southwold Museum. Each week I leave a small essay by the jam jars of flowers and leaves with their names, lore and medicine. I write about verge cutting and agricultural pesticides, about the radical apothecary Nicholas Culpeper and poet-botanist George Crabbe, interview ecologists and ornithologists and the guardians of the local woods and reedbeds.

But still I never meet any people.

Then one year, I joined my neighbours in a campaign, protesting the development of a tourist train that threatened to break the web of the back lanes we lived in. I began writing urgent leaflets and press releases and speaking on the radio in defence of the neighbourhood. Suddenly those words I had been writing about the flowers meant something; I found myself able to talk with everyone. As the planning application went to the council to be considered, we crammed into the village hall and stood up for the land and the birds and the trees. Afterwards we walked down the lane, the people from the big houses and the tied cottages – incomer, neighbour, local, landowner, renter – calling good night to each other in the warm summer air, under the fruiting cherry plums and elm, all historical enmities forgotten in that moment of banding together. It was a good night. Something stirred that night.

I had been walking myself back into the land but the land was taking me somewhere else.

In 2007 I had another tidal wave dream: the waves were going slowly along the coastline, sideways, like a massive long shore drift. Mark and I were standing on the bridge down by the harbour, watching it approach. That year we had been holding an open dialogue with the wild coastline, the woods and the fens, that began with a question: *Who is the self that walks this territory? What effect does the land – its moods, rhythms, creatures, weather – have on our imaginations, on our memories, on our realignment?*

It was a project to map the mosaic of the waterlands and their relationship with the human settlements along the shifting shoreline. We named it after the sea kale communities that held fast in the shingle banks. Having this kind of dialogue means you don't walk the track you choose. You encounter what is there, going out without a plan, meeting what crosses your path, not just the beautiful things but also the difficult. We began just as the sea asters were setting seed in the marshes. On 9th November there was a massive storm surge. A powerful northeasterly wind ran against the high tide and the estuaries flooded their banks. We ran out of our houses and stood by the shore as the rivers merged with the sea and swamped the houses down at Blackshore harbour.

After the flood people everywhere began speaking about how to protect the land. Small bands collected together, stacked sandbags against the river wall, spoke out for the birds and the spirit of the place.

'Just a few cows', we were told by the greysuited men from the Environment Agency in Reydon village hall. The agency were refusing to mend the broken banks of the Blyth as the government announced its retreat back to the metropolis. The defences of the rivers and harbours were being abandoned along the territory of the sea kale – the Blyth, the Ore, the Alde, the Deben.

The cows in the water meadows didn't count. The birds didn't count. The land didn't count. The people in the coastal sea towns didn't count. Suddenly I realised I was living in a different time. A time I did not know.

It was business as usual in the hotels in town, down at the pier, at the fish shop (*The show must go on!*) but some of us were beginning to ask why.

We walked the coast line from the statue of Neptune at Lowestoft, towards the Martello tower of Aldeburgh, from November to the following late summer. We stood on the beaches with 1700 others making a human SOS protest at Walberswick, watched an adder slither by through the sea peas as the police and activists outwitted each other at Sizewell power station, watched the sky burn as the reeds caught fire at Easton Bavents.

We swam in the ocean, with the seals, in all weathers, watched the sea shift colours, the waves tipped with the fire of sunrise. We swam in the wake of Roger Deakin, and walked in the footsteps of W.G. Sebald. Above us the sky raced with clouds, the wind blew sharp and salt, and warm, scented with heather, hail clattered on our heads. The land pulsed with light. Stags roared in the reeds. Seasons came and went. At night I looked out of my window, across the marshes, and where once only moonlight reflected on the sea, oil tankers floated in the darkness, waiting for the oil prices to rise, like giant neon sharks.

To belong you need a story, and to have a story you need a territory. You need a strong taproot to keep you anchored in a hard time. Sometimes the territory you find yourself in is not the place where you think you belong. It is not the lovely bluebell wood, or the rose garden where you sit alone with your thoughts. It's not a tropical ocean or an Aegean island cove. It's a windy English beach with people and houses and oil tankers on the horizon, where you encounter a thousand difficult questions about power and nature and exploitation. And the story you need now is not the story you were born with; it's a story you have to discover, that you are challenged to go walkabout and find.

I wanted to stay on that wild ecstatic shoreline with the flowers, with the birdsfoot trefoil and centaury and harebell, to put all my attention on birds and stones and light, to retain an outsider position of the artist and dreamer, but that shoreline kept taking me to the people, to face those awkward questions: to the protesters at Sizewell, to the campaigners in the village halls. It took me back into journalism as I found myself writing an article on our project for a local community magazine, the first I had published in 20 years.

The walking didn't take me to paradise, it took me straight into the heart of the struggle.

The Dye Garden

❧

'I'll go,' I say, 'but if they ask us for feedback, I am walking out.'

We are sitting in the garden at midsummer, debating whether to go to a neighbouring market town to see a documentary film. Hosted by a group called Sustainable Bungay to introduce their 'community response to peak oil and climate change'. It is called *Life at the End of Empire*.

The cinema is housed in an old-fashioned theatre and sparsely attended. The film is two hours long and unrelenting. Its narrator travels around the US on a personal odyssey, showing how agriculture causes the destruction of the planet, how everything in our ordinary lives, from the car that brought us here to the plastic that shrouds every supermarket purchase, is made possible by oil. At the end the filmmaker walks towards Lake Michigan in the rain, giving his antidote to the dire situation in which we are fatally embedded: learn medicine plants, he says, find your people. When the ship begins to sink, secure the lifeboat.

When the lights go up, contrary to expectation, I do not walk out. I am seized with a sense of excitement I haven't felt for years and launch into the audience discussion about how we can 'power down' and become less reliant on fossil fuels.

Unwittingly, I have become a community activist in a small market town in East Anglia, as the glass falls across the world.

This is the way it starts: the film is about the Power of Community. It begins at the 11th Hour at the End of Suburbia. You go against your wishes, lured by a love of documentary, and find yourself talking animatedly amongst strangers about Life at the End of Empire, asking whether you can come to the next core group meeting. In these films there is a moment when you realise that life is not the fairy tale you have been taught to believe, that everything is hurtling towards collapse, that everything you use, from your toothbrush to the clothes you are wearing, is made of oil and none of this is going to change just by hanging out on the touchline. It's the moment you join a movement that challenges the status quo and moves towards another future.

We will build the lifeboat together, we declared that midsummer day. It was the day we joined a community-led movement known as Transition Towns that will absorb both of us for the next six years. In Transition I got smart about the industrial-military complex and realised that the future was not just about me: it had to be about us. Breaking out of our individual silos was perhaps the most radical move any of us could make, coming together in a group, our most urgent challenge. But more than this, it gave many of us a leverage in the social world and brought us right out of a silent, shadowy realm, where we had no meaning onto a platform where everything we had experienced up to that point had meaning. We found our voices, our position, and most of all our fellow players.

We stormed the stage.

Transition

The Transition movement began in the small market town of Totnes in Devon. It started with a documentary called *The End of Suburbia* and the publication of a bold twelve-step 'energy descent action plan' for communities around the UK. Its core tenets were to build resilience into local economies and culture that were at this point of global capitalism extremely fragile. It was a bold statement, modelled on permaculture and a visionary architectural manual, with tools and resources online for locally-based groups, known as initiatives, to meet and explore the ideas set out in the plan that included food growing and policy work with local governments. The movement burgeoned in Britain after the financial crisis of 2008 and then around the world, firing up working groups in city neighbourhoods, bio-regions and villages.

We were a small group of local people and incomers, all ages, across the political spectrum. The energy unleashed by our meeting within this frame, emboldened us to give talks, to go to civic institutions, to start up community projects. In this town, we found ourselves no longer outsiders but engaged, like thousands of activists, thousands of communities, across the world, in a social work: reclaiming the fields; swapping seeds; pressing apple juice in the rain; serving giant saucepans of beans; teaching children about bees; making plant medicine; having a conversation where none existed before. This is not an interchange you would see in mainstream media, or hear in conventional circles, but it was happening nonetheless.

For a long time, it was the only thing I cared about.

Psyche and the herd

Psyche's second task is to face a flock of angry rams and gather wool from their golden fleeces. If you asked me which out the four tasks was the hardest it would be this: to face the herd and emerge without being trampled by their fierce and golden hooves. The rams shine and stomp their feet, they butt each other in the head. Psyche hears the clash of bone and horn and thud of hooves and weeps.

Beside the field where the flock graze and fight is a reedbed. There Psyche hears the small rustling voice of a slender reed who tells her the rams are made angry by the light and heat of the sun. By night they will be asleep. She advises Psyche to wait beneath the shade of a large plane tree and when the sun has gone down to gather the strands of golden wool left behind on the prickly bushes and briars.

The beehive

It was a bright November day with a sharp East wind. In a church hall people were gathering and taking their seats. They were not here to worship or go down on their knees however. They had come to hear about growing and distributing food from city growers in one of the most intensely farmed areas in Britain.

I stood at the back of the hall with a giant teapot in my hands, the church kitchen behind me. Josiah was on the front of the stage. After the speakers had finished, he instructed the audience to form into circles and discuss how we could get together and work out how to grow more food locally. The hall began to buzz: people sat in circles and exchanged information, ideas, and experiences; they discussed how to transform and renovate public space, start allotment projects, community projects. If you had peeked through the window at this gathering from the outside it would not have appeared significant. There was no one glamorous or rich or famous inside. The food on the table was ordinary: parsnip and squash soup, organic apples, home baked scones, tea. An inconspicuous event in a small market town in the hinterland of East Anglia.

And yet if you had come inside you couldn't have helped noticing a feeling. A feeling that came from the sound of people talking to one another about plants and the land, the warmth in the room, a sense you could get together and start again. It was a feeling that stayed with me for weeks afterwards. It reminded me of something. And then I remembered what that was. I had gone next door to my neighbour who had just bought a nucleus of honey bees. She was about to take them back to her London allotment. We stood in the garden before a wooden travelling case and there were bees flying out amongst the flowers, the bistort and sunflowers, shining now in the late summer afternoon. Listen, she said. I bent down and listened. The box hummed with the sound of hundreds of bees. It was warm and sweet-scented, and harboured an intensity you could feel even though you could not see it. We stood there for a long time together.

Some part of us longed to be inside that hive.

An alchemical space

I am curating a garden. It's a small walled garden that sits in the courtyard of the local library. The back bed harbours perennial flowers, spring bulbs and small fruit trees and the central bed is a showcase for plants that revolve around different themes. In the first year, Eloise and Gemma launched the community beehive group and planted bee and butterfly plants: lavender, lemon balm, hollyhocks. Last year this garden was hosted by Lesley who filled it with food plants: climbing beans, potatoes, currant bushes and artichoke, and the produce went to the Happy Mondays community kitchen and to a series of 'give and grow' seedling and produce events. The year before that Mark grew medicine plants: yarrow, vervain and burdock, and held surgeries on their curatives leaves and roots, hosted workshops on making tinctures and teas, led a spring tonic walk around the town streets and churchyards. The garden is a teaching space and a breathing space, a showcase for the growing plants we need to re-engage with as we build a low-carbon economy.

This year I am planting woad, indigo, dyer's greenweed, yarrow and St John's wort for a Dye Garden. Each plant will be an exploration of our relationship with them through time: the fashion industry (cotton), the use of colour (madder), the rural economy (hemp). We are surrounded by textiles, wrap ourselves and our rooms in their colours and design, and yet we never consider them. What would the world look like if we did?

The technological world goes so fast and furiously it's hard to have time to look deeply and truly at the wonder of ordinary things. The humble leaves of woad can be a doorway into the fabric of the world. The plant, once grown across the whole of East Anglia, takes you back in time, to the archaic and medieval worlds, it puts colour and yarn and imagination and belonging back into your hands. Takes you into every shade of blue.

Some part of me knows that unless we can engage as a band or network we will lose hold of the places and plants we love, that to connect in the spirit of regeneration we need conversations and gatherings, an alchemical space where things can turn around and we can forge another identity for ourselves as a people. Where we can let go of the arguments that divide us paying close attention to what we hold in common, in the small places, at the edges of things, in the spaces where there are no agendas.

What breaks up the false dominion of monoculture is the presence of diversity and kinship. The meadow, Darwin once observed, is resilient because of the beneficial connections between each plant, insect and organism that flourishes there. To thrive in a hard time we need to know ourselves as that chalk land meadow, as an old growth forest, as the network of mycorrhizal fungi beneath its leafy floor.

Walking

Here I am in the backroom of the Green Dragon with a giant roll of brown paper. We are drawing a map of the town for a series of 'wellbeing walks' we will hold this year. Everyone is getting animated with felt tips and crayons. Our kindergarten imagination finally let loose among the stern cobbled stones and tiled roofs of the 'fine old town'. Our walks will be short and attentive. We will walk on sunny and rainy days noticing the flint walls, the colours of the old wonky houses, orchards and garden, marketplace and river, crossing the wooden bridges over the surrounding water meadows, standing ecstatically under churchyard cherry trees and allotment poplars. It was the living breathing version of Christopher Alexander's seminal work on private and civic architecture, *A Pattern Language*, a joyful navigation of alleyways, doorways, benches, marketplace and courtyard.

Follow me: I am going on a wellbeing walk with the group and others from the town. This landscape could be a painting by Samuel Palmer, the apple tree laden with blossom in a quiet garden, the winding lane, the great harvest moon swinging above the surrounding fields of barley. You could see this place through political or historical eyes, as a landowner, or as a dispossessed people – a cruel and unfair England. You could see it through scientific eyes, the eyes of a disappointed environmentalist, noticing the dead poisoned soil and razed hedgerows, the threatened ash, the disappearing songbird.

Or you can see it as we do now, like the artist, and notice the round beauty inherent in all its forms. You could hear the blackbird singing on the rooftop, feel the soft south wind soughing through the leaves, the scent of summer rain, the land that is always here, rooted in deep time.

This evening I went walking with ten people along the river Waveney that loops around Bungay Common. At one point I jumped into the river and swum amongst the damselflies and yellow lilies. As I looked in front of me, I saw the people in a line walking through the long water meadow grass on this midsummer evening and as I went to join them, I realised why recognising the link between a line of people in a Palmer painting in 1830 and one that takes place in front your eyes in 2013 matters. Because if we can recognise and return to the place where we belong, where we become part of the living, breathing planet, we can stand by it and by each other.

You think living in seclusion amongst the dragonflies and damson trees is the radical move. But it's not. Being amongst the people in another spirit is the new territory.

The people in the room

It's an ordinary evening in an ordinary town. I'm standing on a bench in the Green Dragon and waving a black handbag by Issey Miyake: 'You have to guess what three designer items I am wearing,' I say. Everyone laughs as they look at my wintry gear: yak jumper, cashmere jumper, alpaca coat, zigzaggy pony-skin belt.

We're at a Green Drinks night in a free house beside the printing works. It's a monthly event held across Britain to discuss environmental issues within a frame of social change. Tonight I'm the 'expert conversationalist' and the topic is 'Give and Take Fashion'. We're looking at the world's second most polluting industry (after oil and gas) and the plants that supply its textiles. Each spring we've been hosting a 'Give and Take Day' where the community brings stuff they don't need and takes home something they do, without any money changing hands. In this run-up discussion, I'm telling everyone the story of how I once used to be a fashion editor and now just wear give-and-take second hand clothes.

Being wealthy in this grassroots culture you discover has little to do with money or consumerism: it is measured in sacks of potatoes and log piles, stored apples, pickled cabbage, seeds, honey, hand tools, coats, our informal exchange of goods and skills. Knowing the people behind provenance of all things: the raspberry canes from Rita and Nick and Jeannie, the apple and cherry trees from Gemma, the vegetables from seed swaps, our clothes and our furniture from Give and Take Days. Everything in my house and larder and woodpile, in my relationships with neighbours and local shopkeepers.

There is a pain in the heart, looking back at those nights now, because that configuration does not exist anymore: the people in their ordinary lives still live here but we no longer meet in the library or the Green Dragon, as we once did. It was an ordinary group but the future made it extraordinary, the way we were configured to be different, think along different tracks, be generous, share. I will realise, with the *douceur* of time, that it was an experience, a transition in itself. Learning how to be in a group, becoming part of the territory, re-enfranchising ourselves.

Sometimes we caught each other's eye. The feeling in the backroom was dark and warm. We sat silently together around a small table and close. It was one of those moments when the crack of the world opened, as if we knew we had met at a certain time for a certain reason, like a flower that has reached its height of beauty, just as a single petal begins to fall.

When I look back – we are caught at that table. It wouldn't get better than that, only sourness would follow: one of us would go crazy that summer, one would move away, another buy a cafe, another start a business; two of us would stand by witnessing the decline of an enterprise that still held its form but where the heart of the thing had drained away. Old men would come with sharp critical voices, with their odour of dissatisfaction. The women of the town would continue to decorate the tables with this season's flowers.

We wanted to believe it could go on forever, that our small events and projects would enter the traditional fabric of the place, but at some point the vision falters and you are forced to confront the conventionality that is wired inside the social psyche, the sobering truth that these community events are more about feeling good and belonging than the radical shift you understand is necessary. At a meeting to discuss the future of the library garden, I realised that even though I had curated this space, swept its leaves, planted, pruned, watered it all these years, no one had noticed I had been there.

'It's a teaching space,' I protested, as one member began to suggest pulling out the 'weeds'. 'Doesn't look like much of a display,' grumbled the treasurer.

I had become what I had feared. The Woman Who Does the Flowers. And badly.

I took some of the plants with me when I left: madder, mallow and thyme. The currant bushes were pulled up and replaced with rose bushes, Coffee mornings were held, hanging baskets were erected.

In those community activist years we gave things up. We got poor. We wrote about our experiences, we talked to the Job Centre frontline about climate change. We talked to our local MP about climate change. We hosted regional gatherings and seasonal meals, talks and conversations and picnics. We lost our car when we skated off a back road in a blizzard, someone invited us to share theirs. We had no ladder, we borrowed one from our neighbours; my shoes wore out, three people gave me their boots. I still wear them.

On Car-Free Day we found ourselves canoeing down the River Waveney under the stars at autumn equinox with Graham. You can stay the night with us, said Nick and Josiah and Elinor and Gemma and Daphne. After Green Drinks, Margaret drove us home, Rita and Kate picked us up to go to the Lowestoft Anti-Cuts meeting. This was the question:

Do you want control, or do you want relationship?

When a food magazine editor came to interview the group about our Happy Mondays community kitchen, I tried to explain how the learning and teaching we do is not formal. It struck me that there was a time too when I didn't know about any of this knowledge-sharing, workshop-giving world either. I didn't know what a facilitator was, or a go-round, or people who said it is not in my remit, or wave their hands in the air and bring lunch to share. There was a time when checking in had to do with the hotel, rather than a circle of strangers in some dusty church hall.

When you enter these grassroots collective spheres, you find out that human beings like doing practical stuff together: digging gardens, bottling jam, making biodiesel, mending jumpers, laying a dead hedge, chopping wood, without feeling entangled socially, or obliged. We liked the feeling of agency that these reskilled actions gave us, the sense that when the storm hits we could be all hands on deck and to know the ropes.

None of this would have happened without that Transition frame of the future. None of these activities would have happened without this small band of people, their kindness and heart. We would never have met. History and consumerism and the class system would have kept us separated from one another. The library community garden would be bare brick. The bee-friendly wildflower meadow at Flixton would be unsown. I would not be writing this chapter. You would not be reading it.

Except that it happened and had effect: and it's worth knowing if only to remember that these seeds were sown in a time when everything seemed set against us and all life on Earth. Those seeds are still inside us.

No glory

In March in that last year, as part of the No Glory campaign to challenge the celebration of the First World War, a speaker from Norwich Stop the War Coalition came to the library and talked about the millions of young men who died in the trenches of France and Flanders. This was not a wellbeing walk, a Give and Take Day, or any of our usual events, nor is the Transition movement political. And yet we gathered in a space so that a history that still caused a collective grief 100 years later could somehow be addressed.

Quietly and slowly after the talk several people told of their grandfathers and great-grandfathers who had survived the war and yet never spoke of it. Some finally spoke – or sang – as they lay dying, remembering their comrades on those muddy fields. The Great War is a trauma that runs very deep in the English psyche and the loss of whole bands of men from the surrounding villages can still be felt.

I realised then that no matter how many seed swaps we organised, or community meals we cooked and ate together, if these things are not done in another spirit, in kindness and with full awareness, they will affect nothing.

To restore the wasteland demands more from us than event managing or clever talking. For regeneration the conditions have to be right.

If not, the superficiality of our minds and our unfeeling wills will trample over the statistics of men and beasts killed in the name of Empire. Our hearts know differently but keep silent, because we have been bullied for centuries not to utter a word. Soldiers famously lost their ability to speak in the face of the horror at Ypres and Passchendaele. And still now it is hard to speak out loud about war or factory farming or deforestation, even among our fellows. We don't want to look at the industrialisation of the planet, and our implicit agreement in the slaughter. We want to be polite and well-thought of, and for nature to be our solace. Something beyond our friendly social gatherings and projects has to happen. An alchemical container is needed that could not be wrought at that library, no matter how well meaning our endeavours.

I am at Ipswich station waiting for the London train and there are soldiers everywhere on the platform, dressed in wool khaki. 'What are you doing here?' I ask one of them. The boy gazes into my eyes and something like terror and grief jolts through me. He hands me a card that reads: Rifleman R.G. Cole. London Regiment (Queen Victoria's Rifles).

'Oh,' I say, 'you cannot speak!' I don't know it yet but this is a performance being acted out in railway stations all over Britain to mark the Battle of the Somme. It is a show, except it does not feel like it.

In the carriage the ghost riflemen sit silently among the passengers. Opposite me the poet Luke Wright, famous in Bungay for his rollicking political satire, looks up from his computer screen and watches them.

A hundred years ago on this day 19,240 young men died in a war that is remembered as much for its poetry as for its bloody sacrifice. Thousands from the small villages of Suffolk boarded the trains to France and did not return. You can still feel their absence in the fields when you go walking. Loss is not a personal matter anymore. I have learned that too in these waterlands, where time becomes unmoored.

I look at the card in my hands and shudder: *we are here*, it says.

Pattern language

I spent my bohemian youth in a London neighbourhood, living alongside a band of fellow journalists, connected to a whole city. It wasn't until I returned to England after travelling that the word 'community' started to mean anything, as I found myself isolated from the human inhabitants in the Suffolk lane. An incomer, a renter and of no significance to the local rural, suburban – and strangely, feudal – society.

Writers, by their nature, are wary of traditional communities, the status quo who judge and condemn any one who thinks out of the box, who pushes for new life and liberty, who brings our difficult history to light. Where we meet each other is in a shared love of place. We love the names of places, our memories of journeys and encounter, our bodies remembering their curves and gradients, as we cycle towards the library, the theatre, our feet remembering street corners, paths, trees and bridges.

What I learned from that small group was that a sense of belonging doesn't depend on alliances with friends or colleagues. It doesn't depend on having a community you can call your own, or being tapped into the conventional circles made by institutions, by church, school, or family. Being of a place doesn't depend on the people who live in the district, or what they think of you or you them. Belonging is belonging to humanity, to the Earth, knowing that how you act and move and give every day matters.

Belonging is loving the world wherever you are. The damson trees in Cathy's garden, the onions stored in Nick's garage, the rain as it slides down the window. Belonging is something impersonal, and because it's impersonal it's more intimate, more generous than any idea of community. It's feeling at home on a corner in Mexico City, on the long road across America, edged with sunflowers; belonging to the mountains and the desert, to the Thames, to the Ganges, to the California coastline, and now to this grey North Sea, with all its watery territories, all the tracks we make, the people and the animals and the birds, the indigenous blueprint of places, the vernacular of everywhere.

We can talk about carbon emissions and climate change, we can think in numbers and statistics, tell our horror stories and hopeful visions, but nothing will change outwardly, the way we all wish it would, unless we come from this kind of affection for the places we live in. Unless we break out of a rigid understanding of geography, class and history and start tapping into our collective lineage, connect with the people who have been speaking, singing, creating this pattern language for millennia.

Until we start belonging to the trees and the wind and feel our feet on the ground, at home with perfect strangers in all places, all our conversations will be stuck within an old paradigm. Stuck in me and my idea of the world, separate from you.

We have to know the physical world as our home territory, we have to see each other as we really are: native, indigenous to this Earth. We have to know, as human beings, that we are the biodiversity we talk about. We are the heritage seeds of the future.

People of the Butterfly

I t's Friday night in Norwich and eleven of us are discussing climate change. So far we have agreed that to mitigate the effects of civilisation on the planet's atmosphere we will have to powerdown to a low-carbon economy, de-industrialise our agricultural system and bring equality to bear in the human world. You might think this conversation is taking place in a warm lecture hall this November evening, but it's not. We're meditating on the vicissitudes of financial power under the philosophical gaze of a statue of Sir Thomas Browne. We're sitting on a quincunx of (very hard and cold) granite shapes, inscribed with the names of his philosophical examinations upon life and death.

Occupy Norwich is holding one of its evening talks and I've come to spend the night here among the tents at Hay Hill. Like thousands of others I've been following the activities in Zuccotti Park and at St Paul's Cathedral online and I want to find out what it's like to physically occupy a space in the middle of a city in winter. The square is a small wet space under plane trees. Above us looms the Norman castle, an oppressive fort of stone. For some weeks now I have been bringing potatoes to the camp kitchen, sitting on these hard stones, discussing climate change and downturn economics with a shifting crowd of people in anoraks. The year is 2011 and these assemblies are happening in cities all over this island and throughout the Western world. In these squares, on the these steps, in these tent teaching spaces, a whole way of life is under a radical re-examination. Not by the 1% who rule but by the 99% – the people who serve its complex machinery. Ourselves.

Philosophers, since the first Athenian city-state was founded, have provided politicians with rational justification for their red-in-tooth-and-claw deeds.

92

Political ideas, sanctioned at universities, have justified all the Empire's violent acts from the shock doctrine first meted out in South America to the rationale behind the atrocities of the Khmer Rouge. In spite of the call from the 'thinking classes' for a full-scale manifesto of economic demands, the Occupy movement is finding its own directives. New kinds of street university are springing up where people can decide on the intellectual and ethical base behind their actions. Most of us have not met before and certainly not in these configurations. We are strangers bound together by our sudden realisation about the global banking system. We are used to living and thinking individualistically, within a hierarchical structure, sanctioned by the official bastions of education. Now we are coming together and learning to think and come to conclusions as a group. In common with other occupations, Occupy Norwich is using the tools of consensus decision making, skill-share and co-operative agreement.

'What we need is a maximum wage,' declares one of the climate change debaters.

'What we need is a fair society,' adds another.

'What we need is a society,' says a third and everyone laughs. A student called Sam writes everything down. Our names and our conclusions.

It's a Friday night in Norwich. The world passes through Hay Hill: shoppers and workers, police and street pastors, the homeless, the mentally challenged, curious and cynical teenagers, merry pranksters celebrating the end of another hard week. At the FoodCycle Cafe at the Friends Meeting House the long queue for the free weekly meal is dwindling. At the Forum, a Cafe Conversation on Philosophy and Depression organised by the university is winding up. We're just getting going. It's a debate that will go on until eleven and then continue around the camp kitchen until 1:30am.

In 1992 a German professor from the University of East Anglia walked from Norwich down the coast of Suffolk. His meditation on life and death begins with Sir Thomas Browne and ends in the streets of London, following a train of black funeral silk woven in this city of silk-weavers. *The Rings of Saturn* charts the intricate wheel of history as it holds us ransom in its grip. In their seats of power, the 1% preside, like dragons with their hoards, coveting form, bringing death and ruin on the world. As I lie on the cold hard ground, next to Sam and Victor and Nick, I'm wondering what it would take to break that pattern, bring warmth and life back to the people, to get us off the wheel.

Butterfly

In 2011 there was a story about the butterfly that went around the Occupy tents in the cities of Britain and America. The caterpillar keeps munching his way voraciously across the green planet. One day it enters a cocoon and everything it knows about its former life begins to dissolve. In this breakdown, the buds of a new form emerge, as if from nowhere. The old caterpillar forms rise up to defeat the imago that is beginning to shape itself, its wings and new colours. So it falls back. But, impelled to transform, it begins to rise again, and this time the imaginal cells that hold the blueprint of the butterfly link up and hold the line: the butterfly becomes stronger, the old structures dissolve and eventually it breaks out to become a pollinator of the world.

Transformation is a process human beings are born to undergo. As archaic and indigenous people will tell you, this changeover is part of our agreement with the planet. Our caterpillar civilisations however do not want us to transform in this way and lose their dominion over our labours. But sometimes the future is more powerful than the old world. Sometimes the forces of metamorphisis break through our carefully constructed lives, in places that have been locked away for aeons, and our souls quicken. A moment flashes out of the blue, when we realise what matters is not what we have been told matters.

In chaos theory, the butterfly stands for the small move that sparks off a radical transition within the non-linear systems of the planet – in the shapes of clouds, the flow of rivers, the populations of reindeer, the juncture when one element turns into another. When the butterfly appears it signals profound change and a vast switch of direction. A moment of turbulence in which limit cycles are broken, energy dissipates, structures shift and the planet can keep itself in a state known as far-from-equilibrium, so that life can happen. When the explorers of chaos theory looked at what kept everything in motion they found a shape they called the strange attractor. Drawn by the meteorologist, Edward Lorenz, it appeared like owl's eyes, like a lemniscate. Most of all it looked like a pair of butterfly wings.

The imaginal buds of the new butterfly fail when they first emerge from the soup in the coccoon: the great backlash of the caterpillar's immune system destroys all their fragile colour and beauty. At their second attempt however they are older and wiser. They learn to hold the new form of the butterfly by linking up with other buds. This is the story that underpins what we do and sometimes we tell it to each other in the hard times.

The butterfly has no power in the way power is commonly understood by politicians and the people who obey them, which is the power of domination, the way of the castle. Its power lies in the capacity of transformation, its strange attractive quality. The butterfly carries the colours of the dreaming in its wings and in the shape these wings make in space and time, it remembers the infinity present within all finite forms. To know the beauty of the Earth, of the transitions that can take place, requires us to relinquish our devouring of the world, and go inwards and dream. We have to re-imagine our lives. And as we let our former identities dissolve, our voracious small-minded caterpillar forms, we will start to know ourselves as we really are, to see each other in our true colours.

Media

Here I am sitting on those stones, in a red coat, writing notes in a time when I always carried a notebook: pages with lists of names, notes from talks and conferences I went to, interviews with activists, timetables for the collective 'social reporting' platforms I edited, ideas for my own posts, 400 of them in six years. A lot of quotes and meeting notes. Trying to catch a flash of butterfly wing, in the stories that fall between the cracks of our agendas, the ideas that could turn the fate of the world around.

During that time, I travelled to the city, documenting those circles and conversations: sitting uncomfortably on church room chairs and new age studio floors, around small tables in the pub in Alexander Street, discussing the progressive column I now co-wrote with six activists for the county newspaper. I came to assist the work of Transition Norwich 'comms' and for the Heart and Soul discussions that demanded a different attention from our country market town practicalities. My notebooks will lead me to form a grassroots newspaper, to cover the Paris COP21, to write an op-ed for the *New York Times*. It will take me to Joe Ryle in in the squatted greenhouses of Grow Heathrow, it will take me to teach report-age with an Occupy poet called Venus at the Sunrise Festival, it will take me to Manchester to help build a 'Real Media' network that was not dom-inated by mainstream media's fostering of antagonism and consumer de-sire. These were the years of citizen journalism, when everyone had taken to the barricades of the internet, filing copy, sending intrepid reports from Tahrir Square, from Madrid, from Oakland, a charting of all the popular, colourful resistance against those old forms.

It was a time when features about a relocalised culture were also being written: stories about social enterprises, repair shops, community gardens, local currencies, city farms, energy companies, co-op breweries and cargo bikes; testimonies of radical breakouts from individualism, a re-linquishing of a property-obsessed culture to embrace one that celebrated neighbourhoods and shared lives. A heartening tale of big picture vision and small everyday actions, of exchange and restoration and sincerity.

In the old world I am, like everyone I else meet, negligible: a nobody, struggling to appear like a somebody, so some institution or 1%er won't come down on my head and crush the living heart and soul out of me. But in Transition in these years, in this emergent future, you know your meet-ing in times of adversity means something. Those conversations brought a depth and immediacy into our lives that is hard to put into words.

Our skills and abilities that job centres and governments consider negligible had relevance in this context. My own trade of writing and edit-ing, brought many kinds of people together and allowed us to relate our own experiences, where none of us had space before. Communications that could, like the mycorrhizal networks underground, keep the lines open, cross-reference, untangle, make live, feed back.

That notebook was my record. As the world tipped out of balance and thousands of us endured economic hardship, I found my words were my agency. I found I was not alone in my struggle. I never ran out of copy.

Dreaming of Norwich

The caterpillar is voracious and its immune system is strong. You cannot assume that the first rising of the butterfly will be successful. Its flight will be resisted in subtle and unexpected ways. In 2009, as the Transition move-ment began, we would sometimes be sought out by psychologists offering professional help and by academics keen to write theses about community resilience, how grassroots action could affect wider social change. Our meetings often became strangely awkward when these outside investigaters appeared, as ambition and control began to emerge within groups that until then had self-organised around shared principles. On the surface you could not say exactly how this happened but underneath some of us recognised the old caterpillar forms of church and state.

In one of our Heart and Soul churchroom meetings that first spring, I gave a talk about the earth dreaming practice Mark and I had been engaged in for several years. Afterwards I suggested we could use this as a way of exploring our place in the city. It had gone down well among the artists in the group but had been severly resisted by several Quakers. Afterwards, four of us began our own independent project called The Dreaming of Norwich. We wanted to discover how the underlying mythos of a city could hold clues about radical change that our everyday language of data could never capture. Once a month we would meet up for a day, go walkabout in the city and then reconvene and share our findings. We walked along the rivers, through the market, visited buildings, sat in gardens, under trees, by ourselves and together. Helen photographed the streets, Mark wrote notes.

During our first journey, I climbed the steps to the Castle. It was a hot day in July and in the meadow below the ramparts I counted 42 species of flowers and trees. Norwich Castle was built by the invading Normans in 1067 as a fortress and it overlooks the old Saxon settlement and the historical quarters of this now small modernised city. I had just been reading John Berger's *Hold Everything Dear* about the Israeli occupation of Palestinian land, and the image of the watchtowers on the hills kept coming to me.

Same domination, same mindset, different time.

The sanctuary

When the Transition movement was launched, its blueprint for energy descent inspired over a thousand initiatives worldwide and provided an intervention for communities stuck in the rigidity of the status quo. It gave people a chance to meet within an ecological frame for the future and be able to speak, unbound from social and political barriers. However its essentially pragmatic nature meant those changes were mostly discussed in terms of outer behaviours and attitude. What was not addressed was the inner divestment of an old world, or how we could create the kind of culture that could be stronger and more beautiful than the one built and maintained by fossil fuels.

The movement's insistence on optimism, gave almost no space for the unstorying of our lives, for confronting our slavery to the 'inner authoritarian' that dominates our feeling lives and our actions, like the oppressive fort of stone in the heart of Norwich. For the kind of alchemical change that was required of us collectively. Sometimes when the subject of power come up I saw a glint of greed in my fellow activists' eyes, and shuddered.

'They are so powerful.' I am sitting next to Anthony Smith who had once come to our Transition carbon reduction circle and introduced the documentary *The Age of Stupid* (which he helped fund) at Cinema City, just before the COP15 summit in Copenhagen. Things are depressing at climate action campaign 10:10. There is not enough money and the political and corporate climate deniers are vociferous.

'They are so powerful.' I am sitting opposite Ross Jackson, a businessman from Copenhagen, whose book *Occupy World Street* is just about to published. We have all just been to a talk at the Assembly House called 'Guardians of the Future' where he explained his road map for a new economic future. I am talking about shifts that happen on ground level. I have worked with grassroots organisations for years, he says dismissively, what we need is a new political structure.

I am not a politician, an economist or a businessman. I am a writer, who knows human history depends on the decision of a people to follow a storyline, or change it mid-sentence. Trackers of the collective imagination, we have learned to recognise an illusion when we come across it: hold it up to the light and test it against the physical reality of space and time.

Storytellers know that no sorcerer is powerful for ever, that all spells can be broken. At some point the small child, the youngest daughter, the third brother, the fool, comes and challenges the magician, cuts through briars and restores beauty to the kingdom. One day the sister runs widdershins and finds her brother trapped in the lake of reason. He or she doesn't believe in the illusion of power that has been conjured, and so asks the emperor, the fisher king, the boy with the frozen heart the question that breaks the thrall. How come you have no clothes on? What ails you? Shall we go home?

As folk tales and history tell us: you never know when those people arise. The Arab Spring showed tyrants can be toppled, that autocratic regimes can collapse overnight. The Berlin Wall can come down. The big houses along the East Anglian seaboard can fall into ruins. These are not big moves organised by PR agencies or oil barons. These are the moves of small and ordinary people, holding out for something else. They are the spirit of the times.

Maybe it's because I spent a decade looking at the frills and furbelows of the *ancien régime*, documented its predilection for glamour and grand views. Maybe when you are brought up in the ambitious atmosphere of politicians and public schoolboys you can see and feel so clearly how everything is done at the expense of the human heart. Like fairy tale giants, these modern warlords amass great hoards of wealth and compete with each other, in a world constructed entirely of will and ego and its unbearable self-pity and self-importance. How everything depends on the mass of ordinary people, believing in the ultimate superiority of a fairytale elite – presidents and queens, stars and celebrities.

The story we are taught to believe in is the story of power. Power sends everyone in the room and in the world into a trance. What breaks its spell is not to desire that power, nor any of the material things it brings. It is to know deep in your inner core, that those who live out their dragonish nature at the expense of their hearts, never inherit the kingdom. And nor do the servants who worship or despise them.

We had to be the small people in the villages and neighbourhoods, eating in community kitchens, humbly sharing our tools and produce from our gardens. We had to be the people who told a new and ancestral story, living within the generous aesthetic of the heart, and not in the rulership of the will. We had to be the ones who carry the fire, even when it looks as if it has gone out, who know where the medicine plants grow. Walking alongside millions of our fellows everywhere, in all places, in all rooms. The ones who can say we are here. We are not going anywhere. Because there is nowhere else to go. This is where we stand.

Sometimes when we met in these circles and gatherings we experienced of a reckless kind of happiness, an inner drive that sometimes felt out of control and not quite real. We expressed our feelings of excitement in discovering each other, at this chance to begin again, to share stuff we had never said out loud. Possibilities and visions propelled us to meet up and speak together. But this collective moment was short. It raged like a bushfire, like a love affair, and then died out. Convention and control broke up those good moods and fragile alliances. The gap between the global situation we perceived in our minds and the local territory at our feet seemed vast and unbridgeable. Ideas did not make it into physical reality. People found themselves quarrelling without knowing why. There was a lot of talk about community, but not much fellow feeling.

To keep feeling good meant that someone else in the room had to carry the difficulties that came to light and feel bad. Chinese medicine practitioners might have recognised this as a symptom of over-enthusiasm of the heart. If we had been smart we would have looked at the history of new movements and recognised ourselves in the ecstasy of Ranters and Cathars. It was not our fault we skimmed over problems and shut down: we were all raised within the individualistic mindset of Empire, and the sudden awakening of our hearts brought all our resistances to empathy into play. Maybe if we had been smart fewer people would have walked at this crucial shift where the fun stops and the work begins. What made some of us undergo that period of unrest and conflict was not happiness, but something more like *hozho*. A determination to weather the storm in order to secure 'real-world harmony and balance'.

That's when I realised that Transition was more like alchemy than the behavioural change psychologists and social scientists were talking about. And that the first step of alchemy is not enlightenment, but the revealing of the shadow sides of yourself and your culture you have to transform, the dark *materia* of the *nigredo*.

Somewhere along the path I realised we were in the long game.

Kett's rebellion

A group of people are moving with flambards up the cobbled streets towards the Castle to commemorate Robert Kett and the Norfolk uprising that took place in 1549. We stand under the ramparts where Kett was killed, and listen to a professor of social history from the university, talk about the commonwealth and the people's struggle for fairness and liberty in the face of a 'hard-hearted' elite. At the height of the rebellion the camp on Mousehold Heath housed 10,000 people, until it was brutally suppressed by foreign soldiers, under the command of the Earl of Warwick.

Something happens at night when you gather together, holding fire beneath the citadels of power. When you connect its rule across centuries and nations: Mousehold Heath with the Occupy camp at Hay Hill, medieval barons with modern bankers, the clearances of Scotland and England with the current land-grabbing in Africa.

By night we remember something else of ourselves. Something our 1066 civilisation doesn't want us to see. We see ourselves within a deeper broader political frame, begin to access our deep memory of being alive on the planet, beyond the way we have been taught, creating resources for the few. We live in a culture that keeps us trapped in a fearful present, afraid of looking back, afraid of looking forward (is there a future?), trapped in an objectifying, hierarchical world. Our knowledge of History is carefully managed by the custodians of civilisation, worshipped in the form of buildings and possessions and figures of power, whilst the knowledge of how the Earth and the people really are remains hidden from view. But sometimes we access time that does not run in a linear way, in our imaginations that makes connections and see the pattern of things.

'In many ways capitalism began here in East Anglia with the enclosure of the commons,' said the historian, as we stood beside the plaque where Kett was hanged on a freezing December day. As the almost-full moon appeared in the sky.

Dreaming of Norwich: Autumn

In Iain McGilchrist's seminal work on the left and right hemisphere of the human brain, *The Master and the Emissary*, the core struggle is between these spheres' very different perceptions of the world. To engage fully with the world needs both these attentions: the all-seeing right, and the focused gaze of the left. The Master knows he needs the Emissary to carry out the task in hand, but the Emissary believes he is the master of the universe and denies any other authority exists. This is the big problem in the modern world. One the Kogi elders of Colombia calls it the struggle between the Older and Younger Brother. It plays out in ourselves and in our societies. The dominator mindset that refuses to listen to anything but its own voice.

Our dreaming of Norwich showed us that the devouring caterpillar was not housed behind the walls of the castle, nor in the churches or universities, but inside ourselves. To confront the hostility of the old order and not falter is a great challenge that grassroots groups face – the threat of violence that underpins all civilisations, meted out if we do not toe the line. Groups fail because they cannot handle the autocratic defence systems that emerge as the imago begins to form. This happens both within and without any organisation.

The butterfly effect of the 2011/12 uprisings from Cairo to Madrid to Portland, led to public spaces filled with people eager to discuss a different way of organising themselves: all bearing a marked similarity to Transition and Occupy culture. All of them were brutally suppressed as the authoritarian impulse and its adherents spread across the globe. Internally our organisations failed because we had not reckoned with the desire for conformity and power that arose in groups, and partly because we lacked a common lexicon, a prism through which we could understand what was going on.

That's when I found myself remembering a young poet from Belfast analysing the form of a poem. It was a poem by the Australian poet Les Murray about his autistic son, called 'It Allows a Line Scan at Fifteen'.

It

It talks in meetings with a voice like a cyborg. A deadpan voice that goes on and on and wears us all down.

It is made of mind. Data, facts, machines, correct spelling, precise rules and timings, rituals, mantra, constructs of all kinds.

It has an agenda it's sticking to. A secret one it does not divulge. That makes our meetings go round and round, get lost in details, come to no conclusion. Most of all It wants its own way. This is because It has to have control of situations at all times. Everything outside of It is a threat to Its total power.

It has said things to me like: You have to accept the fact you are second-rate and you are just A.N. Other. We don't want to know what you think. I have learned to not go under when It is talking.

It talks of love, but, being heartless, exudes only a kind of passive coldness into the space between us. Even when the heart is angry or bitter it is warm. I have learned in these years to recognise the difference between words and action by their temperature. You could say the rising temperature of our home planet is a response to the coldness of Its empire, the way a fever burns up an infection in the body.

It outwits psychology and sometimes is psychology. Has been the bane of many a wise man, even caused the wily magus Gurdjieff who articulated Its every mechanical move to close the curtains in his flat in Paris and start cooking for his friends.

It appeared in Diss when we all gathered, a pink post-it note in the centre of our problems-to-share wall – it read: *unconscious sabotage.*

It is a big problem in the world. Inside our own heads where it lives. Inside the meetings where we are trying to co-operate and find out a different way of doing things. Dreaming a different dream.

It doesn't dream. It likes to feel good and keep in control. Dreaming means out-of-control which equals BAD. When It feels bad It starts to throw a fit, throw its feelings outwards onto other people in the room. We've been intimidated by Its moods and tantrums, Its bone-chilling voice for aeons, so we keep quiet. It speaks with the power of gods and governments. Institutions and corporations are made of It.

It does well in school, where a lack of empathy with the object of study is essential.

What It hates most of all are poets. Poets see It coming and use their art to expose all its invisible workings. It has a pathological fear of being seen. Of being questioned by the heart. If It has a chance (which it has many times in history) It sends these all-seeing, all-feeling poets off to the gulag, to the trenches, to the Tower. Mostly It wears them out.

Fairy stories warn us about It many times. They are tales of how to outwit the saboteur and his wife, the cruel stepmother, what to do when the mirror enters our eyes and freezes our hearts, when we become trapped in reason, walled up in ourselves, held in a glass coffin, asleep.

It says fairy stories are for children.

We like to think we are beyond our childish games of It too. But It touches everyone. It comes through the young and pretty and clever and the wild man in the torn overcoat who is shouting too loudly in the room. In Transition when It gets the upper hand, people start leaving meetings. Groups dissolve. Good ideas get shelved. Initiatives run out of steam. Dealing with It in Transition means we're having to face people when It comes through. If we're going to succeed we're going to have to find ways of naming Its moves. Not running scared, or becoming enraged or bewildered or worn out.

Gotta get smart!

Dreaming of Norwich: Winter

Our year of dreaming together did not complete itself. By winter, an argument had broken out between us and instead of roaming the cobbled streets together we agreed to meet and deconstruct it, using a method known as 'conflict resolution'. We sat in a small terrace house in central Norwich and Helen showed us her painting of our four Dreaming journeys. It was a circular map of blue and green with a red dragon, a castle, a river and Mark standing amongst the weeping willow like a silver fish outside Julian of Norwich's cell. Dead wood from a sweet chestnut tree pointed into a white space where the circle was incomplete. 'There's a gap.' Helen said. We looked into that howling gap for three hours and It allowed us to shout and weep, to stand in each other's shoes and feel what it was like on the other side of the tracks.

'Storming in groups' is supposed to be solved by psychological means, by the intervention of professionals and wise elders – but unless It becomes Us, unless the Emissary cedes authority to the Master, any attempt at unity will lack the essential agreement to look into the eye of the storm in partnership.

We sat in the small terrace house and the conflict did not resolve between us, or rather how it resolved did not lead to our staying together, or in Transition. Our positions on radical change and our differing allegiances to the status quo and the Earth made it impossible. Our different financial and social situations queered the pitch. Alex said he refused to leave the 'military-industrialistion project' and would reform it from within, and I burst into tears and stared hard at my broken shoes, and said I could not see the way forward. I realised in that moment there was no empathy in the room for anyone's impoverished state, let alone mine. A strangulated feeling arose between us that writing about it now I can hardly remember.

What I do remember is when we left the house and walked into the twilight of the city, it felt as if a huge burden had been lifted. Outside the library there was a vigil for the International Day of Protest in support of COP15 taking place in Copenhagen. We stopped and I lit a candle and talked to a young Transitioner who had just arrived from Totnes. The climate summit that year was also to fail spectacularly. The scores of climate activists who had gathered there with hopes of 'turning the ship around' suddenly realised, as the police advanced towards them, that no one was listening.

The mood and direction of our endeavours would change dramatically in the following decade.

Going home

Sometimes you put your life on the line for a vision. It is a small light that burns inside you on a cold day. It appears to take everything you ever loved away, and then it gives you everything you have ever loved back. Undergoing that process is how you learn to keep the fire. The rulers – gods, government, corporate CEOs – like to govern over the people, but they do not care for the people. They do not care for you, or the fire you keep inside. Some part of you doesn't care for you either. That's the hard part you have to face. Psychologists and mystics can chip away at that part for years, and yet the only thing that transforms that part is doing the one thing It is terrified of: connecting with the heart.

The heart changes the game completely. So we are trained to be like our cold-blooded ancestors, like empire builders, to struggle in a frigid and loveless world, to attack and put each other down: criticise, mock, humiliate, dismiss. To be as successful and cruel as Alexander, as brilliant and heartless as Newton, inhuman, grasping for power, governed entirely by will and policed by terror. To hold the fire, means we have to love the people, though for sure the people do not love us. We love each other as fellows because we know that without these heart connections we fall big time. We end up in a cold sunless universe, without a dream to sustain us, without a voice.

When I stumbled upon the Transition movement, I found I had a vast treasure store of words at my fingertips, and I spent 2008-13 sharing them in hundreds of posts and newspaper and magazine columns. There seemed no end of things to say to about powerdown: about radicalising my store cupboard and working in groups. But after a while the collaborative writing projects I created began to run aground, and I found myself losing heart. As we used to say, the EROEI just didn't stack up anymore.

I thought at the beginning I was in Transition for the long haul. I thought it would shape my life and that I would make a livelihood from it and forge some deep and lasting connections with fellow activists. Then I realised my engagement was a transition in itself. It was a territory that needed to be encountered and navigated, like an ocean voyage, and my texts and photographs were its captain's log. Once I had understood the need to frame what I saw within the ecological and economic state of the world, from a social perspective, rather than stuck in a little individualist cocoon, I could move on.

I had a lot to be grateful for: immersing myself in community activism broke my own disenfranchisement; it broke my silence; it gave me a rough education and skills in areas I knew nothing about, from global finance to splitting my own firewood. But in 2012 at the Transition Network Conference, a moment came when I realised my love affair with the movement was coming to an end: I was standing with my fellow 'social reporter' Teen (also an ex-journalist) in an imaginary High Street of the Future. Everyone in the Battersea Arts Centre was busy building shops and enterprises out of cardboard boxes and string along its chalk-etched pavements. Our printing house was the first to finish and we needed to find some custom. So I went to the Job Centre.

We only have people with skills here, I was told tartly, you need to go to the Bank. Teen went outside to have a cigarette. I stood there holding the real life newspaper I had just co-founded and a feeling I couldn't ignore – a feeling of redundancy, that invisible crushing force normally experienced in real high street job centres. I realised that no matter how many pieces I wrote, or projects I co-ordinated, editorial skills were not considered important in this grassroots territory. Everyone can write blogs, so what is the big deal? 'Comms' in a corporate-shaped world is not true editorial, but a hybrid creature lurking somewhere between marketing and HR (and occasionally filed under 'well-being'). As I stared across the make-believe town and felt the optimism of the room, I remembered Charles Eisenstein that summer on a windy corner on the South Bank, after giving a lecture on the gift economy. He exhaled deeply as we talked, a group of UK Transitioners, eager to share our goodwill stories about downshift and community:

'We are playing,' he said, interrupting our optimistic dialogue. 'Because we still have a choice. We can still walk away. Nothing will happen until it becomes real.'

The Occupy tents at St Paul's had been evacuated. London was preparing for the great corporate show of the Olympics. The reality we all know from a hundred documentaries about ecological crisis is still hard to see, surrounded as we are by the city's lavish restaurants and glass towers, African fusion bands and pleasure boats. The Wave demonstration had flowed over the capital's bridges, to be followed by a decade of climate marches, anti-austerity and student protests, and finally held by Extinction Rebellion with their rainbow-coloured flags as it came to a close. Though it feels like nothing has happened, the allure that has distracted us for aeons is lessening. As our position becomes more stark, the language of the Master has begun to appear at the edges. It does not reveal itself in data or statistics, or political rhetoric, or psychology. It speaks in a language that once crossed every boundary on Earth, that artists and writers remember and still speak, or sing, or move to, or show, or paint, if only in fragments.

I realised I needed to write in another script.

Pharmakon

There's a story cited by Derrida from Plato about the invention of writing. Thoth, the Egyptian god of medicine and magic, tells the king he has created a method that will help the people remember and be wise. But the king tells him: the people will put all their wisdom in the writing and forget to hold it themselves. Eventually he allows it, with the warning that henceforth writing will be both a poison and a remedy. He calls it the *pharmakon*.

What I did not realise was that all the resistance to the writing projects I started in those years was not personal, it was how all governments, all corporations work. The managers of movements want you to write the official story, the new narrative that says they are now in control. They want you to write the press release, the bulletin, the newsletter in the language of the Emissary, but the writer, true to their craft, brings the pharmakon's medicine in the language of the Master.

Transition was no different from any other progressive organisation that wanted to be in charge of a future world. Its organisers were the right people with the right ideas and other people had to change to fit their edicts. But this is not what these times of planetary crisis are demanding. They demand we become a different kind of being and for that kind of change you need the lemniscate strange attractor, the pharmakon.

If you are a writer, this is a hard story to tell but you will endure all things to tell it. You are loyal to the Master in this respect, the Emissary who has not forgotten, who recognises that their presence is both a poison and a cure. Who remembers that as the caterpillar dies, a butterfly is born and all transformation is a struggle between them.

The work of the artist and the writer is to remind the people of this struggle, so we do not follow the wrong god home and miss our star. Somewhere far from this city by a fire under the stars: a man is telling a Russian folktale in a bear mask, a trail of small lights leads us into the woods where a man wearing stag antlers is crashing around the undergrowth and women are speaking in riddles. It is as if all the fairytales I had read as a child have come alive. A crack has opened in my heart to let them in.

Hoek van Holland

I am crossing the North Sea on the *Stena Britannica*, looking out through a cabin porthole at the prow of the ship, having a *Titanic* moment. The superferry is leaving the harbour and the lights of the oil refineries flare from the black land, its decks stacked with container lorries and holidaymakers' cars. In the COP21 treaty signed this year in Paris by the world's political leaders, there was no mention of shipping or aviation, two of the highest producers of greenhouse gases. The oceans were scarcely mentioned in spite of the crucial role they play in carbon sequestration and climate balance, nor was their alarming acidification, their disappearing fish and plankton, their floating continents of plastic. The ship moves into the night, as the feedback loops from centuries of industrial plunder begin to kick in across the planet. The last harbour lights wink red and green. Tonnes of heavy oil churn through the engine room, clanking out sulphur into the atmosphere. The passengers carry on drinking in the bar. The waves are high, tipped with foam, but we do not feel them as they roll beneath the *Britannica's* bows. They are there, nevertheless, moving inexorably toward the shore.

What remains

You could be bitter or disillusioned about the grand plans that fell into dust, what felt like small betrayals between friends and colleagues, but what remains now is neither feeling. The medicine of the pharmakon is bitter, but its effects are sweet. When I look back, when I go to gather the strands of material left by the furious herd, what I remember now is the journey: travelling to the city from a platform covered in St John's Wort and wild carrot, waiting for the little train to take us across the Broads, its shining waterways and misty meadows. And after the meetings, heading back down the back lanes, where the stone walls in spring are green with shepherd's purse and ivy-leaved toadflax, and ancient cherry trees lean out of hidden gardens; then down the Prince of Wales drive, heaving with revellers, music roaring out of the doorways, the bouncers dressed in black coats on a sharp winter's night, and two girls in very short skirts and large smiles leaning out of the shadows, handing me a half-full bottle of champagne. We can't take it with us, they laughed, and Mark on the platform at Lowestoft, waving as I return in the dark. Tell me, what happened, he says.

'Look!' I say, and hold out the golden skein in my hands.

I came to Norwich because that October night in 2009 there were 400 people gathered in St Andrew's Church and I found myself on a Heart and Soul, Arts, Culture and Well Being table, next to Helen, who said after listening to Transition Network's keynote speaker on peak oil and energy descent, she was going to have a problem with last year's trousers. What would she do when she was so out of style? She handed me a dishcloth she had knitted and said it all started here. We looked at the tangled threads and burst into laughter. I am a terrible needlewoman, and she wasn't much better.

I made a terrible rocket stove, I slept on the pavement under the plane trees at Hay Hill, I painted my face blue and opened Earth Hour with Mark and Tom and Chris. I joined an anti-cuts demonstration by the park bandstand on an icy February day. I stacked a lot of chairs and weathered the storm. We went, we met, we had those conversations. I got strong. I learned to hold my own in a group, to value what I could bring, not fall apart when the rams roared out of peoples' mouths. When the bluebeards and wicked stepmothers told me to back off, go home, stop writing. The powerdown years taught me how to hold fast when the rage and grief and terror of aeons rocked the room. Most of all they put a story of regeneration back into my hands and gave a purpose and nobility to our flawed endeavours.

What remains in the ashes of the fire that burned in those years is what matters in the end. This is a story I wanted to tell, what the rams left me, as night fell – strands of gold on the thorn bushes of Colchis.

What's Your Position
as the Ship Goes Down?

❦

What's your position as the ship goes down?

It's the question the man keeps asking us, as he storms the stage and curses the thousand-year-old myth of exile that has wreaked havoc on the planet and the once robust psyche of the human race. Psychotherapy has betrayed us, he thunders: it ignores the Earth, it takes no account of social justice and no longer speaks with the dead. We are divorced from our collective daemons and are paying the price. The gods are fed up! he declares. They do not fit in our heads. They want out!

The man is James Hillman, famous archetypal psychologist, delivering a lecture on Jung and classical mythology. Tall, erudite and very, very annoyed, he beats against his chosen subject like an eagle caught in a snare.

Sometimes you are in a place and you are not sure why you are there. All around me the audience to this Olympian tirade are calmly writing notes for their essays and quite a few of them are making their way to the 'bathroom' and back. It feels as if I am the only person wondering how to answer the question, and another he mysteriously keeps repeating:

What are we going to do now, Jimmy Dean, Jimmy Dean?

James Hillman is dead now, but true to his profession and mine, I have kept the unanswered questions tucked under my own wing. In 1999 I am looking at my night dreams in the city of Oxford and the Indian god Varuna has just visited me. Black-coated, stern-faced, he strode down the aisle of a church and delivered a message:

Consolable grief we can help with, inconsolable we cannot, with the underlying information that *Separation is arrogance.*

Varuna is a primary, Underworld god, ruler of the watery nagas, who carries a noose in his hand in the shape of a snake. He storms through the dark church because he is the keeper of the cosmic law, which is not the law of human beings or their religions. In his 'essay' on myth and civilisation, *The Ruin of Kasch*, Roberto Calasso outlines the relationship between the primordial god and his worldly counterpart, Mitra:

> The civilising sweetness of Mitra, 'everyone's friend', can only exist insofar it can stand out against the dark and remote background of the sovereignty of Varuna. 'Mitra is this world, Varuna is the other world,' the *Satapatha Brahamana* clearly states. Mitra is the world of men; Varuna is the rest, perennially around it, capable of squeezing it like a noose.
>
> When the world only runs according to the laws of social contract, Varuna's nooses tighten around 'those who did not know these were the results of many sentencings under a law no one could decipher anymore.'

Varuna comes before Indra, before Shiva, before all the monotheistic gods and the myth of the Fall. He is akin to the classical Titans, kept trapped under mountains, in stone towers, or banished to the oceans. But no matter how invisible these primary beings are made out to be, there are consequences to ignoring their ancestral laws. And a life lived knowing there are consequences to every action takes a very different shape to one that assumes, so long as Mitra's laws are kept, you are free from any feedback loops.

Twenty years ago, it was the word *console* that grabbed me. It means with soul, with sun. The gods can console the human being, Varuna tells me, but if he or she is inconsolable, this is not because the god cannot help, but because human arrogance will not let the spirit in. If you insist on separation and sorrow, you block the gods' entrance.

The dream was preceded by two others: one took place in a church in which a small boy was possessed by the ghost of a woman who had hanged herself, and the other at the mouth of Hades where Second World War soldiers were wandering out, shouting, 'You are supposed to save us!' In both these dreams I was trying to intercede as an intermediary, and failing because I was stuck in a place of inconsolable grief, among the furious and lost.

To get out of 'hell' we need to ask an Underworld god for help. That's a deal most of us resist because to let spirit in means undergoing radical

change. It means taking on knowledge you would rather not have any responsibility for. But forced to choose between increased consciousness or
oblivion, there sometimes is no choice.

When you discover the world is not as you thought, the heart demands
you make a move: when you stumble upon the reality of the abattoir, the
maize field, the garment factory; when you take the red pill and look at the
graphs of Arctic sea ice, financial bubbles and oil production; when you
suddenly notice the barn owl no longer flies past your window, or the hares
leap in the field, you can respond in three ways: you can continue to listen
to the band and repeat to yourself I'm OK, the ship is OK; you can sit on
the stairs and lament that it is happening; or you can head to the lifeboat.
Obviously, you tell yourself, that is the correct position to be in when the
ship goes down.

But what if you can't make it to the lifeboat on your own? What if
you find the lifeboats were sold off long ago to pay the shipping company's
debts, and you are not, you suddenly realise, a passenger?

Restoration drama

You can do physical things to mollify those thousand-year-old consequences of our civilisation. In these downshifting, community activism years, I
have paid full attention to Mitra: I have reduced my carbon emissions to
four tonnes a year; I forage and cut my own wood, wear cast-off clothes. I
have given up going to supermarkets, I don't use palm oil or buy tomatoes
grown by modern-day African slaves. But, key as those responses are, this
is not the realm that Hillman was talking about on that warm spring night
in Santa Barbara, California as the millennium turned. The place where
Varuna lives in a dream.

To admit the old gods requires a shift to working along the horizontal
axis of feeling and spirit, in a world that only admits the presence of the
vertical – the human body and mind. To be guided by our fiery spirits we
have to feel, in a world designed to prevent us from doing anything of the
sort. Rage, grief, despair, sorrow, are emotional states that keep us in lockdown, wringing our hands and justifying our position on the stairs of our
sinking ship. The heart however can be consoled in time. It is consoled by
life that holds it dear, and because it is never alone.

Jeremy Rifkin, in his book *The Empathic Civilisation*, describes how each age in Western civilisation consciousness expands, relative to its energy production and communication systems. At this point we are moving from a *psychological* age towards what he calls the *dramaturgical*. Empathy expands with our ability to play different roles and thus understand the shared mortality of all creatures. He suggests that unless we learn to empathise and feel together on a planetary level, our ability to withhold or weather collapse will be impossible.

When you track dreams you realise you cannot analyse them psychologically, or they disappear like deer into the forest. You learn quickly that the storyline is not important, nor the fact that your mother or your ex-best friend are once again making you feel like a dishrag. The first key thing in a dream is your position within its drama, and the second key thing is how you move from that position out of the constricting space it holds you in. The third is that, when you make the move, you can see that things change in many dimensions at once. Your dream is not a personal problem, it is a collective state.

Civilisations hold us in repeat dramas, like Sebald's rings of Saturn. We are doomed to keep following the mechanics of the plot, unless we can break into the action, *deux ex machina*, and change its course.

Dreamwork is one way to open ourselves to this radical consolutation. Following the track of myths, as Hillman did, is another way, so long as we do not become more fascinated by our pathology than the world's freedom. The gods, once our way-showers, become easily trapped by our clever 'left-hemisphere' minds, filed under 'Symptoms' and 'Syndromes'. They get mad in there, and we get sick. *100 years of Psychotherapy and the World is Getting Worse*, as the learned doctor once wrote.

When you face the consequences of your unexamined, civilised life, you make moves to restore the world and your place within it. You have a practice, adopt a warrior attitude, you prepare for the future with less energy and money, empty yourself so that you are flexible, free to respond without some ghost or untempered ego in the way, knowing that each small move matters on levels you do not always see. Most of all you can break out of your mind's silo and initiate yourself into the tribe – become one of the people.

But however you move, you know you can't do this stuff on your own. Somehow you have to decipher the law.

Our ways of understanding life in graphs and linear narrative are not cutting it at this point because the planet is not shaped that way. Its laws are not made of words or mathematics. Varuna speaks in winds and ocean waves and his law governs worlds of never-ending chaos and creativity. We can no longer peer into our human problems as if we were Freud, and our 'issues' a hysterical woman from Vienna. In a dramaturgical age, we are all actor and director and playwright, and frequently find ourselves waiting in the wings, spear in hand, woefully under-rehearsed. The Earth, we realise, is our stage. Without it, we are meaningless.

Finding our star

Last night I went to Westleton Common and looked at the stars with a group of local astronomers. The Common was once a quarry and is famous now for its tiny heathland flowers and nightingales. In late summer it houses a small amphitheatre of bell heather and bees. The group has just formed and each month they hold a 'star party' and you can go along and watch nebulas, galaxies and the moons of Jupiter through several large telescopes. We were invited by Malcolm who has a smallholding in the next door village and whose organic vegetables we have been eating for 12 years now.

There is something extraordinary about meeting strangers in the dark (torch light impairs night vision) and it seemed to me, only on a piece of common land among people who are keen to share their knowledge, would you find such a feeling of friendship and ease.

Up above us the constellations burn in the vastness of space and time. They have scientific names like M57 and the Trapezium, and also older mythic names, conjured by civilisations that came and went before our own: Aldebaran and Pegasus, the Crab Nebula, Orion the Hunter, his Dog and the North star by which we set our course. Thanks to the telescopes I now know that the Seven Sisters are in fact a host of luminaries, and that Betelgeuse who shines red at the tip of the cosmic bull's horns is old and dying. The sun will become a planetary nebula too one day, says Malcolm, as he describes the fall of our home star into its final form as a white dwarf. 'And then what?' I ask.

'It becomes a black dwarf.'

'And then?'

'That's it!' he declares and we laugh and go in search of the Orion Nebula.

In some ways you might say that we are short of modern stories to explain our position in the universe: we have looked so far into deep space that we cannot see the blueprint of the heavens, so they might parallel our lives, or the drama of the solar system in which our planet, Earth, plays a distinctive role.

Maybe we need to know that the ship is always going down because that is the fate of all things in the universe, and that our struggle and desire to hold firm and burn brightly in the night sky, in spite of our inevitable mortality, is what makes sense of everything, whether we are a four-billion-year-old star, or a butterfly who lives for three days. That is what gives us meaning and dignity and frees us from Varuna's noose as a people.

To shine means we have to deal with the darkness of ourselves and our collective, which is the 'sacrifice' described by all mystery and spiritual traditions. We have to lose our untempered powers and pleasures, so our hearts may weigh as light as Maat's feather. Civilisations fall because, as native and archaic myths tell us, we fall into matter and neglect our light and fiery natures and our connection to dimensions beyond the one-dimensional here and now.

Though the astronomers can give us facts and the mythmakers and astrologers stories, our life together under this night sky is always a mystery, something unknowable, something you cannot pin down with word or image, number or symbol. But if on a clear night you can let that mystery in and let it move about you, you might discover everything that ever needs to be known. That's a paradox only the human heart can handle.

Sometimes I do not know entirely who I am: there is a lot of space and time now, where there used to be history and culture and closed doors. I am more actor than storyteller, and so perhaps in this brief role as messenger I can enter and answer Mr Hillman's question at this point in the play:

What do we do now, Jimmy Dean, Jimmy Dean?

Open your mind; set the gods free. All hands on deck.

III

SKY

Winter in the South

❧

A shape of life has grown old, and it cannot be rejuvenated, but only recognised by the grey of philosophy; the owl of Minerva begins its flight only when the shadows of dusk are gathering.
– Hegel, The Philosophy of Right.

'*A lors c'est simple!*' laughed Cyril. We were sitting round the kitchen table in Tourette sur Loup. It was deep winter, and the nights of deep frost circled the mountains above us. The instruction was simple but the situation was complex.

We had been invited to meet up with a band of people from France, England and New Mexico. *Come!* Aurelia had said excitedly over the phone, and now weeks later we had all gathered at Egmont's studio apartment in Vence. We planned to set up a community together in the South of France. We had ideas about why we were meeting – ideas about the future, about living in a different spirit on the Earth, working creatively together – but something was stalling.

In the winter rain, we walked around the walled town of Vence looking for apartments. A clown from Arran held a rose mutely before the passers by and sometimes hit them, and two tigers from Siberia and Africa sat in a tiny circus cage. We sat in seaside cafes. planning our lives but at night we lay in the shuttered dark on mattresses, ten of us among a pile of suitcases and Indian instruments and paintings of quince and supine women. We felt trapped in the outsiderness of ourselves and could not speak.

For the third task, Psyche is handed a water jug by Venus and told to climb the mountain to fill it from the source of the river Styx. Psyche, meekly and with a failing heart, climbs the jagged slopes but as she approaches the spring is swooped down on by its dragon guardians. She hides, thinking she should dash herself against the rocks below, as the task seems impossible.

But above her, a god is circling in the sky, the great chief Jupiter in the form of an eagle. He offers to give a hand and taking the jug in his claws, goes to battle the dragons on her behalf and returns with the vessel filled with the dark waters of Hades.

One night, I have a dream: I am on the rooftop with Mark and the goddess Pallas Athena comes from behind a tree, and says this intersection happens very rarely in the universe and not to blow it with a false sense of time. Now is the moment. 'You know you are the wind of change, so you need to change – whatever situation you are in'.

Now is the moment, said the dream. I have learned to take notice of the dreams that come in difficult situations and give instructions, no matter how inconvenient. The next morning I threw open the shutters to the sun and wind and went with Mark and Cyril into the mountains. He took us to a steep valley where a group of Egyptian vultures had returned and another where he had lived in a tipi for several years. In this stony village under the apple trees, we celebrated the winter solstice with another group of people. We spoke different languages and yet we spoke the same language. We sat around a fire and chanted in a temescal and later talked in a tiny cabin into the night of our trips to Mexico, about peyote, about angels, about the difficulties of living on the edge of our collectives, neither rich nor famous, nor with any houses to our name.

And then we all dispersed like dandelion seed heads in the wind.

The owl of Minerva

You can't meet in the spirit of the new until the spirits of the old have left you. The old cling on in the Underworld, amongst the shades, they demand revenge, and your own feelings of injustice keep them hooked to you. For a long time afterwards, I thought Pallas Athena was the draped blindfolded figure at the dome of the Old Bailey, holding the sword of truth and the scales of justice above the courtrooms, seeing the balance with her inner eye. But her message was not about justice.

Pallas Athena is the owl-eyed goddess of Greece, the goddess of cities and craftsmanship and olive trees, the great war strategist born from her father Zeus's head. She arrives in the twilight and sees in the dark because in the realm of consciousness this is where you behold the fabric of things, the truth of the matter. She came, on the roof of the building, perched like the statue, like an owl, telling me that a warrior move was required.

The gods arrive with messages in the twilight when you cannot see the wood for the trees. When we came to France, we had hoped it was the start of something but it turned out it was to say goodbye. We could not see the ramifications of our visit from our small vantage point. All you can know in these circumstances, is what you feel in your heart, what your body longs to do. We had to fly out of the cage of history, and enter another kind of time.

One thing was clear: this was no longer the time of travelling. This was not Mexico where we could dance on roofs to Aurelia's drum, nor even Oxford where people still meet in the woods on a spring night. This was a country that had invisible blood running down its streets, where the expression of the spirit had been annihilated. Though people have 'identified' with the Cathars and been intrigued by the spiritual legends of these mountains, the legacy of the fear from those times is still running in our bodies. As soon as we had decided to go to France, I started to tremble inside. This began to lessen after I had the dream and opened the dark shutters of the house. By the time Mark and I visited Beziers at the end of our journey, it had gone.

Sometimes the narrative of a particular place or people is held in the fabric of your being. It is a collective memory stored within your cells. Sometimes the suffering you undergo when this is remembered is yours to deal with and sometimes not. Sometimes you are simply ignorant or foolish and have jostled something awake. You have in those times to be very sure indeed why you are in a place. When you travel, it is easy to pick up the memories of a place, the history that has played out on its soil or in it buildings: standing, shuddering, on the site of an old workhouse in Oxford, driving through the Black Mountains in South Dakota, in a pool in the Misery Mountains in Australia. In Chile in the desert town where thousands disappeared. The false sense of time Pallas Athena is talking about tells me I am stuck in a cellular history loop and I need to break its hold.

The spirit of the times does not require us to work in insular groups inspired by spiritual ideals of the 12th century. The Cathars, like many Gnostics, considered the Earth to be created by malevolent forces, and themselves as elect and pure, and they were brutally eradicated by the ruling powers for their heretical beliefs. Many people get inspired by their

121

radical ideas, by the troubadour spirit of those times, but these are danger-ous things to be romantic about. We wished to be together but medieval terrors separated us – our desires to be small and safe inside ourselves, our spiritual fantasies, our silent fears of poverty, of failure, of the crushing powers of governments and bureaucracy. We needed to be updated. We needed a change of heart.

The dream was clear. The winds of change come and move you out so you do not live in a false sense of time. I could no longer remain in groups that were only held together by some historical romance. The sword of Athena cut me loose.

Turtle Island

In these travelling years I slept in moon lodges and dreamed of medicine people and Cathars and Indian gods, and I sang and danced alongside a band of fellow seekers as we moved through the great landscapes of the Americas. We were searching for a deeper relationship with the world and our 'hard yoga for the earth', as Gary Snyder once described it, pushed us into some very difficult corners, not least among ourselves. We spent a lot of time dealing with the karma of our families and connecting with indig-enous medicine plants. We thought, foolishly, that the collective shift of consciousness we yearned for would somehow just happen and our meet-ings would assist this. We were coming from the future and had been born into the past. We thought we could travel forever and live in bamboo huts on the sides of sacred mountains, but history and destiny dragged us back to our home countries. The ancestors told us: *those who caused the problem have to deal with it*. And then they disappeared.

The problem, we knew, wasn't going to have a neat solution, like a mindfulness class you could do every Tuesday. *I am another yourself* was not a mantra: it meant going through all the files your cultural history threw at you, being treated like an exile, losing most of your dignity and your spending power, and then having to start over again. Few of us want-ed to go through the emotional mangle that would make us human. Most of us resisted the fall in our own ways and stalled.

You dreamed me, Mark said, what's next? My attention, as if whirled by a Ferris wheel, is thrust out of my hands – I am in a different place. In a place of caves and mysteries, of mountains, of speaking plants, of zigzag patterns of light and colour, of gods who glide through my companions' faces, of inner golden riches and peacock eyes. It feels like home.

For years, those people for whom this place is home seek it out. We seek it in deserts and mountains, in forests, in huge lands that are not our native lands. We seek it in music that comes from the vast primal savannahs of Africa and America. We read books whose words we savour on our tongues because they speak of the vast galactic territories we have now found inside ourselves. But when we return to our homelands these things evaporate like dew. They appear insubstantial, without root. Like glasshouse plants, we are not strong enough to transplant those visions in the rough weather of our own lands. We cannot speak them out. We seek the gods we once saw in each other's faces but cannot, like failed magicians, conjure these things anymore: the jaguar fades from your face, your eternal well dries up, the eagle flies away, we no longer sing together and dance as once we did; when we try the sounds are cacophonous where once there was harmony. It was good at the beginning to be on that holy mountain, in the desert, in the jungle ruins, in the sacred valley, in the ancient grove. The land spoke to us, the ancestors came to us, we spoke with the turkeys, with snakes, with trees, rocks, clouds. Then we went inside the straw-roofed house, into the caves of night, where people have always gone. There was a small fire and ourselves and the cosmos, whirling.

There it was easy, here it is almost impossible. When I seek you again each time I find myself uninvited in your new house. You have forgotten. We do not know each other anymore. I am irritating, a reminder of something that has gone. We are sitting in a darkened room in Minneapolis, in Vence, in London. You came to me shining as gold, like a robin singing in the winter night, yet when I see you here in this place you have your work, your house, your wife and a river runs between us, whose dark Stygian waters I made an oath to, before even I was born.

Now we are ordinary people in a grey jumbled European city and I am the same, only perhaps with a more relentless memory, a memory that torments me at night with its sounds of turquoise cave water, the scent of jungle rain. But this was not the end as I found out, it was the beginning. The truth was that the magician was supposed to fail and we were supposed to be ordinary. And we were supposed to return to these native lands.

So I remember everything; the scent of your body in the jungle night, walking down the peyote path in the dark using my owl eyes, the sky throbbing with light as it lay with the Andean mountains. The peacock. The raven. The laughing. Those who pointed the way. Those we once travelled with. Those who keened on the mountain, who howled with the wolves, whose bodies were made of singing bones and fire. When we were winds and birds and spat the poison of the forest roads out of old selves. The civilisations rising and falling like a sandstorm in the valley below. The orange light in your hands that was the sun falling before us, the grey world disappearing behind you.

'It's in our hands,' I said.

Returning to their native lands my companions vanish without trace, down the New York subways, into the Parisian cellars, into the printing shops of Mammon, into obscurity, into forgetting. We do not disappear. We wandered for years, writing out maps, and then burning them, reducing the remembering of that world to a single focus. A question.

'What's next, now I know all these things are inside of me?'

Alpes Maritimes

'You are my heart!' said the tree and I jumped. Three of us lay in the small stone room in the winter afternoon, listening to a drum, beating out a rhythm into the silence, and a man's voice singing, a deep note that was also a high note. The sound of an ancient world.

Today we went up into the mountains to visit an ancient tree, walking up steep, icy paths toward the forest. The tree is said to be one thousand years old, and is revered in these lands as a wisdom tree. It is so old that it has become empty inside, so all three of us could stand together inside its woody body. We climbed up the chimney of the trunk and sat on different branches, listening to the deer running through the wood, to the hunt that went by and to the eagles that called to one another high above our heads in the open slate-coloured sky. And when I saw all these things again in my mind's eye, lying down in the dark stony room in Tourette Sur Loup, that's when the tree spoke:

You are my heart.

This is no ordinary tree of course. It is a holm oak, one of the Celtic alphabet trees, evergreen brother to the deciduous oak, ruler of the dark half of the waning year. In England the spiky-leaved red-berried holly tree rules the time of descent, but where the tree is native the holm, or holly oak, takes command. At the solstices of the solar year, the light and the dark oaks battle with one another, and one cedes rulership to the other. It is one of the oldest tree mythologies in the world: a myth you can still catch in snatches of song, carol and rhyme – rituals of yule oak logs, need fires and the holly tree that bears the crown. It is a sombre tree as befits the dark half of the year. A grey furrowed trunk and a great crown of shiny oval leaves with silvery undersides and prickled edges. Here it is the principle tree of the hills. Its dark sentinel forms are everywhere. In the alphabet, the holly or holm oak is *tinne* and regarded with awe. It is the tree of the cross, the oak king's challenger, the tanist, and it is to know this energy that we three climbed the mountain today and now lie here, each of us, to consult with the tree in our imaginations, the way people in Europe have been communicating with the wild world for thousands of years. Lying down, closing your eyes, allowing what images come to you in the dark and embrace of cave and stone.

We sit in the small kitchen afterwards, mugs of wild thyme tea in our hands, and compare our experiences. Each of us found the tree initially difficult to connect with. Then we had remembered the eagles above our heads and suddenly found ourselves inside the tree's body.

'I saw the tree from above and it appeared like a cross, like a swastika with tassels of energy flying from each corner. I saw these interdimensional crosses all over the world. Our presence in the trees activates them and us, and also the web of life. When we connected with the holm oak, the hunting dogs got lost. I remember thinking at the time: there's going to be a hunt and the deer will escape.

'The tree told me the following:

'So, at one time everyone will be totally lost. Because you have already been lost, you know the territory, you know what is correct and what is not. But you need to be more strict in these matters, for if you indulge others, it will not be correct. The reason you are not tight enough is because of pride, which brings in these interferences in your mind and wastes your energies.'

'Pride?' chorused the men in disbelief.

'Our pride is in the habitual ways in which we do not take up the interdimensional cross position and be present in the centre of ourselves,' I replied.

'Getting out of pride means we have to remain in these uncomfortable positions without moving, being *actively still* and empty in the centre. This makes you a *living* cross. For this the feet need to be on the ground and the crown needs to be open (which is difficult with the interferences that come from thinking). In this way the human being is connected with both sky and earth. The trees are the root and the birds are the sky connections. The cross meets in the heart. The heart is human, the human is the heart. The tree cannot move. It can broadcast from where it is, but human beings are mobile and can move with this energy. When you come, you are my heart, that's what the tree told me. It's mysterious and also practical. But it's not for tourists. The tree is not for tourists.'

Voila! I said when I had finished my report. *C'est tout.*

And we looked at each other.

Cyril laughed: *Alors, c'est simple!*

We had met Cyril in Mexico in the silver mining town of Real de Catorce where he was living with his backpack full of crystals, making jewellery from silver and amber, investigating peyote. We were loud and exuberant in those days, busily talking with everyone else in the Nagual Cafe, about questions of the spirit. So I did not notice him at first, sitting quietly there in the shadows. He was half Corsican, half Russian, with a wiry body and a strong dark magical face, like a faun, or perhaps a goat. He had the savour of wild things, of an archaic world that existed beyond any town or city. For most of his adult life he had lived in a tipi here in the mountains of Provence and the Alpes Maritimes. After we met we travelled together in many places: in Mexico, France, England, Arizona. We took peyote, climbed mountains, swam in rock pools, talked about the cosmos, mysteries, ancestors, time. Cyril had a particular access to deep time, as he did the wild. Sometimes our temperaments clashed. Once I became furious with what I saw as his dependence on our generosity and threw him out of my desert kitchen. And it was perhaps a measure of his toughness and his grace that we could meet again at another crossroads several years later, and talk as if nothing had happened, to be able to stay here, in spite of our uncomfortable position, so we could be still and decide where to go next.

This is the last time we will see Cyril. We don't know this yet. Perhaps the place does, perhaps the tree does – which is why it speaks so urgently to us today. The small house is built into the ramparts of the medieval walled town feathered with bitter-tasting wormwood. It holds us close in its stony arms, as the mists and the rain fall all about us, its darkness and depth like a lair. Outside the walls of the town there is a path that leads down the hill, a rocky path, that winds past olive groves and persimmon trees and through great stands of euphorbias, with their flowers like golden bells. In the sun and sometimes the rain, I sit for hours among the stones, brown-hooded arums like small monks at my feet. Sometimes we walk down this path, through the fields, to the market town of Vence nearby and are surprised by shining pools of lesser celandine, great veined leaves of milk thistle, the sky blue of an early iris. It is winter still, January, but the air is mild as we are near the coast. You could see the sea in the distance, a vast sheet of blue. All around the town you can feel the alert and watchful presence of the evergreen trees in the wooded hills, umbrella pines and strawberry trees, cypresses and holm.

Cyril took us into the holm oak's land: into the bare *garrigues*, into the deep forests, into mountain valleys, We met several times in Nice, and over rough glasses of wine and *soca*, spoke half in English, half in French about our common experiences. He had to live, like all non-conformists, on his wits. In spite of his penniless situation, his attention was resolutely focussed on spirit and the Earth. It did not matter what had happened between us in the past, because in our hearts – no matter what our fortunes were, up or down, exiled or at home – we were all the same position, still doing the same things. In our meetings that attention came first.

One night he told us about finding the skin of a mountain lion in a Nice fleamarket. How he had bought it and gone into the hills, and lit a fire for the animal's spirit; how he had prayed and buried the skin up there in the wild mountains. Our lives and temperaments were different, but we knew about mountain lions and burying them with honour and about trees that told us we would have to lose our human pride.

Who but ourselves shall bury the creatures, put our hands in the soil, pray, build a fire, mark the passing cycles of time? When you see a snake on the road, said the old medicine man, you pick that snake up and bury him. Because that snake is yourself. *You are my heart.* To be on the tanist's cross, on the cross of the holm, is understood as a sacrifice, but it is not sacrifice. Nothing on Earth demands this. Least of all the trees, least of all the hollow holm, who waited a thousand years for us to speak with him, one cold winter's afternoon in France.

Saranna

Standing out of the rain in a garage in France, Saranna says: I don't want you to go. She is ten years old. We have struck up a friendship made of magic books and card houses and seashore and fashion and questions which I love to answer. She is the best thing that is happening to me at this moment where my life feels as though it is falling through a hole. She is something shiny in a dark place. Saranna has made me promise that when I tire of it I will give her my peacock shirt. I would keep this promise Saranna except that tomorrow I will have to go and I won't know where to send it to. Will you be in New Mexico?

We will leave France without telling anyone, only your dark-haired mother with her Russian wit will guess this. Last night you came into Mark's dream. You had a box of marbles and peyote balls and a treasure without a name. I've still got the peacock shirt and I sometimes think of you and your mama when I put it on. Maybe you dream of us sometimes too. You and I ran down the beach at Juan Les Pins in the dark and for some reason that is the memory I keep of that time: running with you laughing, barefoot along the rim of the dark sea, feeling in that moment free.

I wish I had been able to say goodbye to you when it was goodbye. I wish so many things. I wish the lamb I had to kill in Wales had not died before it had lived. I wish the young writer I once loved had not sold his soul. I wish the lover I dreamed was broken by a tidal wave, was not drowning herself in alcohol. But sometimes we are strange witnesses for one another, in ways only the dreaming part of us can know. In the dream I can carry the broken woman to shore and in France I can leave the tiger's cage. And I could leave because of you. Because though I felt alone I knew I was not alone. And I can wish things were different than they are. And there is comfort this night in that.

Gorge de Verdun

Sometimes you wait and you don't know what you are waiting for. You think you came to find a home but it turned out you came to know how to wait, to know the deep time of the Earth, with the season, with your own season, which is not the time of the city.

The Mediterranean has a different sense of time from Northern places with their clocks and calendars. It is like the evergreen trees that guard the hillsides and the tombs of those who have gone before, whose leaves never fall. It is slow, sombre, sure. When you wait in the Mediterranean, things come to you, slowly, surely, at a certain pace. In the quiet atmosphere of the deep long afternoons, when everyone in the village sleeps, a mythic resonance is awakened inside you, in your bones. Your attention is held in the same way a round well in a courtyard holds rainwater, and you begin to listen to the wind outside the door, that drags the light across the inky sea and sings through the pines. It is an ancient wind that blows, and you listen to it, to its voices, what feelings it brings, as it scrapes the leaves across the terraces of deserted villas, as it whistles through the ruined walls, through the empty stone fireplace, through the olive trees, through the cypress and the bay, through the mountain passes, as it blows through time, remembering you.

Years ago, I learned to wait in Greece, in the port of Pireus as we waited all day for the boat to take us to the island. I watched the olive-coloured faces of the passengers, their belongings tied with ropes, the light on the sea, the changing shadows. I tasted the dry bread that the people take on sea voyages, and the small oranges, and inhaled the scent of fish and salt and oil. That day became embedded in my memory. This is the kind of waiting and observing you need when you sit by a tree in the mountains. This is the kind of attention that can listen to the wind that knows about time because it has always been here.

It is not the time of siesta now but deep winter. There is snow on the mountains all around and a chill in the air when the sun disappears from the valley by early afternoon. Mediterranean winters can be sombre, melancholic, Saturnine in their mood. It can rain for weeks. Though the weather is cloudy I have decided to walk out. There are wild pigs grunting in the oak forests as I walk up the ancient path of Hercules, leaving the little mountain hamlet behind me, the wooden houses with their comforting smell of woodsmoke, where the people from the city came to live years ago, to keep something alive, something mysterious that belongs to this land, earning their keep in the summer season when the outside world comes to visit the gorge below and the river known as the green dragon.

I walk up the path that is flinty, ice-crusted, stopping every few yards to visit the wild hellebores that grow in large arrays under the trees, *les pieds de griffons*. Intrigued by these green winter flowers I lose track of time. Suddenly I look up and find myself surrounded by the austere cold mountains and a misty rain. I am alone. I have the certain presentiment that comes with being in the wilderness, of the Other, a sense that I am not *really* alone. The granite peaks loom high above me, their cliff faces staring down. There is an enormous presence in wild places you rarely contact in ordinary life. It's exciting and unnerving at the same time, and instinctively you seek out a safe spot. *I must find a box tree,* I say to myself in the dripping silence, to steady my nerves.

The little box trees are everywhere, in conical shapes, the size of human beings. They feel like guardians. I seek one out amongst the other trees on the sloping wood. I clamber up the woody hillside and then I sit down on a dry floor.

I realise I am in a waiting place, at a strategic moment in my life, between two states. I have no home. I came here to France to find a home but I know I will not find it here. Something in me has walked away from the village, to step out beyond the reach of human life to know this. I wanted to sit with the box trees on the edge of the town but my feet kept walking.

Box is a slow growing tree. Its pale colour and durability is highly prized by craftsmen who use it for precise work, for measuring tools, mathematical instruments, chessmen. Everything that requires measure and strategy. I know I have come here to measure myself, to sense the structure of my life. That it's time, as told by the goddesss Athena, for a strategic move. These are hard times for the soul, winter times, times of crafting, enduring, of defining, of going to the places that are furthest away from your familiar self, from the comfort of houses. Times when things make their entrance when you least expect them.

As I sit down by the tree, my nervousness goes and I feel at home, even in the rain that has now started to fall more heavily. The tree seems to have taken the coldness of the afternoon away. I think about the box trees in Oxford, carved into the shapes of mythical beasts, griffins and dragons. How when I was a child I had loved its strange musty scent as I explored the geometric hedges in formal gardens, how I had felt at home in their company.

As I sit remembering, something in my body jolts and I jump to attention: there is a man sitting by another box tree further down the slope! For some reason this sight has sent me into a panic and my heart begins beating like a drum. I am not normally afraid of men, it is just that the sight is so incongruous. I felt sure I was alone. *Who is this man?* Not moving or making a sound, I look at him. He is about 30 yards away with his back turned but I can see his profile. He has a small beard and wiry body. *Oh, it's Cyril!* I think to myself. But no, Cyril is in Nice. And I feel sure I would have noticed anyone else coming along the path or as I had climbed the slope.

I wait for a long time for the man to move or make a sound but none comes. I think about whether I should make my presence known in some way. *Why would you do that?* I think. *It's only a man.* But something in me knows that it is not just a man and I am acting in this strange way because my body has registered that something Other is going on, even if my mind hasn't. It's then I realise that when I move slightly to the left the man becomes a piece of wood. *It's an optical illusion!* Of course. But then my body jerks me back into the place where I can see that it is in fact a man. Only not a man I can meet. He is a man from a different time.

Our bodies know things our minds do not because, like the mountains, they are ancient. They were formed millions of years ago, and they resonate to the wind, to the winter, to the world of the box tree. They are archaic and they love the archaic world because they were built for it. Our feet love to walk the icy path, our ears respond to the sound of the wild pigs, our hands instinctively seek out firewood, our tongues lap mountain water. When we quiet our modern minds, and we listen with our bodies, our archaic bodies that come alive in the wild places, we can touch the mystery of time, the mystery that is held in this Earth.

In the wilderness, where the ancient wind blows through the gold-glinted leaves of the box tree, where the green river roars, where the mountains in their mineral fastness face you, time is held in a different way, in a deep way you cannot ever know in the city or in your safe room at night. If you keep still, are quiet in these wild places, not afraid, let your body instruct you, you can contact the archaic knowledge of this world. You can find it in this place and you can find it in yourself. You can know you are connected to life in ways you cannot speak of and do not need to because in that moment you have become part of life's measure, its strategic move. You can know that the faun-like man is as you are, sitting in a certain way by a box tree, and you are meeting across the vast spaces of time.

Did you once sit here and see me in the future? I ask. But the man does not reply. We are in this mysterious present moment together. When I know that, I stop asking questions. It was time to be there, to know I was not alone, in this hard time, in this hard time for the Earth, and then it was time to go.

I never solved the mystery of how this happened. Mysteries are not there for that. I knew that there had been people before, who had lived in these valleys, and that somehow they were still here, although in a different time, and that they too had held out in the hard times. High in the caves, with their seer eyes, they saw into a future, in which I was sitting under the same tree, where they had once sat. They saw that life would continue.

In the Western world people talk of the faraway places where the archaic life is still preserved, of Africa and Australia, but they rarely refer to their own ancestors, to the people who lived in Europe for thousands of years, who left their mysterious marks on rock and stone. Not the well-documented tribes of Celts or Saxons but other earlier people. These other people did not just live here in France, they were in England too, in Ireland, in deep time.

Sometimes if you sit on hills and moors, or an ancient burial ground, under beech or elder trees, their presences will resonate through time. And sometimes on a lucky day, a slow day, unexpectedly, like me, you might see them. These people are not speaking of *justice* or of sacrifice or war. They are the keepers of life; they are speaking of stars, and sun, of plant, and river and tree. They are speaking like me, like an ancient wind that blows through the house, through the box hedge, remembering you.

The River Is a Strong Brown God

❧

The journey
Limehouse Docks, London

I t is said that wherever you are born on this Earth, the water that runs through the territory runs through your soul. The clay of the Thames basin shaped me and the rivers of London flow through me – a deep hidden river that runs under my old neighbourhood, the Westbourne, that becomes the Fleet, along whose invisible grimy banks I worked as a young journalist. But most of all the river Thames which appears in the bends of my life in ways I never expect. These are practical city rivers, but they are also Underworld rivers, whose dark waters of oblivion and grief, I approach, holding a coin for Charon, the ferryman, with caution.

I have not lived in this city for over a decade and yet in these years I have dreamed of its geography. In the dreams London plane trees hold me in their sooty arms. I am shamed by a hundred parties in Kensington. I find myself standing in the hospitals of Whitechapel and among the protesting crowds of Westminster. An acacia tree blooms in a Spitalfields courtyard. Young soldiers from Ypres walk down Regent Street; while in an unnamed suburb Aphrodite waits at a corner for Eros to return. She is so drunk with supermarket wine her eyes have clouded over.

It is raining quietly at Salmonfalls. The lock is closed and we cannot find the key, so the boat is trapped. Charles has gone to find someone. I am standing next to an angelica plant growing out of the brick and feeling the old city of London, canal London, brick London all about me. It's been a long two days in this narrow boat and now the journey is ending, as we turn away from the river Thames into the Grand Union Canal, running from Limehouse to Camden Town. There have been four of us taking

133

turns at the bridge, stoking the wood fire, making tea, navigating the route, jumping down the towpaths, turning the lock.

I am wrapped in a Welsh blanket, huddled like a mudlark on a tramp boat, impervious to the dark and rain underneath this little bridge. This corner could be London in any time, but it is not the glass and concrete place I have seen on this journey, a place I now no longer recognise.

Charles's surrogate father died on this narrow boat and he is returning it to the real son in London. He called us and told us he could not do the journey on his own. I have felt his father's spirit around us. When we stepped on to the boat, moored under the black poplar at Maidenhead, an invisible force hit me so hard I reeled.

Charles felt it too, only he didn't have the words for it. For some reason none of us can speak about this, edged in disquiet, in terror, as it is. We would like to, Chiara and I, but the men cannot speak of it. One because he feels he knows too much and the other because he fears he knows too little. For two days we have guided the dead man's vessel along the river Thames. Along the waterlands edged with loosestrife and willow, in between swans and suburban gardens that run down to the edge, down through the bridges of London, along the mudbanks past the buildings of the city's core.

We called out their names as we went by, like a litany in a mass: Ravenscourt Park, Battersea Power Station, Westminster Bridge, Tate Gallery, St Thomas's Hospital, Cleopatra's Needle. Warehouses where I once danced, streets where I took taxis, theatres where I stood waiting in queues, walking home with friends and lovers under the swinging lights, hotels where I interviewed people, streets where I photographed models, my father's chambers. My whole past going past me as the boat curved through the grey water, battling the tide, as we headed towards the vast rusty gates at Limehouse. Last night we stayed with Chiara in her dead father's house in Putney and I looked at his paintings that hung on the wall of the quiet drawing room and I knew the meaning of them from my past – and yet I did not know them now in this present.

I am saying goodbye to our fathers' city, to the city that comes in my dreams but after this will not appear again. I am saying goodbye to something I once knew the meaning of but now I can no longer know. This is Chiara and Charles who gave us shelter in Oxford and London and Wales and we are returning the favour by guiding Charon's boat back to its quay. It is an exchange we have had for two years but it is coming to its end.

The dead father worlds are pushing us apart, as if our presence together is jolting things awake that the sleeping city prefers not to see.

You go as far as you can and then you stop, or sometimes something prevents you from going any further. At Salmonfalls, we cannot find the lock keeper to make the final hurdle. It is raining quietly. It is dusk.

The bridge
Oxford canal

I stood by the bridge at Isis Lock under a tasselled dark tree, and looked into the water. A rat was floating belly up and half-remembered lines about the Fisher King from Eliot's great poem came to me: an injured king fishing in a dead canal, in lands that should have been set in order, in a culture that is fragmented and dying.

The lock is the end of the Oxford Canal before it meets with the Thames. I have lived beside these waterways for two years now, learning about medicine plants and community activism: defending the water rats and boat dwellers, gathering the hemp agrimony flowers that can bring fluidity to minds and bodies made creaky and rigid by civilisation. The dark tree is an alder, the tree of the spring equinox, that lines the banks, with their Stygian crack willows and poplar.

I looked along the canal, at the thick and churned mud of the towpath, woodsmoke curling up from the chimneys of the narrow boats. A robin sang among the bare trees – and then there was silence. I waited in the frigid, almost-spring air and I heard the words:

It's over.

I jumped – but somewhere inside I knew already. I ran my hands softly down the tree's straight trunk and cut a sprig that held last year's cones and this year's rainbow-coloured catkins and shoots of green.

The sprig was for a table set for supper in a tall house in the canal neighbourhood in the north of the city. It was the fourth in a series of dinners we held that year with an artist and cook called Miche, set around the five seasons of the year in the Chinese Five Element medicine system. We called them the Organ Dinners, as each season in the year focuses around an organ in the human body, that corresponds to a sense, element and human archetype. Tonight I was the host for the spring season: liver and eyes, wood and warrior.

The fourth dinner table is piled with sharp and sour dishes: shoots and leaves, steamed beets, olives, live yoghurt, foraged nettle soup. The six of us talk about the trees we selected, holding sprigs of green in our hands. But when it comes to my turn I start booming about descent and ascent, about water, about bridges, the equinox and Bran the chthonic Celtic god, who gives no quarter to the upperworld. The alder is his signature tree.

Everyone starts shuffling in their seats and yawning. I am way too intense. I am pushing for the conversation to go deeper but my fellow voyagers do not want to go this way. Everyone has arrived late and has some other party to go to. We had been able to meet in the other family organs: the father lung, the mother spleen, the child kidney. But the liver is a warrior who lives outside the family house, and in the archaic world, brings an activating, initiatory force in his wake.

No one signs up for the warrior initiation, a forced breakdown of your old safe ways of seeing, The breaking advances towards you from the outside, in bush schools and medicine circles, by the encounter you do not expect. In the ordeal your self-obsessed consciousness is violently broken open to the primal forces – the ancestral intelligences of the planet – and you are made aware of what being human demands of you on Earth. You are wrenched away from your home and pushed into the collective. You have duties towards life. You are not the same person you were before.

The poet Robert Bly once wrote that young men need older men to push them down into the darkness of the kiva, out into the wilderness into their vision quest. Young men need to grow like trees and become guardians of this Earth, rather than spending their life-force constructing and consolidating power.

But the patriarchs of the civilised world are not the wild men of the woods or warriors.

The young men regard me, like three fair-haired brothers of a folk-tale. Already they carry the karmic sins and ambitions of such men upon their shoulders. Already they are sold downriver.

This is the moment in these dinners, where the exuberance wanes, and those who head the table realise we now face the challenge of the element in question. We are no longer at a party, but held the impersonal energies of a medicine system, immersed in what needs adjusting and transforming in the social world.

You feel incapable of the task.

As I speak, a gulf begins to widen between us. It was not there before. Initiation makes a bridge between the world of spirit and the world of matter. Unless this bridge is forged, you live your life in the world of matter. No matter how intelligent, how ecological, how radical you are, your existence is governed by objects and intellectual facts. You don't have the spiritual technology to cross the river. Your will, your ego, your intellect, your drive for sex and power, keeps you within the world of the senses.

The warrior sees the world beyond the five senses, informed by the organ that discerns what is of benefit to the whole, or not. This room we sit in, full of warmth and light, piled high with cooking pots and books, appears like an island; outside the house the rivers of the city flow, the Underworld rivers of Lethe and the Styx, the gargoyles amongst the towers gape and grin, the leaves of the alder tree rustle quietly at the end of Isis lock.

I gaze at my companions before me, feel the darkness of the night pressing inward. These are no longer the men who leapt carefree into the lake of Cader Idris, laughing among the sycamore branches, men whom I met in the kitchens and meeting rooms at the edge of Empire. These are men with the ghosts of the machine world all about them, pressured by the academic institutions of the world, men indentured to a world that praises only the hard and the heartless, good pupils, company men.

The tree extends into space, unconstricted by the architecture of this world, bursts through its mental abstractions, its economic systems, its roots reaching deep into earth and water. Moored in these elements, you become connected with the ancestral Earth and its implacable laws. You see in the room the world of the city, as it floats above the Earth, sucking its energy for its own designs. You are watching an ancient machinery in action, as it freezes the living beings before you, holds their hearts in its heraldic grasp. It is a sobering moment.

The manufactured world requires everyone to talk as if death does not exist, as if this organ dinner contains no medicine, as if the tree is not inhabited by a chthonic god. But when you hold the alder sprig, you speak its wild language. Nothing can alter what you see.

So I fall silent at the head of the table. A river runs through the room and we stand on either bank. To see in this way demands the loss of innocence and this is not our agreement. Something hairy and wild, has entered into an educated world and shaken it.

It's over. If you want to restore this wasteland, you have to restore yourself first.

The alder marks a bridge in time in the cycle of the year. A pivotal moment when you leave the nourishing dark of winter and push upwards into the light. Tonight I know it is the end of the line. I have no choice but to go through the lock into the river, to leave the city canal behind me. It's over.

The alder is called the 'tear of the sun' because to live in the sun's radiance means you depart the dark waterlands which have been your home. You shed a tear because you loved your companions of those experimental underworld years, and you are a social creature. You loved the ease of communication; you loved these exuberant dinners. The feeling of being together in a band, of sharing the same house, of going up mountains together, cooking together, laughing together. And you loved yourself amongst them, in all that gaiety and conversation.

But now there is silence and a cold and stiff feeling in the room; people are restless, wanting to go to parties. You do not go with them. The solar year is turning. The warrior faces the river alone: your allegiance is to the mysterious spirit of life; you wrestle with the desires of the world, take responsibility on behalf of the Earth. It is a mood and an attitude.

Something breaks through your old world and teaches you this mood: the encounter, the entry into the hermitage, years of travel, the desert, the practices. You learn to build a bridge across the water.

One day you cross that bridge.

Record keeper
Waterloo Bridge, London

In a dark room a voice is telling me about the caves at Lascaux and about the menhirs, markers of prehistoric time, that stand on a windy cliff in Corsica. The dead in the menhir stand in front of the living to keep them company.

The room is part of an exhibition based around the work of the writer John Berger, and these recordings in the room are from a performance he co-created that took place in the abandoned underground Strand Station in 1999. It's called *The Vertical Line*.

The Line travelled down through 30,000 years 30 metres below the streets of central London between Holborn and Aldwych. The journey took a small audience down spiral steps into the depths of the station through a sequence of sound and visual installations.

'We are not underground anymore,' the voice is saying, 'we are inside a body of limestone whose innards glisten. We are inside the tripes of a mountain.'

'And the darkness, the darkness around us has nothing to do with the darkness of the sky, or the darkness of water. This is the darkness of rock.'

Eliette Brunel, who discovered the Chaumet caves, gasped as she turned her torch and found a mammoth, then a bear, then a lion, rhinoceros...

'It was as if time had been abolished,' said her fellow caver, Jean-Marie Chauvet, 'as if the tens of thousands of years of separation no longer existed, and we were not alone, the painters were here too. We could feel their presence. We were disturbing them.'

Outside in the corridor, there were black and white photographs of the writer, looking intense and craggy, his eyes piercing the darkness he has written about all his life – the darkness of civilisation, powered by industrial capitalism, and the darkness of the rocks which he describes as 'full'. 'You can put out your hand and touch it, and through it come the animals'.

I sit down at a typewriter he used to use, which was also my own first typewriter. I type: 'It is a long time since I used a Lettera 22' and a young man walks past with a bunch of dried stalks, emerging out of his backpack.

'Isn't that wormwood?' I ask him. 'Yes,' he laughs. 'It's from the Imperial War Museum. They don't use pesticides in their grounds and you can find all kinds of plants there.'

For five years now, I have lived horizontally in time, in this narrow land, and placed my attention on practical and social grassroots movements. I've focussed on forging a community practice, working in groups, finding ways to be resilient in the face of an uncertain future, in which resources are scarce and an unstable climate challenges us to change our world view dramatically or face some kind of apocalypse.

That autumn I had begun working with a theatre maker called Lucy Neal on a book about collaborative arts practice in times of collapse. As we sat in her kitchen, discussing the people who would help shape it, Lucy handed me a ceremonial dish an Aboriginal artist had given her. It was called a *collamon*, a vessel for carrying fire and water. The bowl contained a piece of chalk from the Downs, some empty honeycomb, and stones from the river bed of the Thames.

'Let's begin here,' I said.

The book catalogued the work of 58 artists which took place, not in galleries or theatres, but in common spaces – bandstands, libraries, beaches, burial grounds, mountain tops and community gardens. These were collaborative projects that could help people break out of cultural restriction and change direction: a project that brought a valley of people together in Cornwall, or tracked the nectar and pollen-bearing plants in a London neighbourhood, that curated a museum of waters from across the globe, or a rhythm to be played by people across continents, like Chinese whispers. That led people down the steps to unearth the small treasures left in the mudbanks of the Thames: coins, fragments of bone and tile and china, sherds of our past lives at low tide.

It is hard, in the face of the darkness of history, to remember that empathy and kindness matter. But the artist and writer show how practice and attention can forge depth in a shallow time, wrest meaning and value in a culture governed by the dollar and the drone. They open the door to worlds that shift beyond the agreed horizon and create spaces for other things to happen. For the people to still be the people.

Afterwards I stand at dusk outside Somerset House, a building which once housed all our records, our births and our deaths, in these islands, and hear the dark river flowing past Waterloo Bridge. For a moment it was all I was aware of. A sense of vast and complex time opened: wormwood time, tree time, river time, flint time, in which all the rushing traffic and scurrying 24/7 city world seemed to disappear.

Berger had opened my eyes to the dark when I was 19, as he uncovered the mechanisms of Empire behind the canvases I had spent my adolescence absorbed in in the city galleries. What excited me was the discovery you could take off the skin of this world by gazing into its workings. You could look at a painting by Vermeer or Velasquez and deconstruct the value and meaning of a whole culture, upheld by the people who sat around its painted dinner tables. You could break the illusion, the power and status inherent in materialism, by paying attention to the material. By letting what lies beneath be revealed under your own scrutiny. John Berger showed how women were seen as objects to be owned – not from a moral stance but as analysis. And so, I had used that pale green typewriter to deconstruct my own bourgeois life with words, interpreting the images that went before me: the chairs, frock coats and party dresses, the exotic piles of fruit, landscapes of luxury and privilege, and still now a consumer world, fuelled by oil.

How do you get underneath the skin of the visual world, to break out of a history-bound world view? Something pulls you back toward the riverbank, to use your warrior eyesight to access to what writer Clarissa Pinkola Estes calls *Rio Abajo Rio*, this Underworld river beneath the river, a door that opens through 'deep meditation, dance, writing, active imagination, all activity that requires intense altered consciousness, by practice of any of the arts'.

When I go to the city now, it feels as if I move through the land of the dead, that I am still on that barge, heading towards Limehouse, and that it will always be so. It feels as if I am moving through the past, my own past and the history of the world, following a vertical line, left by a lineage of writers and artists, travelling into deep time.

Heron
Island, Reading

I am standing as a heron on a dark quay – or at least I wear a heron mask – and there are ducks quacking nervously among the reeds, At my feet a small candle flickers in a red-papered jar, and in the distance a fire crackles in an old tennis court framed by thin sycamores, waiting for the people and the storytellers to arrive.

Sometimes you need an intervention to crack your old world apart. I have learned that this small moment of stumbling in the undergrowth and waiting in the dark is what begins it all. I could write a hymn to the tea light, to the people dressed as crow and badger who are now waiting under these city trees to surprise the people; to the path of tea lights up Hurst Hill in Oxfordshire that spring equinox night when I stumbled upon a group of road activists and read a poem about England out loud, and everyone cheered; that night on Rannoch Moor when I heard the deer roaring in the darkness as I waited, or in a Hampshire wood hearing a man dressed as a deer, stumbling about. It was if a door had opened and everything that I had forgotten came tumbling back, as if I had punched a hole through a flimsy papered wall in time and the fresh air of another country blew through.

You can say that everything that led up to this all-at-once moment only makes sense when you look back in time. Tonight we led the people from the centre of the industrial town, from a park that was once a plague pit, toward this small island, rescued from its dereliction of syringes and bottles, and that this convergence, as all these convergences, happens by old father Thames who keeps rolling on down to the mighty sea.

I once interviewed a storyteller who told old tales around our fire. He said we like our stories to go from A to B but in fact life is not shaped like that, remembering the river doesn't happen like that. Indigenous folk prefer to drop into their stories in the middle of the flow, as they might bathe in one of its pools on a hot day, fish from certain rocks, where others once mingled in the shade. And so it does not matter that this river tale is not this river in its true sequence, running from the Oxfordshire spring, with its soughing black poplars and bright stands of loosestrife, to the mud banks of Gravesend where the sharks and seals gather. And yet here it is again at the end and beginning of things, a record of all our births and deaths, just when it felt as though there was nothing ahead but stuckness, a blank sheet of paper. Here it is as the door to another world opens and a bridge unfolds before me, with people crossing, as it has before, often and always unexpected, on this English spring equinox night.

The river runs softly past the little island, the weir rushes as the people cross the bridge carrying small red lights in their hands, and at some point, when the people are collecting their costumes up, there will be a big cracking as the tarmac bursts open, leaving a large entry hole into the earth.

And you tell me that it is all gone, that everyone has forgotten, in England that has gone to the dogs, on a planet that is burning, and I tell you: shh wait, listen, sometimes you need an encounter with the dark to crack your old ways of seeing apart.

Wayland and the Futuremakers

❦

I am lying on the belly of a grassy mound that moves through the winter silence like a whale. Below me lie the bones of my island ancestors in two burial chambers, stacked one on top of the other, ringed by tall beeches and flanked by an ancient track. We are in the first days of a new millennium. A robin sings in a spindle tree: red breast among pink berries, tiny dots of colour in a sere, frostbitten landscape. The barrow was built at the advent of Neolithic agriculture, a technology that would change the dark leafy face of these hills forever. The place, however, is named after a later technology, the working of metals, and the arrival of bands of Nordic Saxons in the 5th century. It is called Wayland's Smithy.

That night back in the city I have a terrifying dream. I dream I have a giant safe full of treasure but am being kept in a dark house by a group of men. I escape to France, but am betrayed and wake just before I am murdered with a knife. It is then that I remember the sentence that came to me as I lay on the mound.

The treasure is in the living, not the dead.

Sometimes you think you follow the wrong god home, and sometimes you know you have no choice. Wayland is the lamed blacksmith of the Saxon pantheon and forger of the famous dragon-killing swords wielded by Beowulf and Siegfried. He is not the kind of mythical being you would necessarily choose to go on a journey with. He is not an elegant Minoan goddess in a beehive skirt, nor a heroic Greek warrior, nor an exciting blue-faced deity with eight arms standing on top of a tortoise. His maker skills do not bestow wisdom and healing powers like the Celtic or classical patronesses of craft, nor does he promise Hadean transformation or ecstasy. He is a blacksmith who kills boys and eats bears. Like Vulcan and other mythical lamed smiths, he is very rough and very gruff.

143

In 2000 I wanted to connect with the ancestral fabric of my native land, an England I could love with my heart, that was not its modern Empire or bloody history but an ancestor place that would make sense of everything I saw happening in the present. I didn't think much about Wayland at the time. It was just a name that I found myself repeating when I remembered the Smithy during the years that followed.

But when you are stuck and need to break out of the chains you feel all around you, you don't go to the mythos for an elegant or noble solution, you look for the man who has the right tools for the job.

Capture

Deep in the Northlands, Wayland lies on his bear rug by the hearth at the end of a long day. He is dreaming of the swan maiden Hervor who has flown away with her two sisters after nine years in Wolfbane. While his two brothers have gone in search of the maidens, he has wrought 700 rings of red gold for her return. When he notices the original ring is missing from its slender thread of bast he wonders: Does this mean she has returned ? *Will I find her tomorrow retting flax by the lakeshore where I first stumbled upon her?*

Wayland awakens the next morning to find he is in chains, bound cruelly by hand and foot. Over him stand Nidud, lord of the Njars, and his warriors who have stolen upon his tower by the light of a waning moon. The king has given the missing ring to his daughter Bodvild. He then casts the lord of the elves onto an island and commands him to make jewellery from a large casket of gold and fine gems. The queen orders that the smith is hamstrung so he cannot escape. Everyone is forbidden to visit him.

Press

In 1976 an offset litho press breaks down in the English department of Birmingham University Art Faculty. It is midway through a print run of an arts magazine called *Arnold Bocklin* (after the typeface), the first publication I have ever helped create.

Billy Foreman laughs: 'We will leave it,' he says, 'and something will resolve. We'll come back and know what to do.'

Billy Foreman, assistant editor from the bluecollar North, is an advocate of *Zen and the Art of Motorcycle Maintenance*. I am a rookie reviews editor from the whitecollar South, learning how to get my hands dirty. I know nothing about machines or class politics or journalism, but I have read a lot of books by the time I find myself at the Flat Earth Press with a staple gun in my hands. We are all students of bibliography and this is our fieldwork. The literature of England is a land we have in common.

'The problem with Narnia,' says Billy, as he shows me how to roll a cigarette with one hand (so the other can be free to work with machinery), 'is that there are no women. The only woman is an evil witch. It's the same with Tolkien's Middle-earth. They are lopsided.'

I stare at him amazed. I have been immersed in these otherworld tales all my life and never thought to look at them objectively, like an engineer.

'Why do you think that is?' I ask.

'Maybe you should step back and see for yourself,' he replies.

Bridge

For millennia people have known that to walk true in the world is to walk with 'one foot in the logos and one in the mythos'. Our mythologies help our imaginations make connections between the fiery spirit of things and their physical expression. They engineer a bridge between what scientists call the left hemisphere and the right hemisphere of our brains and enable us to negotiate their different territories. Since industrialisation however, these myths have become refuges from the 'reality' of materiality and science, escapist fairy tales that enliven our lives of hard mechanical labour.

We have lost our techné for crossing the bridge. Medicine and initiation stories that once instructed us how to live on the Earth are seen as fantasies or children's stories. At best they serve the psychologist's couch and the self-help manuals that tell us if we deal with our inner stepmothers you and I will be OK.

But we are not OK because the world is not OK. Those agrarian and metalworking technologies have now crawled across the entire face of the Earth. Vast machines dig and shift mountains and forests and seas, imprison and process millions of creatures. We look at the living world through pixelated eyes, talk like machines and defend our industrialised, scanned, irradiated, genetically modified culture with a tiny fraction of our consciousness.

Wayland the barbarian stands at the edge of his folktale, his eyes grim as a snake's, resisting any Freudian and Jungian readovers. He is not an archetype you can befriend in a workshop. He is smarter, older and more ruthless than any hero or goddess you might fall for or identify with. He knows exactly who has captured him and what he has to do to make his escape.

I'm not a lover of Norse sagas, to be honest. I am not thrilled by thralls moving through Mirkwood with their shiny white shield bosses. And though I can breezily tell others to let the barbarians into the city to bring a new narrative, I am not sure I want to let this elven smith into my worldview any more than anyone else.

And yet his capture speaks to me. Because he is kept and treated the way all makers, all creators are, hamstrung by elites and forced to produce glittering objects and fables to enhance their glory and supremacy.

Somewhere in my bones I know that to get the barrow of time, to return to the ancestors, you have to liberate yourself from the sovereign who has fettered you and for whom you have toiled against your will. You have to stop making the jewellery that delights and empowers them.

You need to tell another story.

Flight

Wayland seizes his chance. Lured by the casket of red gold and gems, the king's greedy-eyed sons secretly visit his island forge. As they peer into the treasure he strikes off their heads and hides their bodies under his soot-blackened bellows. He then fashions a brooch from their teeth for Bodvild, jewels from their eyes for the queen and makes drinking vessels from their skulls for Nidud.

'Where are my boys? What has befallen them?' asks the king, as he drinks from the grisly goblets.

Wayland tells him that he will reveal their whereabouts if the king swears an oath he cannot break on his treasured tools of warfare:

> *Oaths first shall you all swear me,*
> *By ship's-keel, by shield's rim,*
> *By stallion's-shoulder, by steel's edge,*
> *That you will not harm the wife of Volund.*
> *Nor cause the death of his dear bride,*
> *Who shall in the hall bring up our child.*

The king agrees. Wayland then reveals where the sons are, their teeth and eyes and skulls, and that his child now grows in the belly of Bodvild. His line has entered the kingdom.

W.H. Auden and Paul Taylor's translation of the Icelandic *edda*, *The Lay of Volund*, ends with the king's daughter confessing that the story is true. She is indeed great with child, though it is not clear whether or not this is of her own choosing:

> Against his wiles I had no wit to struggle.
> Against his will I did not want to struggle.

However, Wayland's story does not end here. He has fashioned a pair of wings from swan feathers and, as he ascends into the sky above the kingdom of the Nijars, he laughs triumphantly.

Some say he flies to Valhalla where Odin and the swanwinged Valkyrie gather the warriors of Middle-earth for the final battle of Ragnarok, the twilight of the gods. Others that he flies to the British Isles and sets up his smithy alongside the Ridgeway, where every 100 years he shoes the hooves of the White Horse of Uffington.

Either way this Saxon saga is placed on top of a vaster and older story and hides it from view, in the same way that Daedelus' Cretan labyrinth obscures Ariadne's hive-shaped dancing floor. The Smithy appears 4000 years after the first Neolithic burial mounds were established on this grassy hill. For a long time now, sitting beside this story, I have been wondering what I should do with it.

Then one day I know.

Chronicler

In 1991, I break away from the glossy magazines I have spent my youth working for as a chronicler of master carpenters, designers, jewellers and craftsmen. I switch off the television, unplug the radio and walk out of the city. I go in search of a world where the Earth is sovereign, where myths are still tools that help us open the door to other dimensions. I forge practices that can link the world of dreams and visions to everyday life.

In 2007, I change tack and begin to write about a grassroots culture that is breaking free from fossil-fuelled technology. As the corporate world tightens its grip, I chronicle the people who are saving seeds, making their own bread, keeping bees, foraging for medicine, exchanging skills and knowledge, learning how to split wood with an axe, gaining sustenance from the trees and hills again: people who don't want to live in smart houses and hyperreality.

But in 2015, I am encountering a limit.

The limit isn't in this physical world, it is in the mind. No matter how many changes we make in the way things are produced or shared, we are still seeing the Earth with our left-hemisphere, rational minds. We are still stuck on the island of Saeverstod. How can we see the world through mythological eyes, where each thing – each cupboard, knife, pair of boots – has its life history embedded within it, its counterpart in story and myth? How can we fly free?

That's when I realised I needed Wayland's sledgehammer.

Flint

I live in flint country now, far from the rolling hills of middle England, where large glassy stones crouch in the agri-industrial fields like birds. On the cliffs beyond Pakefield I sit and hold a flint that could be a tool from hundreds of thousands of years ago. To the north, 'Gulliver', the coast's first wind turbine, moves slowly in the breeze; to the south the dome of Sizewell's nuclear power station gleams white in the sun. This is the oldest inhabited place north of the Alps, and on certain days you can close your eyes and feel how it was when the hyena and rhinoceros gazed upon a blue tropical ocean, a sea that is still sparkling on this late summer day, though far colder and greyer and emptier now.

Accessing deep time is a clifftop activity. You think it means digging below your feet, a place that physical effort and academic knowledge will take you to, but it doesn't. Time is a broad thing you can feel in your imagination, like the blue sky opening above your head, when the Earth becomes at once larger and more mysterious than you imagined, a space in which all times converge and make sense of this one present moment.

The mind on its prison treadmill prevents our seeing beyond the hostile broadcast of Empire. It keeps us stuck in a history where its rulers are always in command. But sometimes you encounter a strange being, who is neither man nor god, who shows you a way out, though it takes you a long time to realise it.

To make the future, he instructs you, you have to attempt a kind of gaolbreak. The mindset of Empire is a ruthless vampire on the human imagination, and to see clearly, to be free in your thoughts, to live in real time with your feet on the real earth, you have to kill the mechanical thinking that blinds and traps you: self-pity, control, the feeling of doing something wrong, of owing, of being lesser than the people who hold you captive.

Only when you are free can you see. Only when you see can you act, and trust your every action will affect the fabric of the world.

The wind drags light across the ocean. W.G. Sebald walks past the cliff on his way to the Sailor's Reading Room in Southwold. The rhinoceros moves away through the yarrow flowers. Wayland laughs. He is a master swordsmith and jeweller, but his true art lies in flight.

Makers

I wanted to tell you about the things I have loved dearly in this world and the makers who have made them. I wanted to tell you about the teaching house of Tadao Ando in Osaka with its empty tearooms designed in stone and wood and glass, and the history house in Spitalfields where Dennis Severs conjured an imaginary family of silk weavers spinning out their tales in its candlelit rooms. How these encounters revolutionised my relationship with the fabric of places. I wanted to tell you how perception renders our physical lives meaningful, in a way that mere possession of things or virtual realities never can.

I wanted to tell you how Elizabeth David's description of her Sudanese cook preparing salted almonds in twists of brown paper, and the rough technê of my own kitchen – the Opinel knife from France I have used for 30 years and never sharpened, the *molcajete* hewn from volcanic rock I found in the dusty border town of Nogales – have helped me create a thousand colourful meals through these difficult downshifting years.

I wanted to tell you about Sid and Barry and Gene and all the men with grease-smeared faces who mended the cars that once took us to the stony deep time places on this Earth, along the rocky back roads of England and America. But most of all I wanted to tell you about that morning in Birmingham in 1976 when I stood in the shower at dawn and saw my own grease-smeared face and inky black hands in the mirror and laughed. Because I had just printed the first of a thousand publications I will forge in my lifetime, and because I loved Billy Foreman in the way you can only love someone when you are 19 and a student of English literature, and because the smell of Swarfega will forever hurtle me back into that moment when I stumbled upon my craft.

But I can't – at least not in the way I would have liked to. As stories. Because we don't have time for nostalgia: my personal recollections of almonds, or London houses, or my father's deftness with a spade, or my mother's with a rolling pin, gifts that have been an anchor in a sea of choppy times. I don't want to usher you into my silo of memories, I want to break it open.

Wayland brings another technology. Not the kind of hardware that plugs you into a network of virtual worlds and abstractions, but a tool that allows you to access the real network of the Earth. A sledgehammer to break the mind-forged fetters that imprison our imaginations.

The hammer breaks our link to the past, so we can live in the future, beyond the islands where we have been cast; so that we can know other dimensions exist, where the Earth is a mysterious place, full of colour and beauty and intelligences other than our own. So we can forge a story, not a barbarian fantasy that amuses us before we return to our obedient, dull lives, but one that can act as a working bridge between our fiery consciousness and our material selves that house us here on Earth.

Only with this relationship can we be free to dream another world. As a people we are bound by the clock, kept in isolation from our true lands. We are all lamed, one way or another, financially, emotionally, mentally, tied to the market state, indentured to cars and houses and a petrol-soaked economy, unable to leave. In our fetters we forget it is the king, our gaoler, who is stuck because he lacks the art that Wayland possesses and because he is addicted, like all dominators, to the cruel and glittering stuff of power.

But Wayland does not forget. He knows that Bodvild wears Hervor's ring and the king has enslaved him against his will and stolen his sword. His vision is clear. He bides his time and then he makes his move.

꙳

Making a move is the strategy of the imagination enacted in the realm of the will. You make the move by looking at the energy behind the form and then acting. You break the link to whatever or whoever holds you prisoner; you soar into the freedom of sky. Myths are practical things and blacksmiths are practical beings. Every time you break free, you open the door of time and make space for the future to happen. In this space, the tyrant cannot keep his grip.

Our civilisation rests on the assurance of its rulers that the vast populations it holds sway over cannot make these moves. That their everyday actions are hampered, that we will toil ceaselessly for the mechanics that keep their realms running. But some of us have downed our tools. Some of us, impatient to find our way to the future, have stumbled upon a technology still held in the memory of giant stones and small pieces of flint.

Forge

I don't have a car anymore, so most weeks now I have to cycle for our veg box to Darsham ten miles away. Today I am collecting it from Dunwich, which is only six miles from my house but means I have to push the bike along the beach. It is high tide and the wind is against me. My feet sink into the stones, *crunch, crunch, crunch.*

Occasionally I collapse into the shingle laughing, and remind myself I am on the de-industrialising path: no supermarkets, no palm oil, no GM, no pesticides, no central heating, no aeroplanes, no mobile phone, no Facebook, no Amazon, no IKEA, no Primark, but a determination to go a long way for Malcolm's fresh peas and strawberries. Malcolm has built a mini-observatory amongst the rows of sweetcorn and fruit bushes in his smallholding and today we are converging at Dunwich with his local astronomy group. We are looking through solarscopes, a telescope that allows you to look at the sun directly without going blind.

'The thing about H-Alpha,' an ex-merchant seaman called Terry tells me, 'is that it takes time for you to be able to see through it.'

Hydrogen-Alpha is a wavelength deep in the infrared of the electromagnetic spectrum. Solarscopes use an H-Alpha filter to block out all sources of light except this narrow bandwidth. It takes nine months of observation for your eyes to learn to adjust to the wavelength, Terry explains:

'Then you start seeing things you never thought were there.'

At first you see only a red globe that feels shockingly near. But on a second glance you notice the black sunspots and the flares on the edges of the sphere. You realise that the sun is not this round static disc that brings you warmth and light that you take for granted. It is the fire that smelts life. You expect it to be calm and cool like the far distant stars, or Jupiter or the moon. But it isn't: it is a raging furnace, stoked to the max.

Wayland is its blacksmith.

Axis

It is said that Wayland's flight to the Upperworld represents an ancient shamanic journey that soars up the axis mundi to the stars, a flight you see represented by the birds at the zenith of totem poles and standards the world over. Wayland is returning to the constellation of Cygnus, the swan, and his story acts as a door into a world where people are more than mere human numbers trapped in a single moment of history: where we are imaginative creatures who live in many dimensions and our lives and our presence here only make sense in terms of this journey. All civilisations work by blocking our ancient access to this flight, by saying that Wayland and his smithy are just a story, made up by a rough and barbarous people who no longer exist.

But we do exist, and so do the stones on the soft green hills of England, and the three swans who fly past my window on their way to the marsh: *whuh-whuh, whuh-whuh, whuh-whuh.*

The treasure is in the living, not the dead.

Door

If on a clear summer's night you gaze up into the sky towards the east you might glimpse Daneb, one of a trio of brilliant stars, known as the Summer Triangle. Daneb, brightest star of Cygnus, was once our guiding pole star and in the future will be again when the Earth shifts her axis.

I don't know if any move I make affects the world I now live in, except that each time I break free from Empire, from the Machine, from someone who commands me against my will, I feel lighter. There is more space, in my mind, in my feelings, in my encounters. There is more room for everything else, for the plants, for the creatures, for the mountains, for the sea, for the stars. Time stretches out and I can feel as I once did among those Oxfordshire hills, immersed in light and air, filled with exuberance, as if I were flying over them. This is when you realise that Wayland is not just a smith, he is also a guardian. He stands by the barrow built 4000 years before his people arrived with their stories of elves and dwarves and dragons, magical rings and swords.

You can't get to the barrow's treasure chest without confronting Wayland, without unshackling yourself from the civilisations that were at that point in time beginning to build their cities in the Middle East and establishing their technologies here in the form of Neolithic agriculture. The Smithy is a doorway in time and something in us knows that in our bones when we lie there on a winter's day and the robin sings from the spindle tree: *I am always here, I am always here.*

If you are a writer of English words you know that your language was smelted in Wayland's forge, and when you search for a way to show the Earth in her true colours, you use those earth-wrought Saxon words and not the mind-made words that belong to Nidud. You know it takes time to see the fiery red spectrum in everything that lives and breathes on this planet, so you relate what you see to the people with the tools you know best and love with your heart, with words, because this is your own true craft.

You are the key that opens the door.

The Seven Coats

❧

From the Great Above she opened her ear to the Great Below

I am taking off my red coat. In its pockets are seeds, rosehips, bus tickets, notes from meetings. The coat has mud on its woollen sleeves where I have dug festival ditches and community gardens, stains where I have poured tea in church halls and slept in protest tents, where I have chopped wood in my garden, a badge on each lapel that says 'we are the 99%' and another that declares freedom for Palestine. We can turn the ship around, I have been writing these last six years, we can do it ourselves. We can repair, resolve, remember, restore, re-imagine the world we see before us falling apart.

I stand in the corridor, with the six coats upon their pegs, lined up like so many books on a library shelf: my life laid out in sequence. I wanted to write how it is when you leave the coat on a hook, pulled by a line that was written four thousand years ago.

I wanted to tell you about the first yellow coat, as I walked beside my mother down Queensway, London, how it determines all the others. It's made of primrose Harris Tweed, signalling that I come from a certain class of beings who live this city. This is my first moment of consciousness. I am me! I declare and in this moment break away from her.

My mother walks onward past the sawdust floors of butchers and the cool leafy interiors of grocers. It is the end of the '50s. I am a small light in a darkened city. This feeling I realise does not come from my mother, or my father who is working in the law courts of the city, defending small murderers and thieves. I know, even though I do not yet have the words, that this existential moment is stronger, more alluring, more meaningful than anything I am surrounded by.

To be free, to awaken, to be your true self, to know the secrets of life you have to let go first of your mother's hand. To live is to know how to die.

But when you have died, you also need to know how to be reborn. And to recognise that moment when it comes.

When Inanna tricked her father, Enki, of the Me that conferred on her the powers of her office, the greatest she held was the gift of discernment.

FASHION My adult coat was not always red, or second hand. Once it was tangerine and new and caught the eye of my friend Alexander in Rome.

'Why have you got the hook outside of your coat?' he asked.

'It's a fashion detail,' I said. 'It means the coat is by Jean-Paul Gaultier. It's his signature.'

Alexander laughs. We are on the Spanish steps and my friend the seminarian quizzes me with all the force of his Jesuit education; I don't tell him this is the most expensive coat I will ever buy, or why that deep orange embroidered frock coat was the only colour and shape to be wearing that season. Or that why, in spite of all my learning, that I am writing about men who design beautiful things.

'Who is he?' he said.

The question you have no answer for, that holds you to account, is the one that shifts everything.

CLOAK Once the coat was a grey cloak with a scarlet lining with my name stitched is its collar: in blue to signify my house, Ridley, named after the Christian saint and martyr. Inside its deep inner pocket there is a battered copy of *Ulysses*, a book I will silently devour, while the rest of the chapel will pray to a god who spent three days in 'Hell' before rising to the sky realms. The institution has taught me to sing psalms, recite Shakespearean metre, pronounce French verse, and in moments of disobedience, read Joycean prose without a full stop.

I have learned from these texts that the true power in writing lies not in clever argument, but in listening: but only from the last do I learn its greatest trick of all, which is to break the rules.

FUR When I was twenty, I broke the rules of all my class and education and went to Belfast to be with my first lover, and he gave me a coat made of soft grey rabbit skins. He had worn it when he was in a rock band. We stood on the Ards peninsula and watched a hundred swans land on the black sea. It was the middle of the 1970s, and all my encounters were ventures in uncharted territory. From my lovers I discovered how it is to live in the industrial north, in South Bronx, to be a Jew, to be ashamed of poverty, to be a policeman, to be sent to the madhouse, to prison, to fight with god – subjects never mentioned in my father's house.

'How come you are the hero in everything you write?' asked the man I did not sleep with.

I did not know. I was experiencing life by proxy.

BROWN When I go on the road to experience life for real, I will wear a honey-brown car coat that once had a belt when it swung in the Dover Street shop alongside cedar drawers of soft silky shirts from Tibet. My sister gave it to me one freezing winter's night in New York and afterwards we went out like furry twins to catch a cab and to eat Moroccan dishes and drink large glasses of pinot grigio.

The alpaca coat will serve as a blanket in the cold mountain nights in the Andes and Sierra Madre. Now I don't fly anymore,or eat in restaurants, when I think of New York I remember the tramp on Broadway who told Mark: *you have something golden in there in your brain, y'all take care of it, you understan'?*

BLACK 'I like to see you smiling there,' said my father as he lay dying, and the summer storm raged outside the hospital window. In my hand I was holding a raven feather, now buttonholed in a small black frock coat I found in a thrift store on our last road trip to Utah.

I wanted to tell you, how it was when we arrived in Zion Canyon that spring, how it was when my father's spirit roared into the night, the stories held within the fabric of each of these coats, but each time I go there I run out of words and a small quiff of terror runs through my veins.

I am standing in this corridor, facing the coats and realise they are no longer my store of material: not these childhood nostalgias, these bildungsroman, these young rebellious love stories, these glossy magazine articles, these poems about birds and ancestors, treatises on plant medicine, not even the latest narratives about collaboration and downshift.

What next now that everything is written, now there are no hooks left?

The line

In the introduction to her retelling of the Inanna cycle, Diana Wolkstein writes of her first encounter with the Sumerian scholar, Samuel Noah Kramer. Kramer had been working with the 5000-year-old inscriptions for 50 years, a cycle of myths and hymns she will describe as 'tender, erotic, shocking, and compassionate – the world's first love story that was recorded and written down.'

From the Great Above she set her mind to the Great Below.

'What exactly does mind mean?' she asked.

'Ear,' Kramer said.

'Ear?'

'Yes, the word for ear and wisdom in Sumerian are the same, but mind is what is meant.'

'But – could I say "ear"?'

'Well you could.'

'Is it *opened* her ear or *set* her ear?'

'Set. Set her ear, like a donkey that sets its ear to a particular sound.'

As Kramer spoke, Wolkstein recalls, a shiver ran through her.

'When taken literally, the text itself announces the story's direction. From the Great Above the goddess opened (set) her ear, her receptor for wisdom, to the Great Below.'

'The Descent of Inanna' is the fourth and final myth in the quartet, and the four together are understood to be the cycle of a complete human being – specifically a female being. This final part records how the Queen of Heaven and Earth goes into the Underworld, where she is killed by its Queen, her sister Erishkeigel, and then is restored to life.

Inanna has to go through seven gates before she gets to her dark sister's throne room. At each gate she has to give up one of her Me, the attributes of civilisation, from her crown to her breechcloth – all seven seats of her physical and material power. She enters the kur, the Underworld, to know the secrets of rebirth housed there, which are not the physical attributes of Middle Earth but belong entirely in another dimension.

You shiver, because you know you can't follow the words of her myth in your mind. You follow her track the way dancers hand down their choreography through time: by imitation.

The myth and the story

The myth is not the story. The story is extrinsic. I walk out, fight dragons, lose myself in the forest. I return, get married, live in a castle, inherit the kingdom. I do this, then I do this, then I do this, then I hang up my coat on the back of the door and tell you a story. You listen to my tale, gripped by adventure. It fits into the ordinary world we know. Our lives are built around these stories with their happy or sad endings. We are rewarded or punished, the good triumph, the bad die, or do a far, far better thing and suffer both fates.

But the myth is not this. It demands we open our ears to another wavelength. It is a complex, non-linear, and runs alongside the story of our middle earth lives, with its clawed feet in the Underworld and its beaky head in the sky realms. It doesn't fit what we see around us. It lives in caves and out in the desert wind, and sometimes looms up in the city darkness and tells us to take care of something inside us that we cannot see with our everyday eyes.

When the story loses its sense, the myth emerges like the bones beneath the soil. It promises something that makes sense beyond the endings we predict, yet leaves us puzzled by its inscriptions on stone and clay, with its bird heads, its masks and painted bodies. With the goddess who rides on the back of a lion, who is conquered and then transformed.

The myth is intrinsic. It works from the inside out, looping back on itself and lives in all time. In myths, like our dreams, there are savage things that don't make sense. You cut off heads of people who seem to be giving you direction, or asking for help. You eat the things you should not, and open the box you should not. You are married to your father and your brother and your son. You are a strange heroine. Discernment is your greatest gift. Curiosity and a thirst for knowledge pulls you where angels fear to go.

Angels don't lose their clothes, and in the Underworld you lose everything. The clothes are least of it.

I am standing naked, before the hook and my sister's wrath. The myth will kill me and put my body on the hook for three days, which is the statutory amount of time a soul stays in the Underworld before it returns to the sky realm. My ascent will involve complicated deals with sky fathers and loyal servants, betrayals and praise, and someone I love who will take my place. Nobody goes into the Underworld and returns. Except you who breaks the rules.

The ways of the Underworld are perfect. The ways of Heaven are perfect. I am imperfect and incomplete. Like all Earth creatures I bring change by undergoing change. As a people we can change the law, but only through our own journey which demands we give everything away that up to that point has conferred power upon us.

Civilisation tells us we should stay still, be perfect and never change. It gives us coloured coats to wear and says by these outer forms you shall be known. But this is not the life that illuminates our being. You go into the Underworld to find that out the hard way. It takes off the layers one by one, peels them, all your worldly colours, until you stand stripped in the strange twilight of the Underworld, infused by its lamps of asphodel.

Mostly you go to meet your sister, whom you have been told is furious with you. Somewhere buried in this myth from Sumer is a key about the future. And for weeks now I have been waiting for it to appear. The first known piece of writing was written by a woman in 3200 BC in praise of this being – who was not a mother goddess, but embodied the morning and evening star, and her myth of descent is the first of the 'mysteries' to emerge from the city cultures we call civilisation.

It is hard to imagine a world shaped by such a descent, because we live in a world framed by monotheistic gods, who sacrifice their sons to war and Empire, and sentence their daughters to servitude. You have to go beyond millennia of saints and masters and sages into the strife-torn deserts of modern Iraq to find where Inanna first held sway, before she became by association the whore of Babylon, her alchemical moves reduced to a strip tease of coloured veils, performed for a bored tourist in Istanbul.

Embedded in her myth is a way to go beyond civilisation's impasse. Because the life ordered by the Underworld is not the life ordered by Empire: it has another structure and practice entirely. As modern people we like to hold the myth philosophically, culturally, psychologically at arm's length. What we fear is to walk in its tracks, lose control over our lives. We do not like to question our existence at every turn. So we toy with the mythos in our minds, at the end of our typing fingers.

Erishkeigel, we say, is our shadow, and become small professors in the arts of deities and griffins. This means that, we say, with our breasts puffed up like chickens. It's about numbers, and cycles of planting and growing, the seven planets, seven colours of the rainbow, seven chakras. Inanna is a fragment from the matriarchal era. She is Venus who appears as the morning star, disappears under the Earth, and reappears in the evening.

But information is not the myth. Myths are enacted, dramaturgical, protean, existential. You allow the myth to be played out through your being, suffer its effects consciously. The meaning and the expansion it brings happens inside of you, wordlessly. When you stand by the hook, you are scriptless. Libraries disappear, all your smart lingo of Eng Lit and fashion and philosophy. You are in the place without words. The words take you here and then abandon you.

Writers are born with the kind of memory that calls them to go through the gates of the kur. They remember, not just for themselves, but on behalf of the people: we have to undergo change, or we are not people and the Earth is not the Earth. When we make our moves the edifices tumble down, the institutions crack, illusions dissolve like mist.

It comes to me in this moment that I have run out of the storyline. I don't know the ending to my own story, or that of anyone around me. And maybe this life isn't a story anymore. Maybe it's something else. The future stands before me like an empty quarter, like the desert road, edged with sunflowers, like the twilight in the garden after the rain. I take a deep breath. I am here, I say and step forward.

The hook holds what you most fear, which in my case is meaninglessness. The void hits you like a mallet and you tremble. You break apart like a seed pod. Collapse happens inwardly and suddenly.

At the moment Inanna is killed by her sister, Erishkeigel begins her labour. When her servant, Ninshubar, goes to heaven to ask Inanna's fathers for help, the first two refuse. Then the third, Enki the god of wisdom, creates two beings made from the clay under his fingernails who slip into the Underworld unnoticed and assist Erishkeigel in giving birth by sympathising with her pain and glorifying her greatness.

Oh, oh, oh my inside, oh, oh, my outside!

Inanna goes into the Underworld because she knows her sister has something more powerful than any of her Me. That's what pulls her, that's what pulls us, thousands of years later, caught by the first line. We are hooked on that moment.

Some of us have been so hooked on that moment we forgot what we went down there to find in the first place.

Leaving the city inside

The story of civilisation tells us we will be rewarded if we toe the line: but though some may receive a moment of glory, or own a fine house, or dine on meals that slip extravagantly past our lips, none of this will give us kinship with the beasts, or our fellows, or return us whence we came. None will tell us what we need to undergo to become real people – which is to say people who value life on Earth.

The myth tells you if you give everything to life, the Earth will give you everything your heart desires: which if we are writers, means knowledge is given to us – a lineage that stretches back through time, to this moment when our words were first inscribed in clay. That is why we go to the Underworld and face the hook, even at the risk of losing those words that have kept us safe all these years. All those poems and articles, adjectives, and smart lines. All those narratives.

The writer is the one who remembers the myth and keeps telling it to the people. Nothing happens for the better unless we let go and change our forms.

The ways of the Underworld are perfect, Inanna. Do not question them.

What is hard for our duality-driven minds to comprehend is that Inanna and Erishkeigel are the same being, that to turn the ship around we have to follow her mythic track. Rebirth takes place in the Underworld, and in order to reclaim, remember, re-imagine, we have to enter its domain.

And we absolutely don't want to go down there. We want to stay in our cosy colour supplement lives and cling to our ideas of happy families and romantic love, our knowledge of buildings and history, our Shakespearean quotations. We long to keep our shirts perfectly ironed in cedar drawers, to repeat the epithets that fall from the lips of holy men in robes.

Who am I without these coats of class and institution?

Who am I without my work?

Who am I without this newfound community?

When Inanna returns to the Great Above, the person who has not mourned her departure is made to take her place. Her consort, the shepherd Dumuzi, who is also Tammuz and Adonis and Dionysus, and all dying and resurrecting ivy-wreathed gods of the ancient world, and further down the line, the sacrificed man on a cross who does not remember her name. Whose books tell us we don't have to go there, because he did it all for us.

The rebirth we seek does not happen without our descent. The world becomes flatter, uglier and unkinder, determined by the unconscious mass, the untempered leader, the foolish woman, the words that do not set their ear to the Great Below. Venus, the embodiment of love, beauty and a fair fight, steps into the arena to bring new life. She doesn't do that by chanting a new mantra or changing her shopping habits, she does that by grabbing you by the throat and pulling you towards everything you have so far refused to see or hear. She takes you towards the unspoken, the missing information in every transaction, each time you have jumped the consequence and refused to hear the beast or child cry out, your sister trapped in a factory a thousand leagues away.

The unconscious snarls back, rages and rants, complains, resents our every intrusion. It is not polite, or reasonable, or forgiving. You have to withstand its every humiliation: inside yourself and outside amongst the people you love and fear. We think to know the facts is enough, that good behaviour is enough, that to write of our wounds and sorrows is enough. But it is not enough.

To let go of earthly power is a real thing. To be conscious within the realms of unconsciousness, is a real thing. To face your raging sister, to move out of the cycle of history, to liberate yourself from your line, to have empathy for the man, for the child, for the tree, for the fish and the barbarian, these are real things. Not to give up, even when you have given up and the world has turned its back on you.

To die before you die is the core tenet of all the mystery cycles that emerged in the early city states before the father gods took command. It has been a task undertaken by writers in the civilisations that followed – content that we labour conveniently in the Underworld as volunteers and substitutes to carry their shadow and suffer on their behalf.

But Inanna's myth does not end there.

Exodus

It is the moment I hang up the red coat. The moment I expect the hook and find none.

I am on the beach on a warm blue July morning. There is one day a year like this, and today it is here. The sea shimmers and stretches out before us at low tide, and the breeze carries the dusty scent of marram and sea holly. In the sea, the currents move around the sandbar, this way and that, and tumble me into the foam. Every time I put my feet down the sand moves too and small fish who lived buried in the seabed. Everything is moving. I am laughing, tossed by the waves. This is how it is on the tip of the future, as you look at the sun on the horizon, as you look at the empty page and don't know what to write anymore.

I wanted to tell you what that is like when you have done your time in the Underworld, the moment that delivers you into a vast unmapped space, and frees you from the past that has been howling and pawing your coat it seems for centuries. I wanted to say how it was all worth it, though I am left naked on a beach, bookless, featherless, empty-pocketed. Because at this moment I want to be nowhere else but here with the future un-written before me. Because the golden feeling I had in the core of my self when I was two years old is still with me at 62, and keeping loyal to that awakeness is what I steer by more than anything I see falling apart around me, and I know I am not alone in that. And mostly because I remember what my sister told me before I left the city:

'You have been the anchor, you have kept this house together, you have absolved our father's guilt, buried our mother with honour, held our hand, listened to us, grieved with us, written our story – now it is my turn'.

I put my feet on the firm wet sand, on the shoreline, on this beautiful day. *We are here*, I say.

The Red Thread

❧

*T*he stage is bare, except for a beeswax candle in the centre with a ball of red thread and a jar of honey beside it, and a horseshoe circle of small cushions. Lighting is focused on the candle. A chair is at the back of the stage (sideways on). The people enter and sit in the circle, facing inwards.

A female figure enters and takes up position with her back to the audience, hand lightly touching the back of the chair, as if it were a ballet barre. She practices a few pliés and tendus in different positions. She is barefoot and wears a long black skirt with a Greek key motif at the waistband, and a grey furred waistcoat, like a rabbit skin. There is a spiral of blue around one of her eyes.

A bell sounds.

She turns and demonstrates

When you learn to dance you start with positions: first, second, third.

When you learn to write you also learn positions. You sit on the uneasy chair, feeling what is happening in the room. You stand behind the chair looking at yourself having the experience *(stands on chair)*. You imagine being above yourself like a bird seeing what that experience means in terms of the world.

(Moves towards the circle) You tell us you are looking for a new story for this time of endings – a story with a beginning, middle and a happy ever after. That goes in a line from A to B *(arms outstretched)*. But what if the narrative that gives us direction is not a new but an old one, hidden beneath our feet, seemingly broken?

Here is the story about the labyrinth we know: the story of a hero, a princess and a monster. Half-man, half-beast, the Minotaur is kept in the centre of the Labyrinth on the island of Crete – a prison system so complex it has even trapped its architect, the master craftsman Daedalus. It was built to contain a monster who every seven years feeds on the flesh of the young men and women sent to him from Athens as a sacrifice. Except for the Greek hero, Theseus, who has met the King of Crete's daughter. She has given him a thread, so he can find and slay the monster and can find his way out again.

Here is the story we don't know and perhaps can piece together. There is no hero or princess, or any sacrificed young men or women, or any monster. There is a woman who can direct you into the labyrinth, which is not a confusing maze or prison but an underground spiral chamber. There is a kind of death she leads you to, but also a revelation, and then an emergence. She wears a skirt like a beehive, and a band of mushrooms around her head, she is a dancing mistress (of sorts). Her name is Ariadne.

The poet Homer tells us Daedelus made 'fair Ariadne, a dancing floor' and placed a ring of young men and women dancing on the shield of Achilles, as they emerged from a cave.

Here is the story we don't know and perhaps can piece together in a time when our hearts need to find our way back to the Earth, out of the labyrinth of our minds.

Turns round; takes (wooden) snakes from under the chair
Turns to face circle, one snake in each hand, arms outstretched

In 1904 an archaeologist called Arthur Evans unearthed the ruins of a vast palace at Knossos, Crete, and declared he had found the Labyrinth of Ancient Greece. He found me in a series of small household statues and called me Goddess of the Snakes.

I was in several pieces and it was never clear whether the cat really belonged on my head. Still The Archaeologist placed it there thinking well, cats and female deities worked together, right, in Egypt? He called the early Bronze Age civilisation he unearthed 'Minoan' after the mythical King Minos.

All along the walls of the palace he found murals of dancing women and acrobatic men, red bulls and blue dolphins. But unlike Egypt there was no evidence of temples, fortresses, male hierarchy or war. The highly-organised culture was mysterious, its system of writing impossible to decipher to this day.

There is a fragment from later script however that gives us a clue:

To the Mistress of the Labyrinth, honey

So here we are going on a journey: we are not travelling across geographies in space but travelling in time, which means we are going vertically, down into the labyrinth, to find the mystery of life that lives in the dark. Follow me:

There are four steps of the dance that winds in and out of the labyrinth. You have to find your way in, confront what is there and then find your way out. There are conditions and instructions for this dance.

Here is one: keep hold of this thread and pass it to your companions.

She takes a ball of red wool from her jacket pocket, and passes the thread to the audience then returns to the chair.

At the end of each of the following four sections she turns her back to the audience and puts up her arms and demonstrates with her hands and feet the number of the step about to happen; then turns to face them.

Step 1: Leaving

Feet in first position, arms out bent at elbow, index finger pointing skyward

First, feet on the ground, centre yourself.

Now you step away from what you know *(steps away)* into what you don't know and at first it is exhilarating: you are leaving the old world behind – all its mess and disappointment. You are a traveller, stepping out from a tiny island into a vast geography of mountain and ocean and desert, following tracks you did not know even existed. You have no agenda. You feel free.

In 1991 I leave the city of London for Mexico with my *compañero* Mark, a place I know nothing about, and after weeks of travelling find myself in the ancient Mayan kingdom of Palenque, its ruins buried under the rainforest. One morning I take a walk to the Temple of Inscriptions but I do not visit the temple, I follow a path into the forest. And there in a pool discover a man swimming naked under a waterfall. He climbs out and looks at me, his eyes yellow like a snake's.

A goddess swam here once he said and told me he had a medicine for me that would make me see the world as it really is.

Goes to the centre and picks up the honey jar, takes off the lid and passes it to the audience to inhale its fragrance

History tells us our lives go in a straight line from A-Z but our ancestors show us we live in loops and webs, in spirals, and everything that goes out has to come back. Everything has a consequence. Everything that is born and lives comes out of the dark.

So you enter the dancing floor with the shape of Ariadne's double-headed axe as your guide.

Walks around behind the circle, making shapes with arms

The shape of the transforming butterfly.

The shape of infinity, of the strange attractor in chaos theory.

The shape the honeybee makes when she returns to the hive to show the colony where nectar and pollen are to be found, according to the angle of the sun.

In the honey jar there were six large mushrooms. We took them back to our hotel room and shut the door.

Step 2: Encounter / The Fall

Second position, arms straight out, two digits pointing outwards

It was about the door from the start. And time. The second step is about holding fast, even when you are falling.

The thing you forget about mushrooms is that they dwell underground: when you eat the outer fruit then you see the mycelium – the huge networks that are usually hidden from sight. Mushrooms have two functions: they break down what is dead and dying, as they feed and connect the roots of the living systems.

One minute I was in a pink hotel in Mexico and the next we were plunged into a vortex of dimensions, whirling about us.

I forgot everything. I forgot even my name as the world buckled out and everything rushed in: the leaves, the birds, the oceans; civilisations rose and fell on the ceiling of the room. I saw antlers of fire on your head. You turned into a jaguar, pacing the room, and then an eagle. I flew with you, I felt your fur rub against mine and the bars that shut down tight, pressing hard against my body, separating us. I realised I was trapped. Outside, the day beyond the door was bright but in here poison ran through

167

my body, and a terrible thirst and emptiness clawed inside me.

And then at this moment of reckoning, you remember the thread that is in your hands: you remember there is a deal you forgot to make as a human being. You remember in this moment that the animals were our teachers.

The bull we have always known – he was the first we painted on the cave walls and fashioned in stone: as auroch, bison, buffalo. When we stand beside him we can feel him in the dark, his warm breath, his creaturehood, his presence. We don't want to be anywhere else, even though we are mostly mute, enthralled and also terrified.

If I give you kinship with the beasts, he says. What will you give me?

I will give you my mother, my father, my illustrious career, an old house in the city, my nostalgia for the past, my hopes for the future, everything that has protected me.

I will give you kinship with the beasts, he replies. I will give you the dreaming of the mountain, the medicine of plants, on one condition: take me with you.

You realise that the real task was not leaving your old life, but to find a way out of the prison. The key to the door.

If you hold fast this is the moment you feel Ariadne's dancing floor beneath your feet. The hard walls of the Labyrinth vanish and in its place are lines that loop around in an intricate pattern. They are of all colours and intersect in ways you have no words for. There is a humming that you cannot tell is on the inside of you or the outside of you; it burns like a slow fire through your chest, and everywhere there is the scent of a thousand small flowers.

You feel you have waited all your life for this moment.

The door swings open. You follow the thread.

Step 3: Return

Third position, three digits with arms crossed above her head, like antlers

Here's the first thing you need to know about the return. The way back is not the same as the way in.

You think the Labyrinth is something you get free from, so you can live in the bright spaces. But that's not how it works.

You yearn to remain in the scent and warmth of the beehive but you are obliged to face the consequences of your life, your culture, your nation. You move against their currents, like a salmon leaping against the flow of the river.

Hard because our feet now remember the dancing floor, a dance once done in the open that connected us with all beings. Hard because this is the uncivilising move. Where we feel our obligation. Where we no longer have an identity to protect us.

Hard because of the nature of the labyrinth – false passageways, dead ends and distractions. Because now you feel the bars, in everything, now you are aware of the sacrifice, the channels of blood that run down the supermarket floor.

How do you break the bars of a prison? How can you move freely in a world that is made of squares and pixels when time is hemmed by a clock? How do you get your head out of the maze and your feet on the Earth?

Here we are in the labyrinth of our culture, so confusing we are stuck inside, its architects as well as the people born to be sacrificed to the insatiable machine at its centre.

Remember those dreams where you are stuck and cannot speak? Here you make your move.

When you cannot catch the train? Here you make time.

Where you feel trapped and afraid? Here you make space. Here you head for the door where the sun is. And again. And again, until you can bring time and space and movement into any situation.

Each time you move or speak, the labyrinth loses its strength, its power, its hold over you. The stronger the connection with the Earth becomes, with your own heart and all our ancestors who stand behind us.

It's then one day that you find your arms unfurl like a butterfly, like the double-headed axe, you reach out and you move in a different shape...

Opens arms to make butterfly shape

Step 4: Together

Fourth position, one arm up and other out to the side, four digits

The last step is done together. I call it *oloi mazi*. All together, as they say in Greece.

Because you find that you cannot do this on your own. You need to find others who remember the steps.

Ariadne's dance took place on a threshing floor – where the barley and wheat stalks are broken open to remove the husks and reveal the seeds. After the bull's hooves have trampled on you and the chaff, the residue of your life, is blown by the wind. The harvest is complete: the dance can begin.

When Theseus returned from Crete he stopped on the island of Delos and transferred the Cretan mysteries to Apollo. It was called the *geranos*, the dance of the cranes, and was said to mimic the winding steps of the labyrinth and the leap of the bird, famous, like the heron, as a guide to the Underworld. It was danced at the spring equinox.

The killing of the bull marked the end of the female-based Minoan culture and the rise of the Greek. The era of the heroes had begun. The women became princesses who would betray their husbands, their brothers and their countries and be abandoned, kill themselves, or turn into monsters, or snake-holding sibyls commanded by Olympian gods.

The volcano of Thera erupted and a tidal wave destroyed Europe's first civilisation, and it disappeared from view. Or so the archaeologists have told us. The Greek hero myths started to straighten the goddess' looping songs and dances into linear storylines.

The Labyrinth hid Ariadne's intricate dancing floor and her bull became a child-eating monster. The patriarchal maze clung like a varroa mite on the back of a honeybee and infected the colonies of the Western world.

Yet still, the spiral dance of the labyrinth remains on the rocks, and the memory of it in our feet.

Dances around the circle in Greek steps

Segue

In 1977 Joseph Beuys built an installation for Documenta 6 in Kassel. He called it *Honeypump in the Workplace*. Two ship engines pumped two tons of diluted honey through pipes around the museum's staircases and within their snaky embrace were held discussions about culture and the future. The honey, he said, provided warmth and kinship with the creatures and a fluidity which allowed a different exchange to take place. The Free

University was what he termed 'social sculpture' – a demonstration of how art is a liberating force within a collective, among people held captive in heart-devouring institutions of their own making.

And so in spirit of these discussions I hand over to Dougie for the second part of our double bill, *A Dance Called the Anthropocene*: we shall go from deep time looking back to deep time looking forward. Do not forget the thread!

Passes round scissors, with instructions for the audience to cut a piece of the red wool and tie on the wrists of their companions. The circle disperses to the sides as the Dance begins. She takes up a drum.

IV

ANCESTOR

Australia

❧

Follow me: I am cycling down a boulevard in Santa Barbara, California, about to leave for Australia on Christmas day 1997, wavy palm trees overhead, when suddenly I notice people on the beach standing up and pointing at the waves. In the next moment everyone is running toward the sea as one. Without thinking, or knowing why, I am throwing down the bicycle, throwing off my clothes and heading for the waves. We all leap in together and swim out. The ocean is full of leaping dolphins and we are swimming out to meet them. No one has said a word, we just go. A pod of humans swimming towards a pod of dolphins swimming by. We are laughing and shouting as we swim way beyond the places we normally go to and then we stop. There is a marked difference in the energy of the blue water. We are suddenly aware of the presence of dolphins – fierce, wild, free, abandoned, hunting, together, moving, moving, moving. We stop and look at each other, not having any words. 'They are talking!' suddenly yells one boy next to me. 'Put your head under the water!'

Click. Click. Click. The underwater is full of their secret joyous code, their language of togetherness, of intelligence beyond our own. We cannot hold our breath long enough, we cannot speak to them, to each other. Quietly and separately we make our way back to the beach. My heart is beating furiously, filled with an excitement I cannot name.

Earlier that week we gave our travelling car away to a man who rescues injured sea mammals who swim along this coast: dolphins, sea lions, seals. We tried to sell it but nothing worked out. We were filled with a gloom every time we visited a garage. So after having found an injured bird on the beach, I found myself offering the car to the wild animal rescue centre on the telephone. I don't know this yet but the ocean, in the manner of all oceans, is about to repay the gift. With its own vehicle that will plunge us into a sea-changing Underworld and help us navigate its mysterious depths. As I cycle back to the motel to tell Mark about the dolphins I go past a poster for a lecture that evening: it is called 'The Aboriginal Dreamtime'.

Lecture

Stephen Aizenstat runs an institute for graduate psychology just outside Santa Barbara, famous for housing the collections of mythologists Joseph Campbell and James Hillman. The first half of his lecture was about exploring dreams – learning how to open dreams out, to let the images speak, to wait for them to reveal themselves. 'Dreams run away from analysis,' he said. Aizenstat described a way of looking at dreams from five different standpoints. He seemed impatient however to get through these details: 'I know you all want to have coffee and cake,' he said at the interval. 'But I want to go to Australia.'

The second part of the lecture was very different from the first. It was a real story, told not by the expert of the first half – a dealer of neuroses in the modern world – but by a man who loved dreams who went to Northern Australia, in search of an Aboriginal elder who might tell him about the dreamtime. The story was about an encounter with a goanna, a large Australian lizard, the most ancient of creatures, from the most ancient of continents, inhabited by the most ancient of humans. The goanna had chased him and his family – his two children and his pregnant wife – whilst they were having a picnic in the bush.

Being a psychologist and not a warrior, he said, after they had made their escape, he did what all psychologists do in a crisis. He asked himself: What does this mean? Why did it happen to me? What is this creature saying? But none of these questions helped him solve the mystery of why a lizard who would normally run away from a human, ran towards him, pursued him, not once but twice, along a river, over rocks, until he got into the safety of his car.

When he did meet an Aboriginal elder, he was told to go back to where he encountered the goanna and remember the dream that followed the visit there. That night he awoke from a recurring nightmare in which he is running the gauntlet in a Roman stadium; he just makes it through but as he raises his arm in triumph, he is killed between the eyes. Miserable from the repeat of this scenario, the psychologist fell into a half-sleep, and in that space, halfway between dream and wake, something extraordinary happened.

A huge goanna erupted from his solar plexus; it leapt out of his body, turned and faced him in its magnificent dreamtime colours.

Months later when his son was born he would not sleep in his cot. He wanted to sleep in his parents' bed. Not just in the bed, but with the father. And not just with the father, he insisted on sleeping across his father's eyes. And so, like the psychologist he was, Stephen Aizenstat asked out loud: What does this mean? What does this child want? Why does he insist on sleeping curled up on my head?

And his wife turned to him and said:

'Goanna is back!'

The dreamer had dreamed his son. A boy he said, who was not like the rest of the family, who were quiet and introverted, but bold, adventurous, forever dismantling locks of doors, and running out of them, chasing life.

'I am telling you this goanna dreaming because I have to,' he said. After four years, he could no longer keep it to himself. 'I am telling it to you,' he said, 'because one of you may be listening.'

One of you was me. At the end of the lecture as he read a poem out loud about the American buffalo, I felt the room fill with the invisible presences of elders from Australia and North America, and the same excitement I had experienced earlier in the sea with the dolphins started to run through my body.

I ran back through the rainy dusk to the motel room and told the dream to Mark. The next day we began what we called 'the dreaming practice,' looking at our dreams, using the five-level structure that Stephen Aizenstat talked about. When we went to Australia we continued the practice, letting the images from the dreams reveal themselves, opening them out, waiting for the rainbow lizard to arrive. Sometimes for hours on end. And we continued to do this in England, America, Wales, the South of France, and Mexico every day for ten years.

Practice

In an ordinary suburban house in Byron Bay, New South Wales, where the kookaburra laughed outside the kitchen window and the frangipani flowered and the sea roared in the starry darkness, the parameters of the dreaming practice were laid down.

The practice is simple. You tell the dream to your dreaming partner,

asking the questions: what does this say about my daily life, my biographical life, my self on the social level, on the mythological level and from the
perspective of the Earth? You tell the dream out loud. The visitor to the
dream listens and can ask questions but only to prompt the dreamer to
go deeper into the dream. Not as an inquirer, but as a fellow explorer. As
you do the territory opens out between you; you discover its language, its
topography, its mood. Something catches your eye, you both look at it and
it opens up like a flower. It could be an object, a detail, or a feeling. Mostly
though it is a position. Mostly it is a position where you are stuck or held
against your will. Mostly from the past.

The visitor keeps asking: why are you stuck in the jaws of that alligator? I can't move, you reply. Except that now you can, now you are outside
the dream, as well as in it. You are no longer six years old. You can open
your mouth, whereas in the dream you could not. Dreams you learn, as
the psychologist had instructed, flee from analysis. Given time however, as
you weather their difficulty and speak what you feel out loud, they reveal
everything. Agency is returned.

Even though we were often stuck in the 'nightmare of history', we
realised if we placed attention on the underlying darkness of our collective
lives, we could learn to free ourselves and the world. Each dream is carefully
shaped to fit everyone's personal legacies, and yet all of them at some point
reveal a small child, the heart, stuck in the jaws of an alligator, needing your
liberating gaze. Our lives are pivoted around these events and replayed over
time. You want to know why you are trapped, what the alligator means, but
you learn to quieten the mind's inquiry. You're waiting for another kind of
intelligence to kick in. What matters is not finding out what the dream sig-
nifies, but making the move from a stuck place into a fluid open one. Sitting
within the dream means waiting until that move is clear, and then making
it. The feeling is what invites the dream to reveal itself.

The practice taught us the kind of attention you need to look at the
unconscious, the invisible realms. It taught us rigour, so that the mind
didn't interfere with its footnotes and clever opinions. It taught us a language that at first seemed as difficult to decipher as the dolphins' clicks.
But by immersing ourselves in its watery lexicon, day after day we began
to see: how we might navigate the world in terms of frequency, sound and
colour; how the animals taught us about presence; how we learned from
them to stand our ground and make moves out of seemingly impossible

places, how history could be disbanded and ghosts laid to rest. The technê of the practice – finding the feeling within the dream, the moves, the position we found ourselves in, exploring the territory of each dream, placing our attention on it without the mind commenting and analysing – we found could apply to everything we did in the waking world. Part of this was made possible by the rigour of the practice itself, and partly by bringing the dream into physical reality by speaking it out loud and then recording it. Mark wrote everything down and kept the notebooks. After the practice, we would go out into the land, to sit beneath the silvery eucalyptus trees, by the ocean, out into the hills.

One afternoon, by a rainforest pool, I saw a boy fall from a cliff into the water. I sat on a rock beside him, waiting for the shock of the fall to subside. A turtle swam by us and a wind shivered through the gum trees. When I looked up I saw a group of men, women and children standing naked in the water, in harmony with everything around them, and there was a peace and a silence between us that seemed to stretch to infinity. I realised I was looking at the future. The practice was freeing up my mind, so I could see it.

Earth

Everything is different in Australia, upside down, bigger, slower, stranger. The land appears older, emptier, the space limitless. Everything has evolved differently and at a different pace. The lifeforms of flowers, stones, creatures, people look and feel very different from other parts of the world. The marsupial animals are not predatory, they live on trees and plants; the native peoples are not famous warriors, they are dreamers, exchangers, walkers, artists. It is a place where life has not originated in conflict but in co-operation. Time is different there too. There are not the quick-changing seasons of Europe. The rains appear in seven year cycles. In this kind of space and time everything feels as if it is communicating. The birds are brightly coloured and bold. The parrots and mynah birds and melodious magpies come right up to you and speak.

The dreamer tells the story Stephen Aizenstat said because he has to. Part of the dreaming is telling the dream. He also said that once you tell your dream, you are held to it. The Aboriginal dreamtime is a told dream, recounting the ancestors' walk through the land, how they became that land. It is how things originated. It is a world that underpins this one. When it is sung, danced, retold, remembered, the world is kept in balance. This is an act of collaboration between the Earth, the humans and the ancestors that once happened all over the planet.

To most 'modern' minds however dreaming is either understood as some odd, isolated, introverted, not-really-here occurrence or something strange in the brain that happens at night and mostly you don't remember, or sometimes wish you hadn't. But actually this is not what dreaming really is, as we found out. Dreaming is really about perception, about seeing the magnificent energetic nature of ourselves and the place we inhabit. But in order to learn this perception you have to have space in which the imagination can roam, and to have that space you have to break out of the mental prison that civilisation keeps us locked up in, like the transportees who once arrived on these shores.

One of you in the audience may be listening, said Stephen Aizenstat. The dream needs to be told but who is going to listen? You could go to the good psychologist with all his questions but that would be to say that something is wrong with you. Well, you could say, all of Western civilisation is sick but this would not be coming from a knowledge of how human beings were meant to be on the Earth, how things were in balance from the beginning. From the very beginning I was always trying to get out of prison and walk the songlines and find out about original balance. I didn't see myself as sick, or Mark. I saw ourselves as prisoners finding our way out of our Roman stadium minds, getting past the gaolers of our egos. Language pioneers deciphering an arcane and difficult text, from the archaic paintings and scraps of manuscript in the caves of our imaginations. The Earth level Stephen Aizenstat had introduced the night of his lecture had changed the meaning of the dreaming inquiry. It brought attention to the fact that the Earth is communicating to us through our night dreams. And not just the Earth: dreams are also one of the only ways our spirits can speak to us anymore.

Queensland

One night in Byron Bay I had a dream about a map of Queensland. A tall woman with several blond-haired children is escorting me into Queensland. I am crossing a 'bridge' made of a vivid sequence of Aboriginal

180

patterns and dots in rainbow colours.

As I awake, a map of Queensland appears crossed with grids. These take several shapes in layers: a British school ruler that goes around the borders; an Arabian carpet, dark and intricate; Chinese dragons, fighting; spiral 'sun' symbols.

I saw these grids were interferences that needed to go in order to access the land.

The grids in this in-between dream were certain abstract and figurative patterns in space. They were made of the mathematical lines of political rule and the invisible geometries of spiritual systems: law religions, warrior traditions, sorcery traditions – all from different parts of the world. These grids were interdimensional and were preventing a direct connection between the Earth and the stars. They were all dark and controlling, and felt oppressive in various ways. This was in contrast to the lightness and space and integrity of the rainbow bridge.

Visions had come to me before in South America, in Mexico, in England, but I had just received them, as you might have read a book, I had not actively worked with them, and lived them out as part of my destiny, as part of the world.

The practice made us look at dreaming as a fact that needed to be acted upon. Though it often felt like nothing was happening as we moved through the vast spaces of Australia, seismic inner shifts were taking place. The visions I had had before were from a well-charted cultural region – symbols, legends, myths – where I was merely a sightseer. Australia was a place where these things from the past did not exist. In their stead there was a feeling of modernity, of diverse kinds of people gathered under the trees, and from the land, among the eucalyptus leaves, in the water, the sense of a direct connection with an archaic and stellar intelligence. It was an intelligence that was requiring my participation, not just as a human being but as part of the dreaming of the Earth itself.

I had been given a map of an inner territory that would guide us to the future. Although the grids were clearly delineated, it was not clear what it would take to break through them or indeed what they were, or how they affected our lives. The path ahead was going to be an investigation. We didn't even know how many years the practice would take or where it would take us, any more than we knew why we had gone to Australia. I just knew that when I saw the rainbow bridge everything in me wanted to cross it.

I had been given a dreaming map, a task and a vision. I had seen, in physical form, a group of people who felt at home on the Earth, who were new but in an ancient place and I had swum towards them. The next day I had another vision which showed human beings as a series of coloured dots in a square. The dots were complete in themselves and at the same time they were vibrating and communicating with all the others.

We were also at a particular bridge in our own histories. We were saying goodbye to two friends in Sydney and Byron Bay who had given us shelter in these nomad years, goodbye to our seven years of exploration, of living in hotel rooms, writing books on balconies, meeting fellow travellers. We were laying the foundations of a demanding practice that would take us further into the Underworld, and also out of it.

The practice would require a radical rehaul of how we thought, felt, perceived the world and our place within it. This wasn't just about living in a rainbow place by the sea and growing vegetables, this was about dealing with the history that was mostly ignored by the lotus eaters of this coastline, about the strange feelings of gloom I sometimes felt as I swam in some of these Australian pools, knowing some terrible fate had occurred to an Aboriginal or white prisoner there. It meant finding our feet on the land where everything seemed to live on the surface. Driving past the vineyards and hill stations, sitting in the hippy town cafes, I sometimes felt part of a mirage that floated on top of the huge flat earth and I longed to root myself, to remember myself, even if I had to go through those grids to get there.

We held the practice in tiny hotel rooms and bungalows where the sea breezes blew, in wooden cabins in the karri forest, in a train that crossed the vast emptiness of the Nullarbor desert. I collected shells and tree seeds and put them in my pocket. I took my shoes off. Threw myself into the giant waves of the Pacific and Indian Oceans. As we plunged into our dreams, the outside world of people seemed to have less of a hold and what was going on inside was calling for our more urgent attention.

What were our dreams revealing? The dreams of our pasts were grey and threatening. Everyone was miserable, separated, domineering, down on their luck, there was rubbish everywhere. The dreamworld was full of heraldic and traditional hierarchy, demanding our servitude – queens, gods, officials, mothers, bossy friends. So the visions of bridges and dots formed the structural doorway for our emergence from this servitude. At the edge of our nightmares other beings also began to emerge: giant rays and whales, emus and kangaroos, rocky landscapes of colour and light.

In a tiny cabin in a forest outside Perth, an Aboriginal man put his hand through a window and shook mine: We are the action, he said.

Fire

The modern world sits like a mirage over the fiery desert lands of Australia. The Aboriginal way of life, symbiotic, slow, all connected, its dream lines woven across the planet for 60 thousand years, lies underneath and waits. It has a feeling for time that these sea cities with all their restlessness and competition do not know. The fire comes and scorches the trees but afterwards it begins to grow again from the inside. Their roots are sunk deep, indestructible. The seeds rain down on the desert floor, crack and burst open their pods. Regeneration starts.

When you begin to dream, a fire comes and scorches your old life away. A new one begins. It is not the same story you were told. Or rather if you looked at the story you were told, you might find the bones of this life, waiting there among the ghost gums, in the bones of yourself, in your dreams, for regeneration to begin.

In the centre of *The Songlines*, Bruce Chatwin sits in a caravan on the edge of the Western desert, surrounded by small notebooks, fragments and inscriptions from his life on the road. *The Songlines* is a famous account of Aboriginal dreamtime, but this forms only part of its text. The central story is of a man, a writer, coming to the end of the road. In the caravan, he shifts through the scenes of his travelling life: his memories of migrating people, strange hotels, nomad Africans and Arabs, monarch butterflies in New York, quotations from Rimbaud, biblical musings, tatters of blue rag blown in the wind, the dazzling eternal smile of a 100-year-old woman, the scorched remains of a prehistoric fire. He is searching for an answer: Why is man restless? Why is he aggressive?

Chatwin walked through the empty quarters of the world, tracing in his imagination the pathways that exist in space and time. He visited nomads, sleeping in their tents, travelling by foot and in open trucks. He admired their proud and fearless ways, their disregard for possessions, their ready smiles, rigour and generosity. Once walking towards the ancient city of Persepolis, he noticed his nomad guide take no notice of the grand ceremonial tents erected by the modern rulers of Iran, as they passed by.

When they arrive at the ruined city, Chatwin gazes at the megalomaniac inscriptions of its former tyrant-king: I fought, I slew, I conquered.

> Again I tried to get the Quashgai boy to look. Again he shrugged. Persepolis might be made of matchsticks for all he knew or cared – and so we went up into the mountains.

To live as a nomad, as a free man, to go home at the end of a long red road, means you live by different laws. It means you walk a track invisible to the naked eye and so you pay no heed to cities. At the end of *The Songlines* three old Aboriginal men lie dying in the bush, at the conception site of their ancestor, the native cat. They are smiling as they lie under the ghost gums, as they become the ancestor, returning to where they belong.

They knew where they were going.

The ancestors lie in the waterholes: when the sun appears, they arise, they dance and sing, they are the ancient creators of everything; they go on journeys, make camp, meet up, fight, love, depart, go back in. Their tracks across the land make meaning of everything. They are what make you belong. You find them in the mountains, in the clouds, in the animals, in the trees. In the dreamings of honey ants and whales. In your own dreams.

Where you do not find them is in the cities, in the service of the male conqueror: I slew! I conquered! I am the supreme lord of everything I see! The cities fall and are burned away in time. What is left when they go? There is a wind that blows across the desert, singing through the rocks and the spinifex. That sound you follow. *And so we went up into the mountains.*

I heard that sound in the streets of Adelaide one day, though could not find where it was coming from. The didgeridoo, the primordial, ceremonial Aboriginal instrument, is made from the trunk of a eucalyptus, hollowed out by termite ants. It creates a sound like no instrument of civilisation; the roaring wind of the Earth that runs through the interior of yourself, through your blood and sinew. It runs through your bones and shakes them to the core. When you hear it, you know what is missing in your life. What's missing in all of our lives.

The travelling writer does not look inwards, explore the interior of himself, his blood and sinew and bone; the conquerors of cities do not look at themselves, we do not look at ourselves. We are observers, collectors, commentators, patrons, connoisseurs of the Other. Our eyes search outside ourselves, documenting people, placing the world under our control. We amass huge amounts of data, photographs, insights. Where is it all going? Where are we going? Our possessions pile about us, our notebooks, our anecdotes. Our world shrinks. Our bodies crumble. We find ourselves talking with nobody listening. The wind in the desert calls us. The sound of the Earth reverberates through the city streets. But we do not like to look within, to look at ourselves in the mirror. We stare into space, repeating our mantras, believing our right of passage to be guaranteed.

We lack the technology for this endeavour. We lack the law. We only know how to consume and possess the Earth and one another. Our night dreams are what we have left, as city people, of a once vibrant imagination, remnants of our aboriginal ability to live in the ancestral world that co-exists with the physical earth. Tracking our dreams can be a way back to the ancestors. It is a slow way, a hard way. A small tool. A humble beginning. Because we are obliged to face ourselves and all our conquests to clear a space for this way.

After the fire you are free to be new. You can start again, like a green shoot, in all that space and light. Most of all, you are free to dream, to dialogue with the fabric of this world.

After the dreaming practice, we went to the waterhole. We went to a warm still pool where the roots of the tea trees go deep and stain the water red brown. 'Dive down as deep as you can,' Sarah said. 'Then just let yourself float up. Keep your eyes open and look up. Whatever you do, remember the light!'

We all dived down together. I opened my eyes. It was dark brown. Then I looked up and saw a dim golden colour above me. As I floated up from the dive it got stronger and stronger, until it burst into a shower of diamonds as I surfaced with my two companions at the same time, and burst into laughter. Amazing, we all agreed.

Nothing 'happened' at the tea tree lake. It was an intense experience for a few moments, but in those moments, naked, diving into the brown water, bursting through the surface of the glittering sunlight, we had become different creatures. It was as if our modern European histories no longer existed. We were three human beings, in the middle of our lives, on the Earth together, starting again at a pivotal point in time.

Temescal

❧

'Only bitter fare here, my dear,' said Mimi, handing us cups of creosote tea, as we climbed up the mud steps from the temescal. It was November 11th, *la luna de los muertos* and we are in the borderlands between Arizona and Mexico. Francisco Ozuna, *curandero*, has built a temescal in the back of Mimi's ranch, and today will lead a vigil through the night. We will make an invisible bridge between the dead and the living, he tells us, and bring 'the powers of wisdom hidden in the dust' to the surface.

Francisco had worked for several days creating the small underground sweat lodge, shovelling red earth and constructing a roof and steps from mud and stones. That afternoon we had gone to the creek and gathered *palos muertes*, wind-dried stalks of hackberry, black walnut and agave, and curly mesquite wood from the desert for the fire. Huge bunches of wild marigolds he had found abandoned on the highway were set on top of two flanking earth mounds: the fire-coloured flowers offered on the Day of the Dead that grow abundantly in Mexico after the late monsoon rains. Then we drew a circle of ash and amaranth seeds around the temescal and the central fire. When evening came and the people gathered the ceremony began: the flat river stones were heated in the fire, then hauled out, brushed with juniper branches and carried into the chamber on a big spade.

Inside, the small space is exciting. The desert night is cold but under the earth where we've taken the hot stones, naked under moon- and starlight, the heat embraces you. The tea is bitter in your mouth, the osha root is sweet. We are silent and then sing and howl and chant until our bones shake. Afterwards we throw buckets of cold rainwater over each other and dance round the fire. Francisco chants all night. Mark sings beside him.

Modern people don't observe the dead: we shunt them aside with awkward funerals, and this ancestral doorway of the year, once observed throughout the archaic world, has become a children's party game. But Indigenous people (Francisco was part-Apache, part-Yacqui) know the dead are part of the Earth. Once mourned properly they can assist the living, rather than hinder them as forgotten shades.

In Mexico, across the border, there is a tradition of honouring the dead. People go to visit the cemeteries with candles and cakes and sing songs and write the dead messages at this time. But on the American side of the border things are very different. In the town there are very silent groups who come to collect the dead from the mortuary where the ravens gather and cackle on the roof. From our apartment opposite we sometimes see coffins being delivered from the trucks. There doesn't seem to be much singing and dancing going on.

The marigold's name in Nauhatl is *cempoalxochitl*, and their vibrant colour represents the sun, which guides the dead on their way to the Underworld. The strong scent of the flowers attracts the spirits when they return to visit their families on this day, helping them to find their way. Osha, or bear root, is traditionally used in Native American sweat lodges to purify the air as well the body. A bear medicine from the mountains, the root assists a shift into dreaming and connection with the ancestors.

I will remember this night, long after the story of why I was in this high desert fades. Rituals can burn into the memory like fire, open up a portal, so that your ears keep the sounds of a man digging the red soil with a shovel, the sensation in your feet as you climb down the oozy steps and change places with a tarantula, the feel of the fresh night air when you emerge. There had been hard invisible difficulties between us all leading up to the ceremony but when evening came what remains is Francisco laughing as I led everyone in a dance around the fire when things got a bit grim, how our car sloshed through vast rain puddles as we brought breakfast for those who had made the night-time vigil, and that we buried the ashes of a friend of Mimi's who had been sitting on the shelf for a very long time.

I don't remember it as a bitter time.

Crow lineage

'There is a crow who sits on my shoulder,' said my lawyer father. 'It is my conscience.' And then he stared at his shoes in despair. When he died, the crow came to me. You have to tell me everything, I said. About conscience.

The crow sat in the corner of my room in the travelling years when I lived on the edge of small towns in Europe and America. Silently, he observed me write my notebooks. And sometimes I would ask him a question. And he would put his head on one side and peer into the mysterious darkness of the void and declare what great law of conscience he located there.

You have, he said, to deal with the files with your name on and leave the rest.

When we embarked on the dreaming practice in Australia, it was as if all those files had blown open and everything that had been buried from our dark houses and histories came to be redressed: animals faced me in the slaughterhouses, children with metal teeth attacked me, friends and lovers lurched out of the shadows, seeking reparation. It would have been good to sit around a table and come to an understanding, but we soon found dreaming doesn't work like that. Words and good intentions mean nothing, moves are all that matter.

After our long dialogues, Mark and I would go out into the backcountry, or by the sea and watch the dolphins leap in the waves. Here now in the desert, we sit on the roof and watch the sun come up over black mountains, walk the creeks and arroyos, go with Mimi into the canyons, into the wild scrub as the day's heat fades. We are learning the names and the meaning of the flowers in these dry lands, the tough, the spiny and beautiful, the bitter leaves and sweet-tasting roots of ceremony that help us face the journey.

The ritual of the temescal is there to burn out the dross you hold and cede it to the fire as fuel and then as ash to the ground. Ghosts can cling to you, the dead that have not been mourned. Some of these phantoms are yours and some are not. Some are parts of you and your lineage that need to die in order for the new to flourish. To mourn and bury the dead, so that they can feed the living and not haunt the Earth.

Only the elements of this Earth can transform these invisible bonds; only if you are connected to this Earth can you undergo that process and walk that path. Most would rather do the ritual without the suffering and endurance that it demands. For a long time, I did not realise why we were so assailed by ghosts and dreams of the past; then I realised I was in the place the ancient world knew as the Underworld and it was not the native stories or rituals of Native America that would help me navigate it, but a memory of that chidhood book with a pink and green cover: *The Legends of Greece and Rome.* I needed a different lexicon to see and map its mythic territory.

Doors of Hades

You go into the Underworld because the god in you lives in the darkness. To fulfil what some call destiny, the deliberate journey you make on this Earth, you have to go where no one wants to go. Once it was understood that human beings were incomplete unless they took a transformative journey in this place. It was a pact you made with time, with the gods, with the Earth, with the ancestors. In Europe these soul journeys once had collective maps but these were burned, the names of the territories were erased, the entrances to the initiatory caves filled with stones. And yet the people still had the desire to go deep and abilities within to do this work. We were still being born.

The way into the Underworld is the path we are most loath to take. Because it demands you go backwards, into the past, against the flow, widdershins, into faery, into the moon, into the Other, into denial, into terror, into the void. Into yourself. And not the self you know, the one you don't, the one you don't want to know and have always pushed away, tried to hide and not invite to the Upperworld party.

As we sat with the dreaming practice, we were faced with the refuse heaps of our own lives, our families' lives, our tribal lives, humanity's lives, thousands of them, heaped like so many piles of ashes and broken cars, rooted by red-necked vultures and savage dogs, through corridors of forgotten files. Managed by a clerk who has never seen the light of day and a concierge who bears you a grudge you do not understand.

Transformation of consciousness is the hard work of the Underworld. What you transform is the dark stuff, what is known as the shadow: everything civilisations keep throwing outside the city gates, hoping time will help it decay and disappear. Except it never does. Its poison seeps into the sewers of every settlement, into the minds of the powerful, into the terrors of the night.

Releasing the shadow means going through this rubbish heap, through the files the crow brings to your attention – not all of them but those with your name on – remembering what happened, making sense of it all, seeing the pattern, crying the tears of the forgotten, holding the hand of the terrified, of the lonely, the lost; it means shouting at zombies, at ghosts, being raped by Hades, mourned by Demeter, feeling the nightmares that woke you as a child and to keep feeling them until you stop shaking, until the dawn comes, until you are no longer afraid. It means finding a way in and out of the Underworld, because no amount of evangelising or prayer or good intention will wipe our human shadow away.

The shadow exists because no one has been a human being yet; not you, not me, not the man in the rainforest nor the priestess at Delphi. We have all been kind for a day. But living fully as human beings alive together with all our relations, the trees, the fish, the barbarians, the dead?

We have not done that yet.

Psyche and the map of stones

In her fourth and final task, the Underworld is the place to which Psyche is ordered to go. Venus hands her a box and tells her to humbly ask Persephone, Queen of the Dead, for some beauty ointment, and to bring it back to her. Whatever you do, she is told, do not open the box. Psyche, as always, despairs, thinking that her own death is the only way to enter Hades. She climbs a hill intending to throw herself from the summit but a tower of stones speaks to her. He gives her specific instructions for entering and returning from the realms of the dead.

On your return you will be faced with three distractions, he tells her: an old man with a limp, another who clings to the boat, a woman who sits spinning by the shore. They all want your help. Keep silent and do not give it to them. And the tower then tells her where to find the entrance to Hades at the cape of Taenarum in Mani.

The territory of the Underworld is well mapped by the ancient world, its rivers and lakes and fields. Poets have famously described it and what they saw on their guided journeys. But the Underworld is not a fictional place you can play with in your mind, it is a geography that exists alongside the waking one and you have to approach it with steely caution and a cartographic eye. You can fall into *katabasis* by accident, your mouth full of ashes instead of *obols*. Shades cling to your boat as you cross. You have already forgotten the stones' instruction. Or you don't know where to start. For aeons seekers have sought knowing in the place of unknowing, a place where you spend half your life in darkness, your dreams. So I began looking for the entrance to Hades in my dreams. It did not take me long.

Charon

When we returned to Britain from Australia, my dreams had shifted their focus, some of them sparked by visits to places I made as we were searching for somewhere to live in Oxford: by woods, public talks, old buildings. One night in a hotel room, I dreamed that Britain was covered in a greenish glow that was called the seal light. It was like a collective miasma that hung around the edges of the islands. Then a dark ancestral being who was in charge of the burial mounds of England told me about 'proper burial'. Things need to be buried at the proper depth, he told me, to be returned to the earth. Proper burial requires returning everything to its natural place and not keeping anything or anyone stuck in some personal memory locker. This keeping of essences stuck in a place or time was creating ghosts. This included our own phantom selves. The seal light was making the whole land sicken.

Sometimes it felt, as we walked out in search of a home, as if the country itself, obsessed by its own history, was some kind of burial ground in need of a ritual return.

One winter's night in Oxford I dreamed I was at a suburban railway station. The conductor is a black man who says, 'I don't care whether you come on this train horizontally or vertically, this train is only going to NIMROD.' The train is like the 'A' train to Brooklyn. I see people returning from Nimrod. All the seats in the carriages are ripped up, very few people have come back. They are all tattered and bashed up, fragments of people. I realise the train had gone beyond Nimrod into someplace else.

I am trying to cross the border and get to Mexico but am waylaid on the platform by a host of gay men. One is carrying a woman's dress. He winks at me and says, 'I've been to Nimrod and been a woman.' I have lost my passport and am late for my connection.

In the second part of the dream I am running with people, following a shallow water course that runs down a corridor. At the end of the corridor is a little room and the sea lying beyond a window. The room is full of sand and I can't get to the sea. It is in a 1930s building with a slightly abandoned feeling.

I have this dream after going to a lecture given by a Native American from the Ojibwe nation from the Eastern seaboard of the United States. It's a strange meeting, held in the Quaker House in the middle of Oxford. Like many Native Americans the speaker has a look of supreme endurance on his face, as he surveys the timid English crowd in anoraks. One drop of pure water can clean a whole swimming pool of darkness, he declares and holds up some plants – white sage and osha root – which would assist us in overcoming the world of suffering. Someone asks in a small voice about reincarnation.

His stern face relaxes at this point and he laughs: 'We call it recycling,' he says. 'We're not going to be recycled, we're going home.' And then he throws his head back and sings a chant that shakes the foundations of the well-behaved church rooms.

'What am I doing here?' I say irritably to Mark in the practice. I feel I am wasting my time with these corridor and train people. I would rather be going to Mexico and meeting the ancestors. 'You can only recycle paper so many times before it turns into fragments,' I say, 'before it falls apart.'

And we stared at each other in horror.

Nimrod is the mythical emperor who built the Tower of Babel. His astrological tower was destroyed by the sky god Jehovah, along with his people's ability to communicate with each other. Up until then everyone on Earth spoke the same language. All Nimrod's people dispersed across the globe because they no longer spoke the same language and could no longer collaborate. Everything fragmented. The Babylonian mystery tradition that begins with this mythical figure, half man, half dragon, underpins many of the dualist religions that concern themselves with an afterlife hell.

At first in these dreaming practice years, I thought I needed to save people who were stuck in the Underworld until I realised that my actions never saved anyone. I just became waylaid, trapped in the small locked rooms of abandoned houses. I was stuck in other people's stories about their past, other people's secrets, other people's houses, other people's hells, when I needed to move out of these places. I had many dreams of rescuing soldiers stuck in time, caught on the wire, visiting hospitals, going into prisons, all sorts of grim places in history. I met people who were stuck at eternally repeating dinner parties because of their shame. Dead mentors would come and tell me to instruct the living to let them go. Dead children who would ask their mothers not to weep for them anymore. And sometimes I would tell the living these things. But no one listened.

In the Underworld years, I saw dead mothers who were trapped in photographs. I met men who wore dead men's coats to borrow their power and people who kept dead men's teachings in a drawer but did not teach themselves. I saw people hang on to their dead because they wanted the pity of others, because they could not stop raging, because they were full of guilt.

But like everything else in the Underworld, this was about learning discrimination. You cannot be a go-between at the behest of the dead if you want to go home. At some point you realise that no one, dead or alive, is helping you leave. You have to get out yourself. Where everyone goes after life is a mystery. But one thing was clear, where you did not want to be heading was Nimrod and the great recycling depot.

Realm of ashes

Sleeping in my mother's old studio in London under the eaves in an attic room years before the practice, I dreamed about crossing the line of death. Mark and I covered our faces in ashes and tricked the border guards. As we crossed, I fell into the ocean and the great crab mother embraced me in her giant claws, a huge embrace of love, and then she let me go. As I flew into the air I saw a line of people floating towards a spiralling tunnel of light and then elsewhere a blue square surrounded by gold high in the sky. I knew that was where I was going. So I went.

I found myself in a place where everyone understood each other without speaking. We worked together in small groups of four creating extraordinary things. It was a place of beauty and abundance, we lived in straw houses on a flowering hillside that reminded me of a valley we used to visit in Ecuador in our travelling days. The difference was that unlike my earthly life there was great joy and harmony between the other beings and myself. We were in complete telepathic communication with each other. Why did I leave? I left because I went to an interdimensional place like a silvery lake and met a Mexican seer on its pale sandy shore, who told me about time and about the place of time, called Earth. I was so excited you could measure yourself in terms of time, I said: I want to go there. And so I did.

You come because of your great desire. You come because you are curious. You come because of the challenges, because of the experience and the exchanges and the beings you will meet here. You come for all sorts of reasons that only in your soul's language you will understand. Some of these reasons are to be found in dreams. But you only find these clues if you don't get stuck in the realms of suffering. The dimension of the Earth is not difficult because it is physical but because of a human limbo realm, the world of shades, that seal it in a greenish glow and make it hard for us to leave. There are myriad stuck places, astral realms, underground stations, full of beings who have spent their lives conducting the big bands of the Underworld, impresarios of side-shows, the sweepers of the corridors. Hordes of people that are kept in limbo in these Underworld cities that enmesh you in their intrigues. But if you want to get out of the wheel of karma, out of the zone of fragments, you have to be smart and not get waylaid.

If you start helping in the Underworld it means you are not doing your own proper burial. Proper burial means you have to bury your mother with honour, you have to atone for your father's sins. You have to bury your former life at the proper depth, give up the illusions held by your righteous ego. You have to shed your snakeskins, and collect all the fragments of yourself jettisoned in the realms of time. And then when you have finished your tasks, you have to dance, be light, merry, be in life. You can never really talk to the dead in these places because the dead do not listen. They do not care for you. What I wanted to do was speak with the ancestors who know how to be whole, I didn't want to live like a ghost, a fragment, a zombie with a seal light around me. I wanted to go home.

The kist

In the town we wait in the hot afternoons in our apartment, naked, watching the muslin curtain billow in and out in the desert wind. Everything grows quiet at these times. In these intense temperatures, you grow to love the water, climb long distances over rocks to find hidden waterfalls, swim in the mountain pools with little garter snakes, waking early at sunrise to visit the cool canyons full of morning glory and cardinal flowers. It is a state of expectancy you savour, never knowing what might demand your sudden attention, except that when it does, you recognise the moment.

In the desert hotel the Queen of the Night lived in a pot and grew long arms that spread over the painted floorboards of Carmen's room. On the night of her blooming, Greta, Mark and I met and lit small candles there, beneath her six great flower heads, and held three of them in our laps, inhaling the immense fragrance. We talked about flowers. Greta was a herbalist and sometimes stayed downstairs in Peter's studio where we had met her one day as she was hacking up ocotillo roots. Mostly however we sat in silence. The windows of the hotel room were covered in wire, so no moths could come and visit the plant. But the Queen had other visitors: her fragrance wafted all the way down the dark corridor and entered into the kitchen where there was a party going on for a poetry reading that was happening in town.

People came and went out of the room. Mark licked the nectar that dripped from a milkweed flower that hung above the Queen of the Night. Look, he said, it tastes just like honey. Come and try. Nobody did. Some people fled the room, some stood awkwardly and asked awkward questions: Why were we holding a vigil? Why does the plant only flower for one night? But when the poet came into the room, she took up position by the open window and, laughing, told us a story about the Mayan goddess who held a competition to see who had the most beautiful vagina in the universe (it was won by a human woman, helped by a hummingbird who gave her some feathers). 'I'm going to paint the goddess in the underpass one day,' she said. 'This town needs her.'

For a whole evening we sat in the room with the flowers. The poet entered the room and visited the Queen of the Night. She was a lovely poet and the world needs her. It needs the goddess's beautiful vagina. It needs the fragrance of an insignificant plant that puts everything into something beautiful, even though it only lasts one night.

Under the stars of a beautiful night in America the poets came to the pomegranate town, the dreamers and the visionaries. Some of them still lived here: they were quieter than they used to be but they still lived here. They came for the dark blue dreaming stone that lives in the hills among the veins of gold and copper. They came for a different sound that sang out on the edge of the Roman Empire.

The Mayan people sometimes call the United States the Land of the Dead. But it's not just the dead that live here. There is life everywhere if you look, and beauty and kindness. These small things do not count in the world that only counts money, but they count for everything in the Underworld. I know this because when I have been down on my luck, it is the small acts of beauty and kindness that have made everything worthwhile.

It is what stops the world being destroyed.

The poets store up the best of these things. It's not just the words they are doing this with. It's their lives, as they move through this world, through time, a transformative force they carry having been into the Underworld and back. It's the spirit in which they do things, the way that the poet entered that room like a moth and pollinated the flower. It was the dance we all did holding the huge flowers in our laps. In the room this vibration glowed and filled us with an encounter that would last the whole of our lives.

At midnight we left the room. We found the kitchen deserted. There were bowls of chips and empty glasses and a desolate feeling that parties have when they are ended. The night wind blew through the screen door. We kissed each other goodbye and went out, going our separate ways. And when the sun rose the Queen of the Night closed her petals quietly in the desert hotel.

Lethe

When we came back from Arizona, we stayed in Charles's vacant flat in London whilst it was being sold, deciding where we were going to base ourselves. It was in the neighbourhood where I had lived in my youth, its antique shops now being converted into high end fashion stores. Sometimes I saw people I knew from my past in the street and they would look through me, as if I were made of glass. In the empty whitewalled space we hung out our washing in zigzag lines and slept on sheepskins and ate delicatessen food with our fingers. In the afternoons after the practice we would walk for hours in all parts of London: the East End, The British Museum, down the streets of Knightsbridge and through all the parks.

On those spring nights in the city, I dreamed Mark and I passed through the old antique shops where fetishes were cracking and tribal masks were snapping and releasing their spirits. I dreamed I smoked big ancestral cigars in the Underground trains that were crammed with beings who had nowhere to go. There were so many beings down there that they were stacked up in the toilets.

In one of these dreams, a being in charge of the Underworld comes up and tells me the Underworld is too full. I am at a meeting of mediums and trying to present them with a method to clear this 'astral plane' from Earth swiftly. The mediums are old-fashioned and do not want to move from their position. The spirits need to be released, get on their journey, but are being kept in claustrophobic relationships and indulged. There is a girl assisting me in the dream. She gives me a map to do with stones, a round calendar and places a stone on each month. 'Oh, that could really work,' I say. I realise most spirits are no more expanded in their consciousness than the living because they hadn't moved very far from the human world.

The dream came after I visited a spiritualist church round the corner one evening on a whim. It was held in a small dark church among white-faced houses and their gardens full of golden forsythia and daffodils. The medium there gave the congregation messages about small things that the living were not doing properly, family matters mostly, or illnesses. Most of them sounded as though they were in the next door room, like a doctor's surgery, moaning and nagging the living, like right know-it-alls. One dead grandfather was urging his family to hang out the British flag on Remembrance Day to keep up the war spirit. No one seemed in the slightest bit evolved. At one point, the medium declared a white horse had entered the church and was standing in the aisle. 'Can anyone claim this horse?' she cried, half in delight, half in despair.

The spirit of the horse was not claimed however. I imagined it then, standing amongst the pews. Still and very mysterious. Watching us all.

What does it mean that we are made of fragments when we come back? That we are made of bits of people, torn apart, patched together? That the Underground of London is stacked high with dead souls? You need discrimination in the worlds of spirit, to find the wisdom that lies in the dust, in the ashes of the mesquite fire, the dried petals of the marigold flowers.

Proper burial demands you claim your inheritance and let go of what is not yours. You do this because you want to return to your origin, and this is how you earn your passage, the work you have to do at a deep soul level. You do not want to be in that waiting room, at the behest of your relatives. You have come to set the record straight, and the dead you need to speak with are those connected with your line. The truth of the matter is you can only give a hand in life and death where there is an exchange going on.

You get stuck in the world of shades because you think you are helping others. You can lose track of time in the waters of forgetting, become trapped in the punishment of Sisyphus, locked in the eternal regret of

Eurydice. If you weep for others you get waylaid in the vale of tears beset by the sorrow of ghosts. These are the tears that never stop. You are crying for the horrible things that have been done to you, that human beings have done to each other, to the animals, to the planet, but no matter how much you cry, your tears and great sorrow will never be enough. The trick is to know when to stop: to say this happened for a reason for which I am prepared to be consoled by the gods. And when I am consoled, life will go on.

The god however needs to be invited. You need to stand under the vast canopy of stars and call that help in. As you hesitate at the back door, reluctant even to go into the night, you realise you don't desire to be consoled, to relinquish your rightful sorrow and become part of everything. Oh how the great demon of self-pity stalks the corridors of our dreams! Here we are so powerfully and importantly alone and heroic in our pain where no one understands! Not even Varuna, whose salty ocean we weep in our great solitude while shining sun beings appear in our dreams, laughing at our folly, pinching us awake, waiting for us, as we run, tears streaming with failure, with lateness, over the sooty railway bridges of our minds, thinking the train will leave without us. Oh, no one cares, how no one cares!

Listen. The train does not leave without you. How can it? You are the driver!

Widdershins

I am sitting with Mimi and Mark eating beans and tortillas in silence. We have been sitting here for five hours in the rain-darkened adobe house, not being able to speak. Every time we try our minds go blank, the air is thick as treacle, my blood freezes and it feels nothing in the world is redeemable. There is a child screaming around the house she feels she has been exiled from. She wants to eat us with her jagged teeth but being a spirit she cannot. She has lived in all our dreams, sobbed on all our doorsteps, demanded our attention, and now her damage, her abandonment, her suffering is poisoning our happiness together, breaking us apart. Mimi sighs. We are in a place where even the great monks and mystics of the East have faltered. We are in the mirror kingdom: a back-to-front widdershins Otherworld that children disappear to when their glory is sacrificed on the cruel wheel of this world.

'It never changes,' despairs Francisco, grinding his pine bark medicine outside the door to purify the air. 'With these New Age people, they

198

never stop talking and it never stops.'

If you asked me what was the greatest challenge of these Underworld years, it was to withstand the howling gales of history that blew through its corridors. To endure the denied feelings not only of ourselves but of others as they emerged with loathing from the shadows, the vibrations caused by hundreds of years of cruelty done to human beings and other creatures on the Earth. To withstand the sharp pins of the faery places, the ice-cold territories and freezing terrors. The legacy of this felt within my body like poisoned blood, like asphyxiation, as if I were collapsing in-wards; outwardly, as if everyone in the room was held under a sorcerer's spell that made all around us dumb, mindless, unable to move, held down by the crushing silence of family taboos and collective paranoias.

This legacy appeared in the form of a succession of shadow children with pointy teeth and hard eyes who fought with us in dreams, in real life, who demanded revenge though we offered them solace, who treated us like the parents they hated, who were also ourselves, who were English, Irish, Scottish, American, German, Australian, French, Indian, Jewish, Catholic, Celtic, sick, starved, beautiful, scarred, clever, visionary, the children of magnates, diplomats, lawyers, singers, car mechanics, office cleaners, born in workhouses and madhouses, with a silver spoon and a cursed tongue in their baby mouths. It was a challenge to be hated and not hate in return.

We sought in these years to find the treasure we had given carelessly and terrified to our parents, to our lovers, to our teachers, all our golden fragments, submerged in sorrows not of our making. We searched in our dreams, amongst the rubble of time, in the corridors of tears, the locked family cabinets, the ruined cities where once we lived, for the secret we had kept hidden, as we endured our dark nurseries, our terrible classrooms, abandoned, neglected, despised, deep in the broken hearts of England, Europe and America. The hardest to find, the greatest of these, was the part that did not give up, would not say it was different than it was, like all children who keep a secret and will not tell.

What do you keep when all the dramas are over, when all the apocalypses have happened? What is left of your life, when the person you once were no longer exists? What happens when you have said goodbye to everything you have ever known? There is something left in the ashes of the fire, something you hold dear, that is stronger than all these dramas, a small spark of eternity, something that always was, is and will be. It was these memories of the heart I collected as we travelled in search of colour, for the sweetness of life, for the moments of kindness, courage and beauty. Dreamers, like poets, are those who look for the best of everything, the spark that will endure, in a meeting, in a place, in a flower, that we store like honey in the kist of our hearts.

When I emerge finally from the Underworld, I do not take the train to Nimrod. I dance across the line of ashes and amaranth seeds, through the marigold gate. I cross the line to meet Mark, cross the border into Mexico, where the living have taken the dead a gift of light at the beginning of November, where men walk like jaguars, where the goddess Venus walks naked, her hips swaying in the seabreeze, where the morning glory opens his blue flowers to show you a throat full of spiralling starlight.

I open the box.

Pueblo

❦

T hey left great connecting highways that went from all corners of the Southwest down into Mexico, kivas stacked on top of each other in burned layers, huge halls and towers and intricate doorways. They left no words to tell us why they went, or who they were, but they left thousands of sherds along these vast roads: pieces of pottery that shift their colours and design through time, sometimes yellow, sometimes red, sometimes black, like the corn that can still be found, packed in the stone larders and storehouses, in the canyons of Utah, Arizona, Colorado, in the shade of cottonwood trees and desert willow.

As if picking up a sherd from the lost tracks of my old life, I remember a bowl I once held with ochre grasshoppers around the rim, and a story that felt shattered comes together, uncracked, newly fired. The grasshopper bowl was made by a potter we had visited in a place called Mimbres, once inhabited by the Ancient Pueblo people of the Mogollon culture, in what is now New Mexico.

We think we dwell in a place in linear time and when we leave we think that it is over. When we are forced out of our desert home, we know we are not able to return and a heartbreak happens. But the ancestor places remain with us entire. Sometimes they are an outline of a great house we once inhabited, or a kiva we burned to the ground. What we took with us was the culture and these outlines form the structures in which that culture can still be felt and engaged with.

And when there is no language, no script left, no words to tell you how to proceed, that is when you go, to the bone places in yourself, to find the fragments that are left scattered on a desert floor. We were not indigenous to these lands and yet the rocks spoke to us, the plants spoke to us, the ancestors came and spoke to us. And sometimes in a hard time, those are the words you now treasure.

And for a long time, after the heartbreak has gone, you think of those years as a travelling time, a time of inquiry when we held the privilege of freedom in our hands. And then one day it comes back in a way you never expect, clearly, intact, demanding reengagement. You are again standing there in the Chihuahuan high desert by the pool where the lynx drinks at night and the desert wren builds her nest, the scent of the queen of the night fills the air and the stars wheel overhead, the constellations of Leo and Sagittarius. You throw your arms up, like a saguaro. I *am here, you say, we are still here!*

When you have to start again you go to these sherds and build your-self up again. You go into those corn stores, those caches of seeds, where you hid them years ago, and you pull them out. Outside the rain tampers the soil. We will start again here, you say.

The town of pomegranate trees
Summer 2000

I am climbing the red hill at early evening, going through a narrow alley of fennel stalks, up the metal staircase, and passing by fruit trees in vacant lots – white mulberry, apricot, peach, fig, pomegranate. Stones skitter down the hill as I take the narrow track to the summit, as white-tailed deer disperse invisibly through the manzanita bushes and tree tobacco. I pause, panting, by a burned-out house and sit on my haunches to rest. It's still hot and I am adjusting to the altitude of the high desert. I am on the red hill surveying the town, getting my bearings, locating myself in time and space, sitting by a coral bean bush in its high summer glory.

The coral bean bush is a fistful of sticks most of the year, but in the height of the summer it throws out flame-red pagodas of tubular flowers and afterwards, when the rains come, it grows lush triangular leaves and the flowers turn into long brown twisted pods with bright orange beans inside. In the United States the children call them fire beans because if you rub them hard you can make them hot enough to burn your playground opponents' bare skin. Over the border in Mexico they are used for divina-tion, mixed with crystals. I regard the strange flowers. Where am I? I ask myself. What am I doing here?

I am above the town on the hill on the borderlands between the United States, land of the fire bean, and Mexico, land of the magic bean. Carmen calls it the last outpost of the Roman Empire. It was once the home of the Chiricahua Apache, the last tribe of Native America to fight against this empire, who lived among these mountains. When you first arrive in another country, there is sometimes a great freedom that happens. You feel clear, in touch with destiny, with yourself. The social and mythological layers that invisibly constrain you in your own native land are no longer there. The subtexts of the conversations have gone, the land is not cluttered with battle dates or churchyards or familiar signposts. Life feels more direct. In this town people are open, it's easy to make friends, you feel more in touch with the Earth. But there are other invisible dramas that occupy the space and it is good to be aware of them.

I am sitting by the coral bean overlooking the desert hotel where we are now living. The town is made of old miners' apartment blocks and shacks and all the fruit trees and feral fennel and rue plants in the gardens were planted a hundred years ago by the Mediterranean men who came here and dug for the mountain's hoard of copper. There is a highway that passes by the town and the gaping copper mine that is now closed, where the trucks drone past and sometimes keep me awake at night. All other tracks lead, like this one, up into the hills, petering out into dry stream beds, or are small footpaths and fire-escape staircases that end abruptly. It is midsummer and the time of the drought, and it is so hot and dry the craggy live oak trees that dot these rusty-red hills are dropping their blue-green leaves and the wild animals are coming into the town to find water. This house was burned down by an unknown arsonist last week, the fifth one to be destroyed this year.

On some nights Mark and I went to listen to the poets who came through this old mining town and would read in cafes or in the little park under the moon. I watched videos of those who protest against the Empire and are brutally suppressed, I listened to the testimony of a young activist called Julia Butterfly Hill who lived for a year in the arms of a redwood tree. When the big storm came, she asked what message it brought in its wake: *Transform or die*, the storm told her.

'I like a good time,' said the man from the Tohono O'Odham nation in the south, as we sat in a tiny cinema one night in Warren watching a four-hour documentary by the radical linguist Noam Chomsky on the systematic annihilation of the native peoples of Timor. And promptly went to sleep. Dean was big and sick and some people said he was crazy but when we asked him about the rain ceremony we were planning to do for the catastrophic drought that year, he threw his head back and sang a chant that echoed through the town:

We plant the seeds in the sacred places in the secret times, We plant the seeds in the secret places at the sacred times.

That was the night the storm came: lightning danced in the sky for hours, flashing over the black peaks, and turned the town streets into rivers. We stood at the window in the apartment and watched it flash in rainbow colours. I knew then that if you ask the ancestors about rain, they will come. When you go to sleep with a stone from the sea in your hand, or an owl's feather, the dream of the ocean or sky will come to you. When you hold a bone you found in the New Mexico desert and you ask the mountains to speak to you they will find a way. They will come in a dream and present themselves, the deer will present themselves, the flowers will show you their medicine, their instruction for putting a crooked thing straight. We are here, they will say. As we have always been here.

Our human communications in these dreaming practice years were often not clear, full of drama, karma, misunderstandings, difficulties caused by invisible histories, by furious ghosts and gods, but the communications with the Earth were always direct and unswerving. Don't dismiss life, don't dramatise. See the living world before you as it is, not as you wish it to be. Keep looking. Weep when your heart is sore, but do not remain in rage or sorrow.

Everything on the Earth can be discovered by asking, singing, speaking dreams out loud, speaking with others, in a circle, in a deep place, in a meeting place. Transform or die.

The cliff dwellers
Spring 2001

We are on a journey from Southern Arizona to the red rock country of Utah. We don't know this yet, but this is last time we will be in America.

Carmen had told us about this place for years, sending us postcards of the great rocks of Arizona and Utah that rise above the desert lands, the red rocky heart of Turtle Island. We were here to see it for ourselves. We had driven for hours up the road she had travelled since the 1970s, following a trail of motel rooms and picnic places and pools.

We had come back to see the spring-flowered desert, the red earth covered in white evening primrose, the blue haze of lupines on the hills, the roadsides full of California poppy and owl clover, the golden sprays of palo verde, the flowering manzanitas and the great rainbow cholla flowers. We went on the road to share our findings and our dreams of these places.

So following Carmen's map we went by the fossilised rainbow forest in the north, camping under the stars by the great saguaros of the Sonoran desert in the south, driving through the mesas of Hopiland, down to the Mexican coast, visiting the vortexes of Sedona, the pine woods of the White Hills. In Zion Canyon we made a flower essence with the shooting star flowers that grew by the waterfalls there. In a hot spring at night we covered ourselves in mud and talked under the head of a rock shaped like a crocodile that rose above us, about the stars, about our dreams.

Carmen's journey had sometimes sounded like a kind of penance; driving through the burning desert for days to live out here in the full harsh beauty of the red rocks. But it is cool when we come. Spring is opening the land out. The ephedra is in bloom. There is snow edged amongst the pillars of rock and in the branches of the silvery aspen trees. When Mark chants into the crystalline air, a man with a goat pipe answers him. The mountains around us appear pristine.

The postcards often had metaphysical poetry on the back of them, inspired by the spirits that lived in these mountains and the human pathways that wound through them – *these little roads not immune from grief*, she wrote.

ᚴ

On the way back we passed through Hopiland and gave a lift to an old woman who was walking back to her village on the First Mesa. We were silent for a long time in the car together. Our heads full of Sedona vortexes and medicine wheels, the presence of a real Native American was unnerving. 'What you do call that bird?' I finally asked, pointing to a red-tailed hawk floating above us in the giant bare landscape.

'Bird,' she replied, looking toward her village where the coal mine blew out toxic dust into the atmosphere, and said her sister was losing her mind.

The desert is a place where you get real. Where the reality of growing crops in one of the toughest territories in the world comes home to you. This is years before the seeds of the Transition Towns movement are sown on the coast of Ireland, where a teacher of permaculture designs an energy descent action plan with his students for the town of Kinsale. This is years before I come to the end of a walk along the East Anglian coast, and realise that to be any use to the place we call Earth, I will have to look at the coal mine and the world that was driving everyone crazy.

The Hopi nation is famous for making a pledge to keep the world in balance by example. Harassed by the industrialised world to conform, they still grow maize and beans by hand and honour the cycles of the growing year in their kivas and ceremonial dances. Everything has meaning and significance in the life of the pueblo. But the one thing they do not order is the wilderness, represented by the form and spirit of the wild turkey.

You give a place for wild turkey to remind you what comes before the kivas, the plaza, the village, the fields of corn. Our ancestral link to the Earth and the living systems of ourselves, without which all life goes haywire.

When our Hopi passenger left the car, I realised I didn't want to be a spectator, travelling through reservations, asking awkward questions. I didn't want to stand on the monuments of this red rock land like a tourist. I didn't want to follow someone else's pilgrimage, feeling like an outsider, a non-native. We were arguing too much, quarrelling about the route we should take. Let's go back south, I said.

When you are a traveller you have to know what it means to be a visitor, what the place you are visiting demands of you. Sometimes, you don't know until you leave. What was I looking for in this dry and rocky land, collecting bones and seeds, attending to dreams? The answer wouldn't come until one rainy day 20 years later when, waiting for the bus in a deserted library in Lowestoft, my hands fall on a book on the remainder shelf: it is called *House of Rain: Tracking a Vanished Civilization Across the American Southwest.*

Grasshopper bowl

We had met the potter the summer before on a trip to the Gila River in New Mexico. The land is soft there, the golden hills are like piles of demerara sugar, dark-dotted with juniper, and miles of dry grassland stretch in all directions, only broken by a group of red stones known as the City of Rocks. The community she lived in had built adobe houses nearby around several hot springs in the 1970s. But when we visited the place it had a certain emptiness and sadness: it felt like the people had become tired, the dream barren. The City of Rocks however is strange and marvellous and seems full of spirits. Mark laughs at the shapes of the figures in the rocks and then backs into a wall and the car breaks down. A horned owl hoots, the night hawks sweep past. The coyote calls across the vast empty space as the dusk intensifies. It is a sobering moment; I look at the face in the stone: it is rocky red, stern, warrior, karmic.

Wise up is what it says.

In the settlement we sat down by the pool naked, we sat on a raft and drifted into the middle of the still water, fringed by willow trees. We talked of many things, the way you can in places that are watery and slow. The potter showed me her beautiful geometric pots inspired by the first people, sometimes known as the Anasazi, who left their rock dwellings nearby thousands of years ago. The bowls were decorated with grasshoppers and all the creatures that live here.

In the abandoned greenhouse of the commune where everything had gone to seed, I sat under a fig tree and watched a grasshopper and he watched me. They are beautiful, huge, green and pink in the South West, but you don't laugh at these insects. Because, like locusts they can strip the land bare in a matter of hours. The people who grew their corn and squash and beans here lived with the grasshopper, as they lived with drought and calculated the balance in their sacred ways. They did not let him devour their souls.

It is wise to remember this. The ancients went from this land. There are legends that say they just left the cities built into the rocks, like sand martin nests, and went elsewhere for reasons no one can remember. Only their pottery remains. The land is littered with the bones of brave souls who responded to the call of these powerful ancient voices but shattered like vessels, because they could not hold the bitterness and heartbreak and the rage that is held in these rocks. I know I cannot be one of them.

Kiva

I'm sitting at a window in the straw bale house at a writing desk with a cat called Small Being. It's months later, August 2001, a hot afternoon 110 degrees Fahrenheit. There's a storm coming, and we're watching it, the cat and I, as it advances across the desert floor towards us, a thick curtain of rain. Lightning is crackling in the sky islands all around us, huge forks of pink and green and yellow. I don't know it yet but America is about to change its mood irrevocably. This will be the last time I will walk out and smell the world fragrant with creosote after the rain and feel completely at one with the Earth.

Unaware of impending calamity, my body is absorbing these monsoon days, the small things: rain and cats, heat on my body, the sound of thunder, the taste of river water, the way the sun shines through the seed pods of the creosote bush and fills it with light. That scene is so strong in my memory I just have to close my eyes and I am still there. The reason it's strong I would not call happiness. Because, though the afternoon is beautiful, this is a geography of heartbreak, where the exile of Apache warriors, striking miners, illegal migrants from Mexico and El Salvador is written on every red rock. My own too when I am forced to leave. It's not about me and my personal happiness anymore. It's a destiny moment at a window, heralding the end of my travelling years.

I thought I would always be able sit at this table, on a porch under the cottonwood tree. I thought that the screen door of the desert hotel would always be open and there would be people to talk with in Carmen's kitchen, about stars and medicine plants, that Alex's old van would sit in the parking lot forever, that any moment I could just leap in and drive down that long straight Arizonan road, and travel for miles through the desert thorns, through the golden grasslands, over the mountains, that I could stop somewhere and build a little fire and sleep under a sky of stars.

But the story didn't continue like that. And here I am telling you how it was in those years, long after it ended. When I read Karen Blixen's autobiographical tale about her life in the African savannah, I could not understand why she went back to what seemed like a dull and cold existence in her native Denmark.

Now I do. You think return is a choice or bad luck. It isn't. Destiny sends you back. Duty sends you back. Your task as a writer sends you back. You were there as a visitor, for a long while, and the land spoke with you. Then it ended. You had to go back and tell it how it was. What the land said to you. When you live in the flatlands and you remember, the mountains, the sky islands, are still before you, the Chiricahua, the Sierra Madre, the Andes shrouded in mist. How the canyons reverberated with the sound of the mountain lion, the warmth and the stars.

You don't choose a place with a view when you find your writing desk, instructed Annie Dillard. You face the wall and remember.

And then you give it back to the world.

'You are shutting the door,' I said to the man at immigration on our return from a month in Mexico.

'No, I'm not,' he replied.

'Yes, you are,' I said.

It was a good time and it was also a terrible time. During that spring, in those years, we travelled great distances in another person's dream, a dream from 30 years ago, holding a postcard in our hands. I first flew to America on the psychedelic coat-tails of that dream, enticed by its experimental novels and poetry, by its vagabond tales of the open road, the old van that brought the people from the cities to this desert place, looking for a new way of living with the Earth and with each other. I loved America because it was about the future. As soon as I landed, I felt I could drop everything old and stuffy I had inherited from England and begin again.

But 30 years later in 2001, I am watching this American dream go sour. There are still stars at night but there are helicopters whirling above the straw bale and adobe round houses at dawn, searching for men crossing the border. There are still beautiful flowers that grow by the highway but there are also armed black-suited border guards quizzing us every time we look at them, demanding our passports: 'What are you doing?' they ask us suspiciously. 'I am making a flower essence,' I will say, keeping my eye on the green horns of the devil's claw whose pungent scent rises up in the nervous monsoon air. There are *migrantes* who move swiftly and noiselessly down the street at first light in the town. I find young men who have walked all the way from El Salvador wandering in Mimi's desert garden among the pepperweed. They ask me where they are, is there a safe house nearby, a taxi, a train, a glass of water. An 'alien' Mexican man and woman wait for hours by the burning highway. Should I give them a lift? Whose land is this truly? Should I be responsible? I meet a fellow Englishman who tells me he feels huge floods of grief well up in his chest as he drives through this red land. But is it ours to weep over?

Down the highways, men come and poison the flowers. Men in chains mow the highway native grasses, dressed in orange suits with pink underwear underneath, the colours of the California poppies and the cotton flowers, rented out to the County for 50 cents a day. One night in the desert hotel I met one of these men, caught driving just over the alcohol limit by one of the police patrols and sent to prison for two years. He was intelligent and had worked in the town library where he was befriended by Carmen. His life fell apart when he went to prison, he lost his work, his house, his fiancée, and it felt like it would never mend again. He had seen something that is normally hidden from view, that most people do not want to see: an alien civilisation, driving out of control in a car which has not been stopped for thousands of years.

These explorations change you but not in the ways you think they might. I followed the dreams of people who told me their dreams, and took the paths they had taken that did not always feel like mine to take. I witnessed things I would never have seen if I had just stayed in my native land. I met people who had experiences that are normally hidden from view and because I had seen these things, because I knew we were all in the same boat, I could not turn away from them. Like many visitors, I did not have the cultural blinkers to shield this reality from my sight.

Once you see it you can't unsee it. But what do you do when you have seen it?

Wild tobacco

'What are you people doing here?' shouted the border guard across the tannoy down the High Lonesome Road.

'Yo!' shouted Carol and went through the thicket to speak with him.

We were sitting by the wild tobacco down by the wash. The Hopi and the Apache, like many Native Americans, use tobacco to connect with Great Spirit, the animating force of all life. We were doing what we always did in the travelling times, as if compelled by a blueprint we carried in our veins, to gather beside a pool, under a tree to connect with that spirit. Only here the pool was a dry wash and the tree a flowering wild cotton bush. We knew we needed to be here at this time, together, united. We didn't really have any words for it. We sat in silence in the fierce hot sun until it was time to go. The future was in our hearts, though we struggled in our minds. When we met it was a difficult time, in which it felt every kind of karmic woe was wreaked upon us. We knew we didn't want to stay in a grim and heavy past, nor to live in futurist cityworlds. We didn't want our alliances to be with a tribe, or a race, or a governmental state. So we were sitting down by the flowers and beginning something else among the canyons and the peaks. We were burying the hatchet. We were cutting the cotton threads of slavery that bound us all, we were smoking a pipe of wild Hopi tobacco, for the great spirit of America.

If we want to live in the future, we cannot hold on to our battles, our tribal history, our sorrow and rage. We have to meet in another spirit entirely. I learned this bitter lesson in the place where the greatest of Apache warriors, Geronimo, after years fighting for his people's freedom on both sides of the border, gave up his arms and spent the rest of his life a prisoner.

In these Underworld years, I battled with the old ghosts, working to transform a heavy broadcast within myself into a light one. I did this with fellow explorers in America, with Chiara and Carol, with Mimi, as we met in the spirit of the future, though the past was screaming at our backs, and sometimes devoured us like grasshoppers the summer harvest.

Once upon a time, over a hundred years ago, my great-grandfather came to New York as an immigrant. No one knows why he came, or where he came from. But he probably came, like most people, like myself, because the New World offered a place in the future, where he would not have to be constrained by the past. But, like most people escaping from their history, he did not consider the effect this forgetting would have on the place he came to. Because the past is always there, for the generations that follow you, until the ones in the present change it.

I cannot undo the calamity that befell the Native American people who lived among the red rocks when the white invaders from Europe came, anymore than I can change the terrible histories that befell the natives of my own country: the thousands of ghosts of factory children in the North of my mother's land, the ghosts of the transportees in Australia condemned by my father's profession, the ghosts of the young men from the Great War in France my grandfather fought in.

You may feel new but you come through your parents, through an old crow lineage that stretches back through time. So though you may think you are exonerated from the history of invasions, you cannot be because of your line. You don't need to be identified with these things. You need to experience and transform them.

Discrimination is a hard gift that the Underworld brings. You have to know what's yours in the shadowlands, especially when you are travel-ling, otherwise you bear the conscience for everyone. You learn this the hard way. Part of the work of transformation is to make yourself bitter and unpalatable, so no vengeful spirit can devour you. So no ghost, no history, no pogrom, no atrocity you did not have a hand in can wreak its revenge upon you. The way you do this is by knowing bitterness, by experiencing what has been experienced by others and taking these things into your own heart. There is nowhere bitterer than the Arizonan hills: it is as bitter as the dark side of the sun, the black centre of the sunflower, the taste of peyote. It is here at the end of the summer when I will experience betrayal, heartbreak and exile.

To start again, we have to begin from the beginning, to step in a new spirit on the ancient land. It is the ancestral feet that are going to walk down all the little roads of grief and go beyond heartbreak. The past has to be acknowledged, and buried at the proper depth, so no spirits of ven-geance will stalk the land and drive us apart from each other. It means that old ways have to transform and come into the present. It means that the future can no longer exist in the mind but has to land and take form. It means different kinds of human beings are going to walk on the planet, who know why they are here.

Travelling made us many things. Our lands and histories became en-tangled. We were visitors who came from an island shaped like a keyhole in a grey misty sea. It was invaded by many peoples, who then invaded all parts of the world, including this land where we now stand. We were born into a civilisation where our existence has no meaning, apart from our functions within a mechanised society, where we are like devouring aliens on a depleted planet.

But we have also come from a place of deep time, a place of singing and dancing, a mysterious island of explorers and seafarers, dreamers and visitors. When we went travelling with the dreaming practice, we brought these things wherever we went. In the Sonora desert at the end of our spring roadtrip, we stood together under the glittering sky by the sentinel saguaros. A mountain lion was roaring in the canyon. The night was warm, dry, intense, pulsing in our veins, like a hum all around us. We knew we were not just human beings stuck in history. Our feet were on the Earth, as the saguaros raised their arms to the sky, towards the galaxies above our heads, keeping the connection with the cosmos open. And then in our own way, we did too.

Mexico

The last journey we make is to Mexico and we find ourselves in a town called San Miguel de Allende, once a bohemian outpost for travellers and exiles, where we had lived in the 1990s. Everything looks the same – old colonial buildings in their colours of rose and terracotta, ochre and acqua-marine, the wonky cobbled streets, the shady square where people and rowdy *urraca* birds gather at dusk – but it is not the same. It is no longer the time of singing with Ellen in our courtyard, of reading our travel book out loud in the cafe, of taking part in plays and workshops, of voyages to the mountains to take peyote, walking with Robert up the cobbled street, arm in arm, seeing women in men's bodies and men in women's, catch-ing turquoise taxis with Julianne and Susie to the mineral baths outside the town. It is no longer the time of going to neighbourhood markets and coming back to my small kitchen to cook up feasts, perfumed by chocolate and coriander, to lie down in the stormy afternoons, watching the turtle doves in the great pepper tree.

It is a different time because I am different. But it is a different time for the town too. Some of the people we knew then still live in these coloured houses with their orange trees and tiled fountains, but they are talking in a different way. The preacher who once spoke luminously about god is talking about property and lawsuits. The owner of the cafe where we once sang and gave readings is talking about the prostitutes in Cuba. The dress shop owner who looked after our cat is talking about witchcraft and dangerous neighbours. No one is talking about poetry anymore.

In the Mexican town, where the gringos are now building villas in the hills, something is wearing thin. A skull is showing through. 'I call it the summer of death,' said the American teacher who used to sing with Mark. It is not personal this moment: it feels bigger than that, as if this once-bright New Age lifestyle had become endarkened and was fragmenting.

But in late September there are still flowers everywhere you look: morning glories tumble down the walls in midnight blue, sky blue, scarlet and magenta; wild tobacco and trumpet vines spring between the cracks of every building; sunflowers and devil's claw overtake every vacant lot. A vase of fragrant tuberose permeates our rooms in the old hotel. I step across carpets of wild dahlia, zinnias and marigolds on my way to the mineral baths. We are released into endless balmy afternoons: from the hard martial grip of the American desert into the warm and bountiful arms of Venus.

On one of these afternoons I go to a lecture on cosmic time at the town library. It takes place in a room where an artist is quietly at work painting a mural of Quetzalcoatl, the feathered-serpent of the morning star who was banished from the Mesoamerican pantheon, because he had no taste for sacrifice. The Aztecs and the Maya are famous for their intricate calendars of cosmic time which revolve around the axis of the planet Venus. When the conquistadors came they forced everyone to live their lives according to linear time – the time of the clock – rather than original or ancestral time, thus making their rigorous balancing of past and present unnecessary. 'Now' became this monodimensonal moment, rather than a 'now' in which all time and all dimensions are held.

In linear time there are no cosmic consequences. But in Mexican culture, the lecturer informed us, the creation does not begin with birth but with death. Life comes from the bones of the ancestors. There are always consequences. When someone in the audience asks the lecturer about the ancestors he looks nervous and starts to backtrack. It is all right to talk about ancestors as if education has got them under control, filed under history and mythology, but not as if they were still here. Not as if they were real. The conquest destroyed them, he repeated, several times.

But we all knew, even though we could not say this to each other, that the conquest had done nothing of the sort. We were in Mexico after all, not the United States.

We get nervous because at some point you have to pay for your passage here. At some point the ancestors will tell you the past is not in balance with the present, and if you don't do something about it, they will. All ancient peoples know this and make the balance in their own ways, whatever the conquest says.

Ancestor moon

I am in a car, a European estate from the 1960s in a grass-covered car park. The car won't start – it doesn't 'click'. 'Oh, it's still in gear!' I say out loud. When I shift out of gear it starts. Then I realise there are no brakes and I am skedaddling around the car park, out of control.

It's at that point I notice there is a full moon in the sky about ten times the size of an ordinary moon. I manage to stop the car to look at it. As I stare at the sky a huge black woman comes out from behind the bushes. She towers before me: 'What about your obligations?' she demands, 'The dog and the cockroach.'

Mark and I sat under the mesquite tree in the fierce light of the desert and asked ourselves questions: why was the woman not red? Why was the moon so large? What did it mean that I had to get into neutral to start the car? And why on awakening did I feel so light, after months of feeling drained and disturbed?

The black ancestor came when we did not expect her, in the monsoon time, when the houses and gardens become filled with insects. She told us: we are in charge of the gears but you are not driving the car. Fossil fuel is driving the car, millions and millions of ancestral trees; millions and millions of lives lived on Earth. The energy that is coming through time, that runs through your body, through your intelligence, is from the millions and millions of beings who have lived through time: the ones who went before. Your obligations are to them. You need to remember what you are doing here.

In the late summer, animals and plants endure the heat and wait for the rain to replenish them. The clouds advance from the south like great beasts, throwing down curtains of water. At night, the lightning dances across the skies and dry washes roar suddenly in the darkness. This second spring is where the regenerative power of this desert land lies. These are the months when the Pima and Tohono O'Odham and Hopi people plant their seeds and sing to them and to the clouds. These rains bring forth the pumpkins, the beans and squash that feed their people.

Sometimes the seeds of a new time lie deep buried within us, in the secret places, in the sacred places, where the ancestors planted them, and we are just waiting for a certain kind of song and right condition for them to break open.

The dreaming practice gave us keys about living in time – big time, deep time – a present in which all past and all future is contained. The desert house was our crucible, in the rainy season, in a big land, in the year 2001. When I looked at this dream I realised that my obligation was to the ancestral Earth. It was not to hold the unbearable heaviness of human history, but to remember how it had been originally, to live in these mud and straw places, in these round houses, with the storms all around, with this intensity, with these growing plants. To live in the rhythm of time, to love the place though I never owned it.

It's a common assumption that only Indigenous people have access to the ancestors. That somehow, our link to them has gone – indeed if civilised people had them at all. We scrabble self-importantly looking up our family trees, trying to find a link to the powerful of the land through our violent history, a castle, battlefields, our properties. But none of this helps us belong to the Earth, or find meaning in a world held to ransom by a ticking clock.

What brings meaning are 'the ones who have gone before', the primordial beings that form the bones and breath of the earth, its rocks and rivers and sky.

Our rocks, your bones, our sky, your mind, our trees, your feet, our water, your blood.

What the dream reminded us was there is a primal place inside us that remembers a time where feeling was instructive to our beings. It's a sense you sometimes get by rivers, with the desert rains advancing, or walking down the lane in moonlight. That big moon was a doorway. When you go through the ancestor moon you remember everything. It is the doorway of memory. You are no longer fixed in clock time. You get to a sense of belonging that doesn't square with civilisation, or calendars.

Nobody likes to go through this memory moon, because it demands your feelings and losing control, all of which terrifies the rational mind. You have to face the personal and collective forgetting that is kept in the moon's gravity. Because you realise we have put the best of ourselves out with the trash, and what we have now is the life of a dog and a cockroach. A subservient and a scavenger existence in a technological cityworld.

To seek the origin, the ancestor, is to know how to proceed. To go forwards is first to go backwards, which is to know why the ancestors have to be in charge of the car. We want always to go forwards and leave everything behind. But to make changes you have to negotiate with them first. All native people know this, just as they know that all life begins in the dark. But we came into our brave new world without any such knowledge or obligation. We devoured millions of ancient trees, buffalo, lakeland birds, Arctic creatures, seas of cod, we hounded scores of native peoples, skedaddled over the prairie grasslands and still we have not stopped.

In the desert you can know how people once lived for thousands of years, with their vast intelligence, their vibrant imaginations, respecting the primal forces that break open the seeds. They waited for the rain, they looked to the moon, because without water they could not live. They knew how to listen for water underneath the ground in a place that was once the sea. They learned the songs of the water and sung them to their seeds, to the clouds that each year banked up around the sky islands. Around their fires they told the stories of the watery ones who came before, who lay down and made the mountains, the rivers, the bones of ourselves, who knew where the water was hidden and who had been here when the moon was ten times the size it is now.

They knew the black ancestor drives the car.

I am not a driver, but I am always dreaming of cars. Sometimes I am waiting in a car park, or going very fast down a highway. Often I am blind and have no real control. I have to trust I can see without my eyes. In the dream, nothing is working except the gears. Things only get on track when I listen to the ancestors, then I know what I am doing here and now.

The ancestors make it alright. They begin everything again, The ancestors don't live in modern geography, with passports. They are not in this time. They have always been here and will always be. Once they were here when the moon was near and the world was a watery place. We were close once, but then we broke away and became restless, sun-worshippers, in a logos-ruled world. We liked to have our adolescent hands on the steering wheel and go where we wanted, come what may. We could get it right, if we just stopped, for a moment, and waited. If we held a door open they would come, as they have for thousands of years, in our dreams, in the flickering firelight, in the sound of the rain arriving from the south. We'll know what to do when we get out of gear. It's a large debt but it can be repaid.

The ancestors are everywhere singing for everyone, in every land, so long as we have the courage to face the moon and remember. They are reminding us of the seed we carry for the future, waiting for the right conditions to break open and flower. A seed for all our relations. They are singing a song that comes through the timelines, through our bones, they are singing the land anew. In Mexico and America, here in England: in the flinty pathways we walk along the coastline, in the gorse-covered sandbanks that were once rivers. In the wind in the leaves, in the starlings gathering above the marshland. In the lines on our faces. The hands that type these words.

For life you are obliged to give back. I am obliged to remember, to write the dream down that I once had in the desert of Arizona. Once there were dances and songs that showed us our obligations to the ancestors, to the animals, to the trees, to the mountains, to the sea. We saw them in the elders' faces, in their painted limbs, the connection that came down to us through time.

We haven't paid for a long time and the debt is long, stretching back through history. Our dreams tell us this. What we have forgotten, what we have thrown away, what we have become. A pack of English hounds thirsting for the wild red fox, a thousand cockroaches ravening in a New York larder.

No one has said thank you for a very long time.

Letter to Mr. Gurdjieff

❧

Dear Mr. Gurdjieff, I don't know why exactly I am writing to you today in the stillness of midwinter, except the sound of your name came, like a train whistle, pulling me into the kitchen where I first heard it:

Gurrr-djieeeeff!

I am standing on a Navajo rug looking at one of Peter's paintings, tens of thousands of coloured dots on a long vertical canvas, and behind me, Carmen is lighting a Mexican votive candle as she did each evening on her return from Cochise County Library.

'Gurdjieff taught we were bombarded by the influences of the planets, pulled in all directions by cosmic forces inside ourselves, and we needed to be able to handle them.'

And now, here in this darkness in an English forest, years later, watching the sparks of a midwinter fire fly up into the canopy, dressed in a black overcoat and a hat covered in oak leaves, I felt an urgent desire to recall everything I knew about you.

I wasn't interested in your complex cosmic system then, but I liked Carmen's stories about you: how you would send your students into restaurants and instruct them to leave without paying, how you gleefully went about stepping on everyone's corns. I liked that you drank and made everyone else drink and cook and dance. 'Everything in the Universe is material!' you said about your worldly practice, a method of self-transformation in ordinary life, made famous by the mathematician and thinker, P.D. Ouspensky, as *The Fourth Way*. Carmen was part of a Gurdjieff group that had been running in the hills above Tucson for years: she played your compositions on her grand piano in the old miner's hotel, and tried to dance your sacred steps, until she twisted her knee and had to stop.

'I am too rigid!' she would wail and didn't sound too pleased about the metaphor. On the Day of the Dead she would bake three small cakes, *pan de los muertos*, for her Three Gs: you, George, her old mentor, and God. She wasn't pleased with any of you either and battled with all of your pronouncements and demands for a spiritual life. Sometimes I would find her pushing a broom with an intense look in her eyes. 'I am focused on the task,' she would say. I raised my eyebrows. I was not into gurus, and still am not into gurus, or temples, or being a follower of anything or anyone. Sometimes I've avoided the transmission – or thought I have – in my own annoyance with humans grovelling at the feet of great holy masters and their emissaries.

When we returned from America at the turn of the millennium, we found ourselves without direction in a place where we knew no one, and during that first winter we stoked up the fire each evening with elm and birch wood and read the whole of *Beelzebub's Tales to His Grandson*. It was a long book, over a thousand pages. Mark read out loud, I listened, the fire roared in the grate.

'We have to make ourselves at home,' I said. 'We have to start again.'

Being Effort is required.

You see, even though that was 15 years ago and I no longer have your books, I can remember the language, its strange and yet familiar terms, how they helped us do what seemed impossible at the time. Here by another fire, in the dead of winter, I felt I needed to make an account. Only this time it's not personal. Perhaps it never was – I just didn't see it at the time, wrapped up in my own seeming exile and grief. It had felt like the end of the world.

> BOBBIN-KANDELNOST – *the force that exists in the three centres of thinking, feeling and moving within the self; that acts like a coiled spring and can lose momentum and run out by overuse (see also* Die like Dog).

You wrote that *three-brained beings* don't want to wake up to the *terror of the situation*, the realisation we are all asleep and stuck in automatic behaviours, our minds and personalities all over the place, reacting to outside events and never coming from within. The book, the 'First Series' of your *All and Everything* trilogy, opens with a description of a bellringer in a town, who curses the populace each morning as he climbs out of bed, so that their curses would deflect away from his work in the belltower. No one wants to wake up, get out of bed, do the thing they are supposed to do, to be a live conscious being in a difficult time. Fewer still want to ring that bell.

You wrote your masterpiece in the 1920s, as the world rocked towards the Depression. You had arrived in Paris with the *mass psychosis* of the Russian revolution at your heels. People may say, with the clarity and dispassion of historians: well, it wasn't so hard then to be awake; there was less to consider planetarily speaking. But it is always hard, the burning issues of the day are always the *burning issues* of the day, whether the spectre of another war in Europe or a climate catastrophe. You can be awake to that moment in the way poets in the trenches and gulags were awake, you can sacrifice yourself nobly to a cause to change the destiny of people, or you can be awake and not comply with the orders to stay asleep. You can embody an intrinsic inner move that can break the machine.

There is a moment in the *Tales* that struck me: you are sitting in the Paris cafe, where you are writing in several notebooks, dressed in a vanilla-coloured overcoat and a red fez. There is a bottle of brandy on the table and you are surrounded by the clatter of cups and knives and forks to hone your *mentation*, your absolute focus on the matter at hand, as you turn your Saturnian face, with its drooping moustache, towards a woman greeting a group of friends. You suddenly see this scene at the table played over and over through time, through every civilisation and city, and still here the same petty relationships, the rivalries, the posturings of society, the things that take up the minds and hearts of people and no progress made at all, in spite of everything that has been said over and over again by poets, by mystics, by philosophers, by you.

BORED SECRETARY – *the challenge of thwarting the associative mind that goes into the mental filing cabinets for facts or trivia; the pursuit of busyness out of superficiality and lack of rigour.*

Most people remember the dramas and the gossip: whether you were or were not the last magus of Europe, or a carpet dealer and charlatan who slept with your students, whether your teaching really did come from the ancient Sarmoung Brotherhood in the Hindukush; or they mention your famous quarrel with Ouspensky, or how Katherine Mansfield died in your care at Le Prieuré, and a string of anecdotes and quotes and photographs of people in white tunics in elegant dance salons.

I am not a storyteller, I told Lucy and the women as they melted into the darkness tonight. I come from a line of engineers and lawyers, I have a forensic mind and love of structure. We have come here to initiate a network that will connect the women and the trees of these islands. It is a bold project. I know what needs to happen won't take the shape of a narrative that we might already know, that to change really, truly, deeply, we have to let go of all those happy-ever-after stories of romantic love, of reconciliation and redemption. We need a rigorous practice that will break us open. A shock that will push us in another direction.

Your esoteric teachings were all about the musical scale, and though I know now how your name should be pronounced (Gurrr-jieff, gruffly like a Russian bear), I cannot pretend to know their intricate meanings, any more than I understood how all those dots related in Peter's painting. Yet the impression of a cosmic map remained, and one point shone outward like a star you might recognise in the night sky: there is a stage as you increase your knowledge and practice and ascend the scale, where something has to come in from the outside to boost your inner transformation.

These encounters come but we are not ready for them, or they knock us over, or we forget to make the move. I thought I would never get over my exile from that desert place, from Carmen's kitchen, from my life on the road – so I put a hand out and found a book and that's when you came in with your convoluted metaphors, with your rants about tinned food, with your strange vocabulary, part-Armenian, part-English, part-Russian, for a transmission that I was open to without even knowing I was open to it.

I was born six years after you were buried in the Île-de-France, and the circumstances of my *arising* and my own nature would mean, even if I had been of your time, I would never have come to one of your packed lectures in New York, or danced a sacred dance in a white tunic, even with Carmen playing the piano. But here I am, having worked on self-pity and *inner considering* and contending with everyone else's. We still live in times of mass psychosis. The experts continue to *wiseacre*. The world is still asleep.

BEING-PARTKDOLG-DUTY – *twin methods of soul-making and waking up: conscious labours (also known as being effort) and intentional-suffering, the greatest of which is the ability to endure the 'displeasing-manifestations-of-others-towards-yourselves'.*

This wood is made up mostly of coppiced oak trees. An industrial forest in the 18th and 19th centuries, the Wyre sits between the green hills of Wales and the manufacturing sprawl of the Midlands. Sooty-faced charcoal burners once built great pyres in the clearings and made the charcoal that fuelled the iron forges of Birmingham, the smelters of a revolution that would rock the world. Until the discovery of coal, only the high temperatures of charcoal could melt the metal, and even now it is the favoured fuel of blacksmiths and sword makers.

Now the wood has become a neglected monoculture of oak trees, some streaked black with disease, with no space for them to branch out or for other trees to grow. They are sleeping, the curator said when I arrived, and told me his plans for restoration. Except for the yews. The yews stand there like red-armed sentinels from another time, some of them over 800 years old. When the snows came this winter, herds of deer sheltered underneath the white roof of their branches. This morning I stood in their hoofprints and listened to the rain fall quietly around me, listening out for an ancestral tale I might tell around this fire that might spark another kind of revolution.

Charcoal makers lived in the woods in shacks, feared and despised as 'the devil's men'. The work was hard and long and dangerous. They built up a pile of logs and covered it with soil and turf. The process took days and sometimes weeks. The gases produced were highly toxic and still are where charcoal is now made, mostly illegally, for modern barbeques, in the forests of Africa and South America. The work for the women in the forest was also hard, as they stripped the bark from the coppiced trees for the tanning of leather.

The sparks in the fire come from old spruce fence posts and some birch, but mostly felled oak, where they are making space for other things to flourish here. 'Who are we doing it for?' asked the curator. For the nature lover who values butterflies, for the runner who likes to run along a straight path, for the forester who likes good long planks for carpenters to work with, for the charities who own it to make it pay its way when the subsidies run out, which they will surely do someday soon?

When you don't know what to do or what you are doing life for, you build a fire, and you wait for something to spark you alight again. We are in the time of the winter solstice, the day that breaks the circle of the year, between its last outward breath and the first inward pull of air: the place of no breath.

After your first car crash, at the point when Le Prieuré, your school in Fontainebleau, was faltering, you pushed everyone aside and went into the forest and made up a great fire, and for days you sat in front of it. The fire remade you.

How heated do things have to become until we can reforge ourselves, to work the iron in our soul? If we fed the fire all our stories, everything we needed to die to, could we reforge the world into a different shape?

INNER CONSIDERING – *the act of chewing over incidents which you feel guilty about or wish had been otherwise; to be replaced by outward expression (see also* Remorse of Conscience*).*

What you need, above all, is the courage to face the terror that feels like annihilation. There are almost no words to describe that feeling because it is happening in a place that no one has working words for: as if you are being crushed by air or engulfed by flames that devour your memory; as if you are being dragged downwards into a pit and a force is sucking all the awareness and sweetness out of you.

When I returned I needed a technê to restore myself. I fed the fire my travelling story; I fed it my capacity to love a certain place on Earth that felt like home, my capacity to love certain people, my companions. These things wouldn't happen again in my lifetime. Afterwards I found myself in another position, holding the reins of a carriage in my hands.

To get our horse and carriage into shape was core to your teaching. In order to behave like a human being, rather than a machine, we had to gather our wits about us and become fully conscious. The horse was our emotional body, the driver our mind, and the carriage our physical body. Only when these three parts of ourselves were working together could the passenger alight. Not to hail us occasionally like a hackney cab, but to be fully on board.

The technê of consciousness is hard, on-the-edge work. You have to persuade the horse not to bolt at every turn, you have to instruct the driver to have a feel for the horse and the bumpy road ahead. The carriage needs to be roadworthy, kept in good nick. These three parts of ourselves need to work together. Otherwise we are not able to carry the passenger.

Who is the passenger? It is our conscious awake self, our spirit, our intelligence. The 'being-I' who knows what is going on and what we are doing together in this English forest, as the longest night holds us in its embrace and the owls call to each other from the canopy.

In those desert years I had climbed down and worked with the horse. I had become a whisperer of my own feeling being. We are held hostage by our feelings and, like the nervous, imaginative creature who has borne us loyally all these years, remember every blow received, so that when we see a shape we associate it with a dark presence we once knew, we rear up, or we refuse to move. Somehow, we have to unlearn all that fear and trust the driver. The driver has to walk beside the horse, repair her will which has been broken over thousands of years.

I let the horse lead me to regions that were not on the map: to reclaim my heart lost in childhood nightmares, into the forgotten kingdoms of trees and birds and sea to recover my place on Earth. Most seekers focus on the driver and become too controlling, hampering the horse with bridle and whip; others work on the carriage, becoming obsessed with paint and cogs and springs. But I knew we go nowhere in the land of fire without the horse.

MR. SELF-LOVE AND MRS. VANITY – *self-importance; twin attributes of self-obsession which lock human beings inside themselves and prevent influences both bad and good from entering (to be distinguished from the Self Love of essence which brings freedom– see* Life is Only Real Then When I Am*).*

The moment of solstice is exact. The pause between the expiration of the year and its great inhalation. There are ancient stories I can tell about this moment, how the oak changes place with the holly tree, the robin with the wren, how in my country in the east, the men with blackened faces come over the marsh holding firebrands, and the women with hats draped with ivy, who back them playing the music of fife and drum. The dance is slow and heavy, their boots stamping the earth awake, the sticks clash and click like antlers, like flint against flint.

But most of all this is a technê for showing that life can begin again, so long as we relinquish everything we know in this moment of no breath, so long as we can admit none of us know what is going to happen or how. The technê comes through the mouths of people you don't even respect, or a book that falls into your hands in a second-hand store that you open without knowing why.

Or now, as I find myself clicking two sticks of rainforest wood Aurelia gave me that spring night in Oaxaca for a performance we called the Earth Medicine Show. As she drummed and Mark sang, I danced, and Julianne told us her heart that had frozen over in the Minneapolis winter had suddenly melted, and afterwards the five of us went out to dinner arm-in-arm to the square. That rooftop performance was our first and our last, and even though we rehearsed and talked about it for years, only now do I understand that it wasn't the right time for shows. My carriage was robust but the horse was too nervy, the driver prone to flights of fancy. My eye was not on the road.

I don't like to think that every radical move I've made in these years has been caused by outer shocks. To be *inwardly free* – the ultimate goal of Gurjieffian thinking – you have to transform the world's hostilities and not submit to them. Because I was thrown out of America, because I underwent my own financial katabasis and had to face the reality of the job centre, because I had to suffer, more-or-less consciously, the 'nullities emitting atmospheres of unendurable vibrations' telling me I was worthless, knew nothing, or ignoring me entirely, I am here now dancing by the fire.

> SELF-CALMING – *an act of deception we practice to pretend everything is all right when it is not; false assurances that prevent reality from being perceived.*

When I think of you now I see your flat in Paris, where you spent your last years with the curtains drawn. For some reason I imagine it is one of those ateliers, with a crammed larder of jars and sausages swinging from hooks, though it was probably grander than that. You have given up on the world you say and now only teach a small band of women, mostly lesbians, called The Rope. When the Occupation is over you host great dinners and toast the idiots with glasses of vodka. You insist that everyone has to read your work at least three times to understand it.

I don't know the 17 kinds of idiot you need to be to be totally awake (what is a round idiot, a square idiot?). It took me a long time to realise that an idiot was not an idiot, but that in different moments of awakening you appear like an idiot to everyone else in the status quo, to your family, to your best friend, to your culture and nation and history, that to be ready for the passenger to hail you is a great and noble task because you are doing it for the forest and the deer, and all who flourish under their branches. That is no small thing.

I have been a compassion idiot, a seeker idiot, a relinquishment idiot, a community activist idiot, a real democracy idiot. At each turn I imagined that if everyone woke up, got conscious, the world would turn around. Even though when I go to the city (which is not often) it looks as though we have become more like automatons than ever, our attention captured by small lit-up screens. And then I remember that this Earth is a chance to start again and, every year, time gives us that possibility, this moment.

In many ways I too have closed my curtains on the world and stocked up my larder. I have spent too much time chasing *Mrs. Serious Problem* (as you called the demands on you to secure funds) and the book I wanted to write is unfinished. But one thing you learn from being a writer: you are good at waiting, you are good at holding out, you can weather the moment of no breath, knowing that one day the spark will happen, the sentences will tumble out, and that they are only good if the form of their creator is newly-smelted. You wait for a long time, until the fire is hot enough to burn you without consuming you, to suck the moisture and then the oxygen out of you.

You wait for the opportunity, and when it arrives you toast all the idiots you have met whose *common presences* have helped shaped you, put the reins back into your hands. You look at them across the table, on the other side of the fire, and you raise your glass:

Salut Carmen, salut Peter, salut Aurelia, salut Lucy, salut Mark, salut George Ivanovich!

KUNDABUFFER – invisible organ that controls perception and turns any encounter with a disturbing reality upside down; a force that prevents you from seeing the truth when the truth would cause you to lose hope; a filter that requires dismantling.

In 1918, women in Britain finally won the right to vote (though only if you were a householder over the age of 30). In 1918, the young men of Britain did not return to the Forest from the trenches of Flanders. Those who survived went instead to work in the factories of the Black Country. In 1918, your father was shot amongst the throng in the Armenian genocide in your home city of Alexandrapol, and, posing as a scientist, you left Essentuki with a band of family members, companions and pupils and walked through the Caucasus Mountains. It was the beginning of a long journey west that went through Georgia to Istanbul to Paris.

You wrote that humanity was at a standstill and that 'from a standstill there is a straight path to downfall and degeneration', that nothing pointed to our evolution. And 100 years later it seems women are no more emancipated than human beings are more evolved. We have the vote, some of us are kinder to animals and some of us realise the effect of our actions on the living planet – but as a species we appear to be as stupid, cruel and greedy as ever. Our technology has evolved but we are less vigorous, less alive, more timid, more pursued by ghosts and the trauma of history through generations, at a standstill where we feel responsible for everything and nothing at all; where our key fault is still our passivity and suggestibility – our lack of ability to think for ourselves and to handle those forces that battle for supremacy inside and outside ourselves.

Our buffers allow us to say one thing and do another: we lament deforestation whilst sitting on teak chairs, lament the state of the ocean whilst eating its disappearing fish, we think we are enlightened because we have read books, and pretend the slave trade is over when it is worse than ever. We're still stuck in patriarchy, in a dualist Babylonian mindset – the cause, you once said, of all wickedness in the world – and we continue to nurture the 'artificial, the unreal, and what is foreign, at the cost of the natural, the real, and what is one's own.'

But maybe a standstill is a place to start from. Maybe if we just stopped here together, sat with the disturbing reality of that fact, something else would kick in. Maybe if we shifted out of our predilection for stories, away from our desire to grovel at the feet of shiny saviours and patriarchs, our obeisance to the genetic mummy-daddy-baby machine, our longing for the community to love us, to succeed, to be a star, to be left alone – maybe some awakening would happen.

We would need to go against nature and against god as you once said – not against the *Great Nature* of the glacier and the tiger but our own propensity for passivity and suggestibility; not the solar and cosmic forces but the violent gods we worship and pray to in blind faith, instead of engaging in The Work that would make us function at higher vibratory levels, and thus the world, that would break us out of the prisons of our mind and

228

from all our gaolers. That could allow us to be grander and kinder and more intelligent than these small rooms allow us.

> SOLIOONENSIUS – *a time of solar or planetary tension which energises the Earth so people strive for freedom – then turn that striving for freedom into war or revolution, into destruction; a time when old ideas can no longer move the world and new ideas have not yet gained momentum; when certain new directions can be implanted into general culture.*

Sometimes I remember what lay outside Carmen's kitchen and I can feel the blue sky arching forever, and the empty roads that go on forever, the way in late March the flowers of the ocotillo lick the air like the flames of epiphany, and the scent of chaparral permeating the world after the rain. How I used to feel with the women in Mexico, as we sat beside the water, our colours and laughter and fluidity. I remember the space and that feeling of freedom I can never sense in my own country. How this lightness, this liberation, is what we all look for and yet here we are on this crowded island, in this sleeping forest, my muddy lane with its power possessor driveways and toxic runoff from barley fields, threats of development on all sides. Dispossessed, precarious, unnecessary. This is the territory I have to wrestle and contend with after the hope-for-something died in the high deserts of America.

You have to make yourself matter, become an active agent in the fabric of the world. If you are versed in myth and story, in the beauty of the bird and the flower, it is easy to feel at home on the Earth, but being at home amongst your fellow human beings is a task once you forgo the lullabies and cradle songs of Empire, and awake to find a bell rope in your hands.

We wield great terms above our heads like axes – social justice, transformation, shift of consciousness, power of community – ready to split enemy heads apart with their force. But still we are asleep, reacting, neglecting The Work down among the people in the petty shops and tearooms, enduring the unbearable vibrations of the office bully, the *personages* who control the boardrooms and parliaments.

A network is not a community, I told the women. We stand on miles upon miles of mycelium networks, connecting the forest, nourishing the roots of all beings underground. The community gathers the people together round the fire, it looks inward. The further you are inside it the warmer and more connected you feel. Outside a cold wind blows and you push and jostle to be in the throng.

A network is not concerned with belonging. It is self-directed and interested in the connections it makes. It works outwardly, focused on the matter at hand. The more the network is resonant and alive, the stronger it feels. Living networks depend on living breathing plants and creatures and microbes that are everywhere around us. We are an industrialised, neglected wood – asleep – but there are networks communicating beneath our feet and ancient yews amongst us, and men who make space for other things to happen. And here a band of women unafraid of the dark, standing with the forests, with our sisters of the world, and one of us, remembering you, in the flicker of a fire.

And if time is the great mystery of these islands, of this Earth, we are surely not alone in this moment, in this time of destruction, because if we step into this ancestral moment, in the presence of all beings, all creatures, all trees though time, then this is the moment that things can turn around.

Outside, the Earth waits in the stillness, as glaciers crack and tigers move across the snowline, as the roots of everything are ready to stir in the cycle of the year. Of itself, Great Nature can do nothing to effect our change, except we awaken, open to the spark of the sun inside ourselves. Of itself, the sun can effect nothing, except that we allow it into our physical forms, let it mould our selves anew.

After the fire, I will follow the women back up the track to the barn, as we feel our way with our feet in the dark. Tomorrow we'll get up at dawn, light the stove and move out into the orchard in silence. We will stand under dripping hazel trees at the edge of the Forest, with the apple trees in front of us and the oaks standing behind us, and pay attention to the moment. Somewhere deep in the forest a deer will wait underneath a yew tree, as she has waited since the Ice Age in these borderlands. The sun will rise, even though we will not see it through the cloud.

The light shifts imperceptibly and a hawk flashes past, its scimitar wings cut the air. We hold our breath.

The Time of Stones

❧

'T he dead lie in layers beneath us,' said Tony Dias, 'and influence all our actions.' We were in a schoolroom in Ry in northern Denmark, and I was teaching a class about deep time. The students were sitting in a circle, each taking up position in the calendar of the year, discussing how each station affected them. It is the end of October and the writer and philosopher is sitting in the position of the ancestors, also known as Samhain or Halloween. I am at winter solstice. We are holding a conversation about the end of things, as the oldest people in the room. I talk about restoration and composting the past and he talks about the oceans, how oil has come out of an anaerobic process, so doesn't break down and feed life. 'It is a zombie fuel,' he says.

Afterwards we will climb into canoes and silently cross the lake to the woods where the class will fan out and encounter the wild spaces on their own. The copper leaves of the beech trees will shower down on our endeavours to connect with the living, breathing planet. A lot of the students will have problems getting beyond the whirl of their technology-driven minds.

'Everything is hitting against that zenith of the summer solstice and resisting the fall,' remarks Tony. 'The violence and destruction happens, so everyone can jump the process and begin again.'

For the last two weeks I have switched off the computer, and tried to look back at the tumultuous event of 2016 from the perspective of where I live, a small lane in East Anglia on the edge of England. Most of my working and social life is done via this machine, so when I go offline the world and its headlines vanish. The physical place comes closer, and with it a depth of perception that all the buzzy discussion about politics and celebrity, about money, about the end of globalisation, never allow in. You get a sense of the mood of the times.

One thing is clear: you can't skip the fall, no matter how much you try.

Nigredo

In 2016 a lot of words I used to use in the travelling years, like transformation and chaos, became a way to look at the string of political events that had crashed the world views of the privileged. The shadow had reeled into the open. Nigredo is the first stage of alchemy, bringing to light the dark materia that needs to be transformed. The nigredo is a scary moment. You have to know how to negotiate it. When the hidden rage of millions is unleashed – generations of people humiliated, derided, told they are worthless and have no future – you have to hold fast to your humanity. Here be dragons. You can't be righteous and float above this scary territory, because that fury is in you and me. No-one in the system escapes its hostility. You can refuse to carry the shadow of your culture only if you have dealt with it yourself, only if you are not still blaming mummy and daddy and your first boyfriend and that prick in HR who doesn't recognise your true value. Only the system wins in the system.

Nigredo is all about the reveal. When the US election result is announced it feels less scary than in 2008 when everyone was whooping with joy and hope about the future. The pantomime villain, the bad cop entered stage right to loud hisses from the gallery, but the exiting good cop with his suave saviour style had been less easy to discern. However, all cops are cops when it comes to 'full spectrum dominance'. The Empire is the Empire whatever country you now live in. We are all Romans and all slaves.

This key alchemical moment has nothing to do with social justice, or environmentalism, or any of the grassrootsy stuff I have found myself advocating during the last decade. Nothing transforms if we are the same people inside, if we haven't dealt with our stuff – as we used to say in the '90s – if we haven't uncivilised ourselves, made contact with the layers of dead under our feet, with the sky, with the rivers. If we haven't stood with the Lakota, or with the yew trees, with the rainbow serpent, with the glacier, with the tawny owl. If we haven't found a way to dismantle the belief systems that keep us trapped in the cycles of history. If we haven't dealt with our insatiable desire for power and attention and found ways to live more lightly on the planet, we are not going to make it through this stage. And it is a 'we' because, in England at least, we are on a very crowded island and no matter how much we say we don't like our neighbours, they live next door.

ϟ

When I boarded the boat train at Harwich, coming back from Denmark, I breathed a sigh of relief. It was a moment of homecoming that I never had when I was a traveller, when England was a country I wanted to get away from. The carriage was shabbier than any in IKEA Europe, and the air on the platform smelled of winter, of salt and rain and green. The conductor walked down the passageway and three men who were travelling together and drinking beers laughed out loud. No one had laughed on those Dutch and Danish trains and no one had made an entrance like that, a deliberate music hall swagger down the aisle, like a rolling English road, like the curve of the Oxfordshire hills, almost, you could say, *hobbity*. Not of this time, nor of this dimension.

A door that seemed shut in the schoolroom in Denmark suddenly swung open. A joy ripped through me. The mythos was still here!

You can look at nature, the writer Richard Mabey once wrote, as a tragedy or a comedy. It depends on your point of view. The character of a people is not the same as a society hamstrung by a corporate global economy. In times of crisis, it is worth bearing in mind that the drama changes tack the moment we give up our high tragic roles and become ordinary players. It's true, comedy is used to paper over the dark things, to make light of serious matters; the Empire has used entertainment to distract people forever. Britain is not very militaristic, as George Orwell once noted. We're more interested in theatrics, which is why we are such dismal suckers for Punch and Judy politics and royal parades, even as the joke is so often on us.

That's the way to do it!

However comedy is not just about laughing, or poking fun, it is seeing life from a certain perspective, with heart. It gives an agency to situations where tragedy can only offer a solitary death, it reminds us above all that life is an ensemble act that brings affection, even in the hardest times. We are in this show together. Tickets please, ladies and gentlemen.

In spite of everything, I realised I wanted to go home to the lane. Though the Empire will keep telling me I do not belong, I know that I do. And no kind of politics will take that relationship away. I am not going anywhere else. I am not a nationalist, a flag waver, a patriot, but I can love this place, these marsh birds, these oaks. I can cohere in a fragmenting time, I can remember in a forgetting time. We don't need a grand vision, another story right now, we need to get through the nigredo, the seismic shaking of the jar, and allow the seeds we hold inside us to break open their coats.

Afterwards will come the albedo, the deep memory of water, and the rubedo, the solarising forces, the warmth and light of the sun. We will unfurl ourselves then. All is good, all is return, all is regeneration in alchemy. We just have to have the stomach for the work. We have to trust that whatever happens in our small lives, whatever move we make to undo the unkindness of centuries will affect the whole picture, that we are not on our own. Everything matters. The ancestors are behind us: all good comedies end in a dance, they say.

Return

When I returned from the vast spaces of the Americas, I discovered in England another dimension that is the vast depth and mystery of time. I walked for miles across the land, recovering myself as a dweller of these misty islands, as someone whose heart could still leap at the sight of the sun rising. I wanted to belong, not to society, not to culture, but to a land shaped by ancestral forces. I wanted to become native, so that no one could tell me I did not belong to the Earth or to life.

In my pocket there are eight stones and a fire roaring behind me. The stones mark the eight spokes of a clock, a clock that has been in use for thousands of years across the Neolithic world. In these years I have become a teacher of time and places without knowing it. I have found myself leading groups of people into moors and mountains, into the Cheshire Hills, into the water meadows of Norfolk, into a silent forest in Sweden, at the turns and twists of the solar year. These doors are markers in time. Each one growing roots in the fabric of place. Taking on the light of the sun, teaching us to become the ancestors of time.

At Imbolc we climb the South Downs: we fan out, each of us sitting under a hawthorn tree or in the frosty light on the chalky hill. It is the beginning of the year. Afterwards the people speak about their encounters and make a map. We share a meal and wish each other good speed. On May morning Mark, Josiah and I go to a tiny meadow of frosted green-winged orchids, marooned in an industrial prairie of barley, and watch the sun come up and cook up a breakfast of beans. At summer solstice, I sing with a band of writers I am teaching with Lucy on the borders of Wales. We jump over the fire. On Spring equinox I feast with a company of travelling players. We toast each other and sing into the snowy Cumbria night, devising a show that will follow the track of the fastest river in Britain, crossed by the world's first industrial pipe system, transporting the wild lake water to the city of Manchester 100 miles away.

Afterwards we sit around a fire, in the dark, and speak of our dialogues with the Earth. We talk of what happens when we bring the creatures and mountains, rivers and valleys into this room. As if they stand behind us. It's a different conversation.

Rannock Moor
Samhain 2015

On the road to Holt in Norfolk that October a man came across a killed deer as he was speeding homeward. It was a fully pregnant doe. The man did an unprecedented thing: he slit open the belly of the dead creature and delivered a live fawn.

I am holding a copy of the *Eastern Daily Press* where the story has just made the front page, in spite of all the world's terrors and hostilities clamouring for attention. The tiny fawn looks calmly outward, suckling on a bottle of milk, held in the large tattooed hands of the man.

When asked what made him stop he said: 'It is perhaps something you will never come across again in your lifetime and I am just thankful that I knew what to do.'

The instructions were simple. *Catch the 16:21 train from Glasgow to Fort William. Get out at Corrour and follow the stag.*

Some part of us knows that beneath the noise and strife of the modern world, beyond the headlines, there is a deep place where our presence on the Earth is not for nothing. That when we come across it on an empty road at dawn we will know what to do. For thousands of years our negotiation with life was understood in terms of our relationship with the horned beasts we once lived alongside, and a mythical being, sometimes known as the Mistress of the Deer. In Scotland, and particularly in this part of the Highlands, she is known as the Cailleach. Samhain – All Souls, Day of the Dead and Halloween – is the time when the Cailleach, Queen of Winter, takes over the mantle of Earth from Bridget, the bright one, in a similar way the Oak cedes to the Holly at the summer solstice in England.

The instructions were simple. 'You're going to be the Cailleach,' said Dougie, 'and dance to a piped lament on the moor.'

'It will be dark then,' I said.

'Yes,' he said. 'Very dark. And maybe raining'.

So that was how it was when we set out on a moonless wet night: Jack (the Stag), Wilf (the Wolf), Dougie and I on 30th October to walk the track toward Corrour station. I will bring up the rear, Dougie said. Martha (the Cook) remained at the hostel to hold the hearth. I was left on the hillside with instructions to light the fire (rags soaked in citronella) and start the music (in a box hidden by the rock) and do my thing.

I don't really know what I am going to do of course. I have a red velvet dress on and a furry cape and a large fashion hat I have wreathed in birch twigs and barn owl wings. A midge veil is covering my face – not that there are any midges at this time of year, though there are roving and rutting stags. One is out there. We have just seen him. He was massive and did not move away when Jack flashed his torch. I have done some challenging gigs in my time, but this has to be the mother of all of them.

'Carrying the Fire' was originally a small gathering, created by writer and performer, Dougie Strang, on the Scottish borders, shaped in a similar way to Dark Mountain's Uncivilisation Festivals – workshops, music, performance, discussions, and storytelling fire. This year's was for a smaller group, built around the festival of Samhain and located deep in the heathery heart of Rannoch Moor. We would be based at a wooden hostel, once the boathouse of the shooting lodge, beside Loch Ossian at the foot of Beinn a' Bhric, the Cailleach's mountain. The nearest road is 18 miles away.

Its structure was woven around three mythic stories embedded in this territory, which Dougie would tell over the weekend: on arrival beside the crackling stove with mugs of cocoa, by the Samhain fire, and on the platform of the highest station in Britain as we departed. On Saturday we would be taken by a wilderness guide called Neil up the mountain trails to do a *Whakapapa* – a walking exchange, derived from the Maori practice, where pairs of people share life stories and geographies. On Sunday I would lead a workshop based on our Earth dreaming practice and send folk out into the hills on their own. They would come back and relate what they experienced with each other in groups of four and then draw a collective dream map.

Like many of these Carrying the Fire events, the fire would be a focal space where people sing and tell stories and pass round a bottle of malt. This part is mapped out. What is unscripted is the moment when Gavin will pass quartz rocks around, so we can make sparks in the dark; that Ben and Darla and Tamsin will teach us a Georgian song taught to them by Ivan who uses a giant staff to protect orphaned children; or that Jonny will read a passage from a book about the last wolf making her trek across the snow fields of the north where the swans sleep. And out of the darkness a skein of whooper swans will fly over the loch, calling.

The instructions were simple. You go out and stand in the land, you come back and relate what happened. What you say, what you do with what you know, is the thing that the Earth waits for. Your gift. What is that story? You forgot it. Ah. Here is a hint.

Arrive in the dark.

Follow the stag.

Wait for the people to come round the hill.

When Jack comes round the corner his flambard has gone out. Luckily I can see a tiny infrared beam from his head torch. I leap into action – light fire, switch on music – and begin to sway, arms moving about like antlers and birch trees in the wind, boots anchored on the slippery rocky slope. I can't see or hear anything through the veil. I don't know whether anyone is there, or whether they have gone past. I keep dancing until I hear people howling and laughing in the distance. They have discovered Wilf! I gather everything up and go to find him. I feel exultant.

'You looked about ten foot tall!' exclaims everyone, when we walk back in (without costumes). 'And then you would disappear! And reappear. It was scary. It was magical!'

'Is dance your practice?' asks another. 'You were so rooted!'

'No,' I laugh, 'but I do love to dance'. (I didn't like to say I couldn't move my feet in their massive boots on that rock in case I fell over).

Samhain is a door. It is a door to the ancestors, and this is what we are doing up here, connecting with the ancestor that lives in our bones, out in the wild places. The Cailleach is the ancestor creator of these high places. Out of her creel she once tossed big stones that became the peaks that now tower above the golden deer grass and shiny lochans of the valley floor. She brings the cold sharp winds of winter, commands the weather and wildness. Her face is blue and sometimes veiled like the mist. In the spring she washes her plaid in the Corryvreckan whirlpool between Jura and Scarba, and then she turns into a rock.

We walk over this springy rocky rain-soaked moor, sprinkled with the flowers of heather and milkwort like a fading summer dress. I pocket the last of the year's bilberries and bearberries and Martha shows me some fragrant crackly leaves from bog myrtle, and says she will make a tea from them all. A tea that will have the bitter taste of farewell.

Samhain is a door. Sometimes you need a set and a setting, a space, permission to do things differently: to dig deep, to sit alone, to dance in the night with a veil over your head. You don't know what will happen except something will happen. A small thing that makes sense of everything. That expectancy, that sharpness, that not-knowing is part of its territory.

I could tell you about the people who came, and the laughing around the tables as the feast of venison and pumpkin was served, or the sight of 20 pairs of boots hanging from the rafters, or how my Whakapapa companion, 18 minutes into his 20 minute story, told me that something dark happened on the mountain when his friend slipped and fell to his death. There were always hills and mountains, he said, that came at a pivotal point in my life, that changed the direction of everything. The Dales, Mont Blanc, Glencoe. How all our life-changing territories and encounters that we recounted on our return to the house that made some kind of collective pattern: woods which were torn down for houses, a tsunami in Sri Lanka that nearly drowned a family, a broken road in Iceland that snapped a connection between people, housing estates in Britain where art and writing reforged them.

I could tell you how I woke to find Venus and a sickle moon in a clear sky and swam into the cold waters of the loch. How I watched the sun creep downwards from the peaks, turning the dun hillsides gold, the mountains like beasts crouching, attentive, so alive I could almost touch them. How the star Sirius rose over the mountain, as it has always risen over the mountain, heralding winter.

When Donald of the Brown Eyes hunts his last deer he slits open the belly and finds a ball of wool. It is the beginning of sheep herding in the Highlands and a domesticated relationship with the creatures. In modern Scotland deer are killed on the road, deer are shot by blood-hungry elites and deer (and sheep) chew every last tree standing. When the wolves and the Cailleach roamed on these mountains and the people met around the fire everything was held in balance. Something of that balance, what is sometimes called medicine, is contained in these old stories and in, we are hoping, this event.

Carrying the Fire's name is taken in part from the dystopian novel, *The Road*, where the father explains to his son that the purpose of being human is 'to carry the fire' and that if that spirit is lost the art of being human is also lost. The Cailleach is not human: she is a mythic being that lives deep in our bones and sinews, the parts of us that resonate with stones and wild weather. She reminds us of human beings' original bargain with Earth. Sometimes we need a reminder that she is still there, so we can carry the fire, come what may. So, in spite of living in a 24/7 world, we can mark time; in spite of living in a world where we are told we do not belong, we can make ourselves at home.

I took eight stones out of the loch and laid them on Jack's deer pelt. Here is a medicine wheel, I said: the blue stones represent the Earth cross and red stones represent the sun cross. The eight work like doors, marking gateways you go through. In the Americas the medicine wheel is about space and the directions that bring different challenges and riches. The north is where the ancestors live.

'The wheel of these British islands however is all about time. The stones mark a clock on which you can measure the time of the year and your own time and the time we are all in now – which is a time of breakdown and decay. What old forms need to go and what ancient roots need to hold fast in this time? What are we all doing here together at this moment with the ancestor mountain behind us and the lake of the bard before us?'

Everyone leaves and goes out on the pathways toward the hillsides. Some crouch down beside the loch or the roots of the birch trees at the back of the hostel. Some walk out of sight. I go out and sit on a rock striped with white quartz, and sing a chant to the mountain: it is a song that comes from the Andes, that comes from the Sierra Madre, that comes from a sky island known as the Place of Many Springs. No one taught me that song.

Sometimes you contact something from the dark peaty layer, as Dougie calls the Cailleach's territory, that bursts through the dimensions, through time and space. It calls you to attention: the part of you that knows what to do when you find a dead deer on the roadway. You can deliver the fawn, you can do your thing in the dark and the rain. You can remember. Remembering can take you away from the light of the fire and the kitchen, and yet in the dark you feel you belong, you matter, in a way no culture, no family, no work, no political ideology, can ever make you feel. I am not sure I can take you there with words. I can show you the stones. I can dance. Everything else you walk yourself:

'It was not a psychological or therapeutic setting,' wrote one of the group, Caroline Ross, afterwards, 'but a deeply connected almost mythic space, as I have only seen properly described in the words of Riddley Walker, or perhaps the books of Ursula K. Le Guin. People are not the only people there. Land, rocks, mountains and lakes, beings and heroes of the past, forces and gods are at the fireside too...

> 'If you showed me a far-off society where Samhain was celebrated as we did at Carrying the Fire, I would go into exile from this country to live there with those good people and become part of that culture. Ceremony, gathering together and marking the passage of the year and of our lives are so lost in the wider human culture in Britain from which I am mostly alienated, and manage to evade by living moored beside a tiny island in the middle of a river.
>
> 'My heart was at home over Samhain, I was at home both culturally and geographically. People are made refugees every day and must leave their hearths for uncertain futures. Even within this country, Britons are displaced from the beneficial aspects of their culture and nature, by the market, homelessness, delusion and a thousand other causes.'

But the deer are still here, and so are the mountains, and the wind, and there is still enough wood to make a fire. There are people who can still remember the stories that make sense of everything, and the movements that are the shape of antlers or a tree moving in the wind. And if on a winter's day in the Highlands you hear a raven croak behind you, you might find the Cailleach still there to show you her misty, snowsprinkled face that is sometimes blue.

Winter Solstice
Dartmoor 2018

'There are two ways to grow a movement,' said Sophy. 'You push outwards and expand the number of people involved. Or you go inward and deepen the core.'

It's December and from Sophy's kitchen table I can watch the sun as it appears above the dark curve of the Devon hills. It's day three of a convergence called Deep Dive, an exploration into the process of 'Deep Adaptation', sparked by the emergence of Extinction Rebellion. Sophy is one of the organisers and I'm asking her about the intent for gathering.

It's a beautiful morning, just before the winter solstice, and tonight I will face my death, looking into the face of an eagle. I don't know this yet. You might say not knowing is the M.O. for all explorations – except that having an intent gives you a thread to guide you there and back. You can go into a territory to see what is there, or you can go into the territory to find something you and the world cannot live without.

That's a different journey.

Encounter

That winter I had begun to write a performance called 'The Red Thread', a reworking of the myth of the Labyrinth at Knossos, where the young men and women from the city are not sacrificed to feed the Minotaur incarcerated at its centre, but instead encounter an initiatory force that will reveal the mystery of life and death in the darkness of an underground chamber.

Two things I know about entering the core: intent is what keeps you from being blown apart at a solstice moment, as the seeds burst their jackets underground, as life quickens amongst the dead, and the dead parts of you fall away into the earth. The second is that artists and writers are the ones who can hand you the thread.

In progressive circles there has been an urgent call-out for a new story, now that climate change and species extinction have taken all the happy endings away and the wicked stepmothers and magicians have taken over the castle. 'Creatives' have been challenged to come up with a positive narrative that will break the spell of neo-liberal economics and get us out of the maze. Writers however are reluctant evangelists and propaganda-makers: they flourish in the territory of the existential, where their ancient skills of travelling into other dimensions are highly prized.

Because it's not the storyline, the *fabula*, we should be looking at here. Writers – those who guide us in the non-linear worlds of the imagination – are more interested in *le sujet* (or plot in Russian formalism), which is to say the way of telling the story. Although it looks like the story – this and that happened in linear time – is the point of everything, its real function is to be a container for a structural non-linear refit, once known as meta-morphosis. The story is the sugar that holds our attention and the sujet is the medicine. The difficulty for us as modern people is to look at what the sujet is demanding of us as a people, without everyone splitting off into their own personal narratives.

Threshing floor

There were words spilling everywhere around the room; on giant pieces of paper and small blackboards, altars and tables, we tabled the three R's of Deep Adaptation (Resilience, Relinquishment, Restoration), shared our thoughts on breakdown and extinction, our imagined stories about the future. We looked at how to swerve past blocks of denial, how to wail and rage inside a 'grief mandala', exchanged experiences in 'open space' and mapping sessions, hosted an open mic session and a ritual in the dark at the brink of the year. When it felt like everything was going horribly wrong, we held a constellation and danced to Le Freak by Chic. Occasion-ally I filled up the tea urns and trundled a wheelbarrow full of tealights around the winter garden and breathed in the wet winter air.

In a council meeting we spoke for the beings who were not in the room. Choosing from a collection of photographs and objects each per-son stepped into places and situations we did not know: we spoke from the deserts of Africa, the cotton fields of India, the streets of the East End of London, as ancient women and small children, as refugees facing floods and forest fires and war, as sharks and rocks and maize plants that have fed a whole continent of people for millennia. The walls of the hall buckled open.

Encountering the Other demands we let the outside in. We want to run away to the hills, back to the safety of our small room, our medita-tion chamber. But the threshing process breaks you open to liberate the seed you hold inside you for the future and throws the chaff of your life into the wind. If you are from an urbanised, industrial culture, this pro-cess winnows pretty much everything you have been told matters. At the same time everything that has been left out – which is the living breathing Earth, the sun and all the cosmos, all the invisible people and skeletons hidden in your family's and culture's closets – rushes in. Afterwards you are assailed by dreams, by memories, by bodily dysfunctions, you feel you are losing your grip, your friends look at you askance. For some this is a moment from which they reel, for others months, or years.

However this encounter comes, one thing is clear: change is not something you tell governments or other people to do; you have to undergo change to make space for the world to enter. The 40 or so cultural activists gathered in these school rooms have all been through the wringer one way or another: some have built practices, some have created art or taught, others live in the forest, or at the edges – all of us have accepted that collapse is underway and have a capacity to 'stay with the trouble'. We've been in this room before; when the frequency has gone pear-shaped, when the men talk too loudly or the women cry too much. We know the feedback loop is a key component of all non-linear systems and there are consequences to the actions taken by ourselves, our relations, our nation which we now have an obligation to rectify.

There is a deal you make with life and this Underworld encounter can tell you what that is. It's a deal we made a long time ago with the beasts and with the plants, only our civilisations buried it in sand to power their own interests.

I'm not sure how we can remember this deal together. The links between us, like many grassroots relationships, are fragile: few people here are dependent on each other in their ordinary lives: we are not related, or beholden in any way. We may rally around a cause but we find it hard to meet on a stage that goes beyond the material and political. We might say 'ancestors' shyly in the circle – but we don't name them. Our metaphysical knowledge is mostly something we have found individually in books, or in moments of deep reflection. And we will need, god knows, more than a poem by Mary Oliver or Rumi to hold the centre and not fragment when push comes to shove, to not lose our hard-won coherence and fly off into some small panic room, prowled by monsters.

We need our dancing feet on the ground.

Mythos

Something happens as we sit by a fire and chant for an hour, or we decide to take a step into the darkness of the kur or kiva, when our dancing feet take up the shapes of spirals and lemniscates; something deep and ancient

stirs our bone-memory of being here, the ancestors begin to listen, the animals come nearer in our dreams, we are no longer alone. A door opens to
the future we did not even know was there. The words vanish. Words are
for looking at what happened afterwards and telling. The encounter with
life is a full-body immersion and exchange.

And maybe that is why after all the words we wrote on the walls,
on blackboards in the classrooms, on flip chart paper, on coloured labels
hung on trees, the excitement of all the talking over lunch or tea, what I
remember most is stepping into the Land of the Dead with Deepak close
behind me. We stood there in the stony alcove, with its boughs and bones,
as the night wind blew through the apple orchard, and the small candles
guttered. And we looked over to the people by the fire, who seemed to
be a long way off, even though you could hear them singing and the fire
crackling. Some part of me didn't want to go back. And then I realised: the
ancestors could hear us when we gathered in that spirit.

I chose these myths (or perhaps they chose themselves) in times of
increasing restriction because they provide a technê – tools and method
and instruction manual – for how to negotiate our place and relationship with the Earth, beyond the story told by our civilisation's power-
possessors and priests. They can help us uncivilise ourselves: break out
of the labyrinth of our rational minds and navigate the wild oceans and
forests of a non-linear planet. The female myths are about tasks, about
rigour and courage, and about calling and receiving help in times of crisis.
The three R's of Deep Adaptation are tasks, they demand we leave a lot of
our identity and cleverness behind, our comfort zones, our egoic insults,
the traumas we cling to like antiquated gas masks, long after the war is
over.

These ancestral steps help us move dramaturgically into different
positions: to realise that our insistence on woundedness is a way of avoiding responsibility and breaking out of our separateness. We are not going
to make it on our own. We feel stuck, faced with the impossible, and need
to find a way out: a pile of jumbled seeds, a labyrinth of dead ends and false
passageways. With the myth in hand, you can make a move: you step into
others' shoes, you alter the role, you go through the door, get yourself off
the hook and then the world. The artist teaches the steps, holds the space,
takes up the chant, asks the questions. This is the moment when a kindly ant appears, or someone hands you a ball of thread, or a jar of honey,

or two beings fashioned from the dirt under the fingernails of a god slip through the keyholes of the Underworld undetected.

Our task is to recognise them.

Spring Equinox
East London 2020

'Where is the fracture point?' asked the interviewer. We are in the black 'Rebel' tent at the Byline Festival on the edge of the Ashdown Forest on the hottest day of last summer. The subject under discussion is, 'Where Does It Fall Apart? How Our Civilisation Will Disintegrate', and the panellists are Rupert Read (political spokesperson for Extinction Rebellion), Nafeez Ahmed (author of the documentary *The Crisis of Civilization*) and David Wallace-Wells (author of *The Uninhabitable Earth*).

Anita McNaught, ex-Middle East correspondent and no stranger to the collapse of nations, leans forward and keeps pressing the question. Will it be oil, or water? Will it be political, agricultural, financial, biospheric, spiritual? In systemic collapse the break can occur anywhere and affect everything at once. No one is able to predict where or when it will come. Except that one day, it will.

In a year where biblical calamities have rained down upon the world – as floods, bush fires and locust storms – this fracture has not emerged in the highly stressed natural world but from within a globalised human society. After ignoring the cries of Cassandra for decades, the horse has finally entered the gates of the cities, releasing billions of tiny invisible lifeforms that are no respecters of age, gender, wealth, position or race.

The fracture point is what many of us have been searching for in these last years. Because, as every storyteller knows, the crack reveals everything that needs to be told: the flaw in the character that can bring down whole kingdoms, the chink in the prison wall that speaks of liberty, the wake-up call to a cruel fairy tale that has enthralled you and generations before you. And maybe the crack is, as Buckminster Fuller once described, the moment the chick, struggling for space as its food runs out, catches a glimpse of blue sky beyond the shell – and not apocalypse at all.

ॐ

The crack comes when you least expect it and turns your safe world upside down: the moment when, in Cambridge, Massachusetts, I found a copy of the psychologist Alice Miller's *The Drama of the Gifted Child* and my host yelled at me for not sharing her chocolate ice cream and neglecting her needs. I had just seen a documentary about the AIM activist Leonard Peltier and the Wounded Knee siege of 1973, and looking back now these three things appear synonymous: the bulimic woman whose family had escaped Auschwitz, a disputed murder on an indigenous massacre site, the children whose lives were torn apart by inherited violence.

It was late at 36 to have found out that our true selves are not related to the role we have played within our family or culture. It is late to find out that human beings are not meant to live in denial of the barbarism that underpins every civilisation. Most of all it is late to learn how to weather these encounters with reality and replenish the Earth we have so long taken for granted. To find out, as fear now grips the world, how to hold the line and not fall apart.

Jumping the fire

I have a book open on my lap. It weighs almost four pounds and is 1000 pages long, a testament to the iniquities of Empire: from the genocides of Africa and Tasmania to the famine in Ireland, from the British slave trade to the European Holocaust. On the left hand page there is a list of the nine Ogoni tribesmen hanged on 10th November 1995. On the right are the names of the Shell executives who allowed the executions of the activists to take place, so they could continue their company's devastation of the Niger Delta for fossil fuel. All their names have been redacted. Among the nine is the writer Ken Saro-Wiwa, who wrote:

> ... the stories I tell must have a different sort of purpose from the artist in the Western world. And it's not now an ego trip, it is serious, it is politics, it is economics, it's everything, and art in that instance becomes so meaningful, both to the artist and to the consumers of that art (from Dan Gretton *I You We Them*)

This morning, as a pandemic rages and the world disappears inside its lockdown cocoon, I am writing a piece called 'Outbreak' and it feels impossible to say anything that could count as a message, or speak for the people or a country in the way Saro-Wiwa was able to. But if a writer has an obligation, it is to keep the door to the transformative Underworld open, so the living systems, in which civilisations embed themselves like parasitic worms, do not shut down. And sometimes the way we can do that is to document our own passage through those fracture points, to reveal what powers the world we live in, whether this is George Orwell going into the Yorkshire mines, or Dan Gretton walking to the site of Buchenwald; my own small slide into the kur in times of climate catastrophe.

I thought there were three R's we needed to learn about for Deep Adaptation. But in 2019 there appeared a fourth, Reconciliation, which inconveniently brings the rest of humanity into our individual restorations, and the thorny territory of social justice.

Reconciliation, writes its author Jem Bendell, is not only with your death or anger or regret, but

> reconciliation between peoples, genders, classes, generations, countries, religions and political persuasions. Because it is time to make our peace. Otherwise, without this inner deep adaptation to climate collapse we risk tearing each other apart and dying hellishly.

The real crisis we face is existential: who we are as human beings, and what our presence means on this planet at this time. Ancestral myths address that crisis, not as a tragedy, but as material, as a moral imperative to put a crooked thing straight. Shifting a paradigm is not an abstract phrase you can wield in a lecture hall or workshop, but something that happens concretely, in the depths of yourself, in your relationships in the real world. How to configure that change is encoded in the ancient myths and fairytales, in our encounters with wildness, in the tracking of dreams, the way the Earth can still speak to us through the jangled frequencies of our minds.

I thought I would never be reconciled to the dark forces that were revealed in my own life. How could I remedy anything I had witnessed, or read about? 'Who is it who can walk down these little roads of grief?' Carmen once asked of the tracks the Apache nation had left behind in their exile. And yet we do, willingly, for this is the task ahead of us. I don't know if we will make it to any kind of liveable future, but I know it exists on the edge of time. And on a good day, I can see it and I wish it could stay forever.

I wish for so many things as the skies darken. I wish the girls we once were had not had to shoulder that hard legacy from their fathers. I wish that the creatures in the forest fires of Australia and America had not been burned. I wish that the massacres I am reading about in this book had never happened. I wish my country had not divorced itself from the mainland of Europe, and this plague and decades of hostility had not driven everyone into hiding. I wish I could have reconciled the people who came into my dreams in those years, that we could have sat around that table and found a happy ending. But I have to know that it was enough to speak out their names in the clear morning, under the peeling eucalypt, under the mesquite, under the oak by the curve of the Suffolk barley field.

I did not want to lose my beautiful life but I did. I let it go. I did it to make the world lighter and kinder, to leave a track the way the people have always left tracks for us to follow, in the rocks, in their dialogues with creatures and plants and planets, in their art, in their beauty.

At equinox I will light a fire with the branches of the elm that fell in the winter storm, as the year shifts from the time of the Underworld to the light-filled upperworld of spring, as my ancestors have done in these islands, across the world, since we can remember. I will jump over the fire as I did on leap day with Lucy and Mark, in a ceremony we held in a courtyard in Brick Lane, and a hundred people followed in our footsteps, banging drums and saucepans, shouting these words in Persian, in fellowship, with our kith in the East End, in Tehran, in city streets across the world:

Zardi-ye man az to
Sorkhi-ye to az

O fire, I will give you my sickly yellow and I will take your fiery red!

May you have the courage to jump the fire. May you disobey your forefathers and open the box. May all your helpers come in time. May we all sing before the storm as it advances, as Eros approaches us with his great wings. May we have loved this Earth and each other enough for this not to be the end.

Afterword

❧

You open the box. You always open the box, even though your culture and your conditioning tell you not to. If you weren't curious, compelled, you would not have gone into the forest after dark, or asked the question no one else thought of asking; you wouldn't have climbed over the college wall to meet Eros, or gone to Belfast during the Troubles, or South Bronx where the buildings were on fire. The myth says you wanted to know what would make your more beautiful than Venus – but a closed box always begs to be open. So though you follow instructions, you also disobey. This paradox in your nature is your good fortune.

I am always writing the same poem, said Pablo Neruda at the end of his life. And this is true, I think, of most writers. *What matters is that the message is delivered.* I am always writing that for the change you desire you need to go into the Underworld and come back. I would like to write that you get scooped up into Eros' arms at the end of things. I would like to say after we jumped that spring fire in Spitalfields, and the cities closed down, everything worked out for the best. But the world did not return in the same shape as it was before. Like everyone else, I stopped travelling and disappeared from view. Our lives went online. Mark and I were evicted from our wild reserve by the marshes, and went to live in the woods, in the shadow of two proposed nuclear power stations. I recalibrated. I stopped writing. This is the world, that has not been normal for a very long time.

I would like to say there was a marriage feast on Olympus, that we flew there on butterfly wings, but as I write this the plagues continue, the floods and fires increase in ferocity, and the people keep being torn apart. And though I wish I could promise you a happy ending, if you do make it out of the Underworld, there are no guarantees. We are connected to the fate of everyone else as the hourglass falls.

But if you do find yourself with a handful of seeds or facing a herd of furious rams, you will know what to do. You will know what steps to make and how to disobey. That is the business of writers, to leave a trail behind you, so others can follow, words written on paper, figures etched on terracotta or rock.

There is only one story, the Anglo-Saxon lecturer told the first year English Literature class. Man goes into hell and comes back with riches. It is the ur-myth. It was a long time ago, I was 19, but I never forgot the instruction. I just stretched it back and forwards in time: a woman goes into the Underworld and comes back with riches.

It's still the only story worth telling.

Acknowledgements

❦

The pieces in this book come from publications and platforms I contributed to between 2007-2020, including EarthLines *magazine, This Low Carbon Life, The One World Column, The Social Reporting Project (Transition Network) and* The Earth Dreaming Bank.

'Varanasi' was published in *Dark Mountain: Issue 14 – TERRA*

'Lilies' is an unpublished chapter from *52 Flowers That Shook My World*

'What's Your Position as the Ship Goes Down' was published in Dark Mountain online

'The Seven Coats' was published in *Dark Mountain: Issue 6*

'Wayland and the Futuremakers' was published in *Dark Mountain: Issue 8 – Technê*

'The Red Thread' is a performance text from an essay published in *Dark Mountain: Issue 10 – Uncivilised Poetics*

An extract from 'Temescal' was published in *Dark Mountain: Issue 19*

'Letter to Mr Gurdjieff' was published in *Dark Mountain: Issue 13*

'The Time of Stones' is extracted from online pieces published by Dark Mountain 'The Reveal', 'In Search of a Lexicon for the Deep Core', 'Dancing the Cailleach' and 'Outbreak'

I would like to thank my fellow Dark Mountain editors for polishing these pieces over the years and making them shine: Nancy Campbell, Nick Hunt, Paul Kingsnorth and Tom Smith.

Thanks to our fellow publisher John Negru of Sumeru Books who designed and produced the final text, and generously encouraged this new partnership with the Dark Mountain Project.

Thanks to Meryl McMaster for sharing her wonderful artwork and Christian Brett at Bracketpress for designing the cover.

And finally, the greatest thank you to my dearest compañero Mark Watson for sharing this long, challenging and beautiful journey every step of the way, and for proofreading all the pieces. This book, literally, would not have happened without you.

About the author

❧

Charlotte Du Cann is a writer, editor and co-director of the Dark Mountain Project. She also teaches collaborative non-fiction, and radical kinship with the other-than-human world.

In 1991 she left her life as a London features and fashion journalist with a one-way ticket to Mexico. After travelling for a decade, she settled on the East Anglian coast to write a sequence of books about reconnecting with the Earth. The first of these *52 Flowers That Shook My World – A Radical Return to Earth* was published in 2012 by Two Ravens Press.

Charlotte has published five works of non-fiction, ranging from a collection of essays about food and society, *Offal and the New Brutalism* (Heinemann) to the travelogue, *Reality Is the Bug That Bit Me in the Galapagos* (Flamingo). More recently, she has written about activism, myth and cultural change for the *New York Times*, *The Guardian*, *Noema* and *openDemocracy*. She co-founded the grassroots newspaper *Transition Free Press* and edited *Playing for Time – Making Art as if the World Mattered* (with author Lucy Neal), a handbook about community arts practice (Oberon Books). She is presently working on a collective Dark Mountain book about the ancestral solar year called *Eight Fires*.

About The
Dark Mountain Project

❧

And so we find ourselves, all of us together, poised trembling on the brink of a
change so massive that we have no way of gauging it. None of us knows where
to look, but all of us know not to look down...
Our question is: what would happen if we looked down? Would it be as bad as
we imagine? What might we see? Could it even be good for us?
We believe it is time to look down.
 – *From* Uncivilisation: The Dark Mountain Manifesto

The Dark Mountain Project is a network of writers, artists and thinkers whose work attempts an honest response to the crises of our time: climate breakdown; social and political unravelling; the death of the myths of endless growth and human exceptionalism; ecocide and mass extinction. The project was founded in 2009 with the publication of *Uncivilisation*, a literary manifesto which called for a new kind of 'uncivilised' writing and artwork that tells new stories for an age of endings. The first issue of *Dark Mountain*, a hardback anthology of essays, short fiction, poetry and artwork, was published in 2010 and attracted attention – and controversy – from within the green movement and beyond.

Since 2014, the Dark Mountain Project has published two books a year: a regular spring anthology, and an autumn special issue on themes that have included technology, poetics, the sacred, travel and belonging, fiction and extractivism. From its origins in the United Kingdom the project has grown internationally, with contributors and subscribers from the United States to New Zealand, India to South Africa, Canada to Ghana, Sweden to Australia. From 2010 to 2013 the annual Uncivilisation festival brought together many of the writers, artists and storytellers who featured in the early issues, and inspired further events in the UK and beyond –

including smaller festivals, book launches, workshops and performances. The Dark Mountain Online Edition (dark-mountain.net) publishes new material every week and is read around the world.

But books remain the project's core, and over the years the issues have featured a diverse array of writers, artists and thinkers whose contributions – including fiction, non-fiction, poetry, visual art and interviews, as well as work that is entirely non-categorisable – have all attempted to navigate the troubled, uncertain times we are in. As the manifesto says: 'The end of the world as we know it is not the end of the world full stop. Together, we will find the hope beyond hope, the paths which lead to the unknown world ahead of us.'

Everything Dark Mountain has published has been made possible through the support and generosity of our readers. Take out a subscription to Dark Mountain and you will get each issue as soon as it comes out, at a lower price than anywhere else. You will also be giving us the security we need to continue producing our books.

To read more about the different levels of subscription, please visit: dark-mountain.net/subscriptions

Ingram Content Group UK Ltd.
Milton Keynes UK
UKHW040505100523
421505UK00004B/57